What Makes Us Human?

What Makes Us Human?

130 Answers to the Big Question

With a Foreword by Jeremy Vine
and an Introduction by Phil Jones

First published in 2021 by
HEADLINE PUBLISHING GROUP

1

Cataloguing in Publication Data is available from the British Library

Hardback ISBN 978 1 4722 7251 5
Trade paperback ISBN 978 1 4722 7252 2

Designed and typeset by EM&EN
Printed and bound in Great Britain by Clays Ltd, Elcograf S.p.A.

HEADLINE PUBLISHING GROUP
An Hachette UK Company
Carmelite House
50 Victoria Embankment
London EC4Y 0DZ

www.headline.co.uk
www.hachette.co.uk

CONTENTS

Contents

Contents

Culture

Language and Literature

Contents

Emotions

People and Family

Contents

Society

Equality

Contents

Contents

What Makes Us Human?

The essays in this book were first broadcast on
'What Makes Us Human?', a feature on BBC Radio 2,
between 2013 and 2021.

FOREWORD

JEREMY VINE

Born in 1965 in Epsom, Jeremy Vine is one of the UK's leading broadcasters. He presents *The Jeremy Vine Show* on BBC Radio 2: it is the nation's most popular current affairs programme and includes the weekly 'What Makes Us Human?' feature, inviting different guests to share their response to that question.

I picked up the scissors, carefully lifted the corner of the page and cut a line from the paper's edge to the first word of the letter: 'SIR — .'

This, I thought, is one I want to keep.

That day's copy of the *Daily Telegraph* was in my hands. The letter was from one of their readers, David Lavelle in Coneythorpe. The Yorkshireman described how he had been helping his teenage daughter with some homework when his wife texted him.

'What do you want from life?' her text read.

Brilliant! Mrs Lavelle's question – sent during a shopping trip – was so unusual, so different from the everyday messages we all send each other about errands or office gossip, that David and his daughter were jolted from the ordinary. They set the homework aside to consider a proper response. 'We debated various answers – wealth, fulfilment, love, all three,' he wrote to the paper.

If there was a trigger for Radio 2's 'What Makes Us Human?', the feature that first appeared on my programme in 2013, with Chief Rabbi Jonathan Sacks as the debut guest, it was our search for what we might call the Mrs Lavelle Question. Something to jolt us from our own everyday ordinaries. We sense – don't we? – that all of us tend to spend decades avoiding the hardest questions because the easiest seem so much more pressing. At the weekend, for example, I texted my wife 'Do we have carrots?', because the question 'Do we have a caring relationship where we respect each other and the sex is still good?' just seemed too much for a Saturday.

Life is chock-full of mundane questions, a news programme even more so. Since I began presenting my midday show on BBC Radio 2 on 6 January 2003 – the opening salvo was 'Is some rap music too rude?' – I feel I have made enquiries into almost every subject. 'Are you someone who likes to walk around barefoot?', 'Should car dashboards be fitted with breathalysers?', 'Do you miss pick-your-own-fruit?', 'Have you ever been locked inside a building?' and so on. And on.

Yet it is possible to read the entire list back – 'Is bread bad for ducks?' was a particular favourite – and realise that we had found out everything and learned nothing. We needed a Mrs Lavelle Question.

Perhaps we could also take a leaf from the book of Bethany McLean? In March 2001, the young financial journalist looked at the rocketing share price of an American energy company called Enron and refused to accept the assurance of a Goldman Sachs investment expert that the firm was worth far more than all its competitors because, 'like Michael Jordan', the supreme basketball player, the firm's success could not simply be analysed using a mathematical formula. Bethany disagreed. But, in response to her enquiries, Enron, which was reporting dramatically increased profits quarter-on-quarter, simply showered her with detailed information. She was sent pages and pages of numbers and might easily have given up.

Instead she formulated a question that was breathtaking in its simplicity: 'How does Enron make its money?'

The response from the company was suspiciously brutal. The CEO Jeffrey Skilling said her question was 'off-base' and she was unethical. They demanded a meeting – the Chief Financial Officer Andrew Fastow flew to New York to explain to McLean and her editors why the question could not be answered. But Bethany McLean persisted. How *does* Enron make its money? Gradually, it became clear the corporation had no answer. Her resulting article in *Vanity Fair* was headlined 'Is Enron Overpriced?' and caused the company, still one of the most valuable in the world on paper, to collapse. On 2 December 2001, Enron declared bankruptcy. It emerged that Skilling had earned $132m in a single year. He and Fastow were jailed.

It all came back to that single, six-word question. And maybe to the fear we all have, that if we suddenly ask the biggest questions – 'How does Enron make its money?', 'What do you want from life?', 'What is the point of any of us being here?' – we will, ourselves, face total collapse. A psychiatrist once told me he wondered if his depressed patients were the only ones who saw life clearly – if it was just serotonin and the Rolling Stones that stopped the rest of us from realising there is no point in existing. 'Why do we bother, Fawlty?' the major asks Basil in *Fawlty Towers*. 'Didn't know you did, major,' comes the nihilistic reply.

Yet we are all different. In the TV show *Catastrophe*, the strangely intense Chris (played by Mark Bonnar) takes Rob Delaney's character to one side. Rob has been waxing lyrical about becoming a father. Chris gives him the following bug-eyed warning: 'I saw my son coming out and it was a f***ing warzone. You see a little troll tobogganing out of your wife's snatch on a wave of turds, and part of you will hold her responsible.' It is their first meeting. If asked, I am not sure Chris would say anything makes us human at all.

However, if Mrs Lavelle is reading this, she may be feeling embarrassed. The reason her husband wrote to the *Telegraph*, you see, is because of the second text she sent. The first had asked 'What do you want from life?' and was ground-breaking. But the letter I was cutting from the newspaper did not finish there. Soon after husband and daughter had got stuck into their fascinating discussion about fulfilment, money and love, his phone pinged again. The first question had been a victim of predictive text, explained Mrs Lavelle. 'I meant to ask *What do you want from Lidl?*'

And so we stick to carrots. All of us, never looking up from the bottom drawer of the fridge. We ask about ducks and rap music. We argue about nothing – I tweeted a carefree picture of me on my bicycle and the first reply was something like 'SCUM IDIOT NOT WEARING A HELMET'. I was then, more fool me, drawn into a discussion of the safety merits of cycle helmets with a keyboard warrior in Truro.

I freely confess my own fascination with the trivial, having been particularly concerned for some time that the door to our downstairs toilet will not shut. When I watched the DIY fix on YouTube, I learned that the latch – the bit that protrudes from the edge of the door – needs to connect cleanly with the catchplate, the metal housing in the door jamb, and I discovered ours did not; so I would have to remove the catchplate, stop up the existing screw holes with matchstick shavings and wood glue, wait for it to set and then drill new holes about five millimetres to the left and . . . wait, was that you snoring just then? The upshot is that I have spent more of my spare time repairing a door handle than asking what my life is for.

Which is why we decided to ditch the latch-and-catchplate on Radio 2. We junked the duck's bread just for a day and put the rap records back in their sleeves. We gave up on breathalysing dashboards and barefoot fruit-picking in rooms that had been locked from the outside, and we asked the Mrs Lavelle Question. And we never looked back.

Imagine, if you will, a political interview. The female interviewer has been on our screens for so many years we feel we know her mannerisms intimately. We know the angle of her shoulder just before she asks the killer question, the way the plumb line of her hair will accentuate a particularly menacing tilt of the head. We know the gritted smile the politician will deploy just as he starts to panic. He, too, has been a fixture of our lives for years. He has been a shadow minister, a junior minister, a Cabinet minister. He is grey now, grey with the burden of a thousand unanswered questions and a hundred secrets. We cannot remember his brief, but it is something to do with employment. Ah, now he is being asked about jobs in the north of England. We have an unemployment crisis. The female interviewer has prised apart his defence and forced the minister to admit most of it is his fault and he has no idea what to do. We reach for the remote because we have seen this so many times before, and then our finger pauses. What has she just asked?

'I will put it to you again, minister. What makes us human?'

The camera zooms in on a bead of sweat sliding along the man's forehead. He blinks, tries to remember the party manifesto, the advice of his wife before he left for the studio, the names of his daughters . . . no, it is all gone. The game is up.

'I do not know what makes us human,' he says. 'I have never thought about it.'

Would we forgive the minister? Probably. We would wonder what had possessed the interviewer to stray so far from the topic of employment in the north. There would be talk of 'an ambush', questions asked about why the programme had not cleared this line of enquiry with the minister's press team. He would protest afterwards that 'it was preposterous to expect me to answer a question like that'. The presenter would apologise on Twitter; her editor would assure us it would never happen again.

But why shouldn't it? Why don't we ever ask each other what we are all doing here? Even the Archbishop of Canterbury seems never to be asked the biggest question of all, but gets pressed on betting regulation and the banking crisis (strangely similar subjects). If the biggest question can never be asked, what are we doing, toiling away in those jobs the minister would like us to credit him with creating?

*

Foreword

What was gobsmacking to the Radio 2 team about 'What Makes Us Human?' – apart from the fact that no one can pronounce its acronym, WMUH – was that people from all walks of life pounced on the invitation to answer the question. Not only that, the answers were so different as to be astonishing. What makes us human is silliness. What makes us human is seriousness. What makes us human is that we are destroying the planet. What makes us human is that we are trying to revive the planet. We had a politician who said what makes us human is dancing, an Olympic runner who said what makes us human is jazz, and a wealthy businessman who said what makes us human is giving things away.

**People from all walks of life pounced
on the invitation to answer the question.
Not only that, the answers were so different
as to be astonishing.**

Many of us resort to the drummer's answer to the question, if you'll forgive the personal shorthand. At home I have a drum kit, the plug-in sort, which puts all the sound through headphones. To everyone else, you are making no more noise than if you rapped your knuckles on a selection of hardback books, but to you, sitting at the kit with the headphones on – oh boy! Your ears are battered the way they would be if you were backing Muse at the O2.

Although I will never be very good at drums – I gave up getting better when someone tried to explain how to paradiddle, and I decided it was not for me – I still love to sit and thwack the problems of the day away. But if you asked me 'what makes us human?' and I said it's playing drums, I think you would be within your rights to tell me off. 'The key word,' you could say, 'is "us" not "you", Jeremy. Not everyone plays the drums.' Correction accepted. I cannot say that what makes us human is having size twelve feet if I seem to be the only customer on Shoes Direct searching for that size. But still people do it: the scientist says science, the musician says music. The wart removal surgeon says the removal of warts. I'm not being critical, just questioning. Might it be questioning that makes us human? But of course I *would* say that – it's my job: I'm an interviewer. Once again, the drummer's answer.

But what if I took my drummer's answer and expanded it a little? What makes us human is being able to find a beat in everything, to catch a rhythm in the air and make it real. What makes us human is that, in a traditional four-beat bar, we have a whole continent that put the beat on the two and the four, but then a small collection of islands that chose to put a single beat on the three and watched it spread around the world . . . in short, the difference between rock and reggae. And then someone turns up and gives you a syncopated beat, and at first they call him insane, then they name the music 'jazz' and it fills all the gaps where rhythm had not existed. What makes us human is that difference. What makes us human is that 167 guests have given me 167 answers to the question.

Sometimes I feel bad, listening to those guests (and watching them – pre-Covid, they would spend about half an hour with me in the studio, which is quite a lot of time in which to observe each other). I feel bad because I have never yet disagreed in the way that interviewers are supposed to. The 'But surely you must accept . . .' question somehow seems out of place in this feature. Isn't it great, for once, just to hear what the other person thinks without the host kicking off? Caroline Criado-Perez, the feminist campaigner, started her essay by pointing out that when she says 'Imagine a human', every single person, *including her,* imagines a man. That was showstopping, and probably the best opening we have had.

When I appeared on *Strictly Come Dancing,* I had a most peculiar revelation about the human condition that I will share with you now, having not yet mentioned it to a soul on the grounds that anyone who heard me say this would think me off my rocker.

Foreword

You have to imagine fifteen hyperventilating celebrity contestants, all arriving to dance on a programme which is the BBC's biggest. We are all excited; not all of us can dance. The first night was a magical event, with screaming, shouting and bright lights – and that was just the food station. I remember bonding with Carol Kirkwood, the weather forecaster, and agreeing that we had both done nothing like this before. We were trying not to giggle as we said it.

Slowly the magic seduced us. It was normal to have a thousand retweets on every social media message, read complete fiction in the newspapers ('Carol Kirkwood is FIGHTING BLINDNESS to compete on *Strictly*') and be asked for autographs by a small crowd in the hotel. At no point did anyone notice that each week, one of our number went missing.

Now I look back, there were signs. At the end of each show there was a vote, a red light went on, and someone cried. Then the person who cried was not with us any more and we all recorded interviews praising them. And we got on with the next programme.

But then, one day, it was us – it was me, it was Carol – who became the person to suddenly disappear. And the strange thing was that we were not expecting it, and it was shattering when it happened.

Suddenly, outside the programme, cycling into Radio 2 in the rain, I had cause to consider what had happened. I must have briefly lost concentration as I did so, for a black cab pulled out on me from a side street. We had a brief altercation – friendlier than it might have been. Then, as I cycled off, I heard the cab driver shout: 'And your dancing's shit as well.'

But here is the lesson I learned. *Strictly* is like life. Here we are in this magical place – Planet Earth, I mean – and we seem to think the dancing will actually go on for ever. Why else would people say they found a hobby 'to while away the time'? What we can never admit is how short time really is. People go missing around us, one by one, and still we dance. We are in denial.

Foreword

People say 'the difference between animals and humans is that animals have no conception that their lifespan is limited, no concept of death', but the opposite is true. Every time I walk towards my gloriously timid cat Wally, he scampers away as if scalded, eyes bulging and fur on end, as if I am planning to serve him up for supper. By contrast, humans live in blissful ignorance. A friend of mine wanted to publish a book on gravestones. 'No one wants to read about death,' said his publisher coldly, and the idea itself ended up buried.

Like the contestants in a dance contest, we simply cannot envisage a moment when the red light comes on and we disappear. This, surely, is what makes us human, amid a thousand other things – our delicious inability to stop the world and ask the biggest question of all, for fear that the result will be the end of our beautiful dance.

On behalf of the team at Radio 2, we are sorry to spoil the fun. I shall blame my editor, Phil Jones. He tells me he had the idea 'while cycling home after two-and-a-half pints' (the half may be significant). He had a radio programme playing through his headphones but was not listening until the fragment of a sentence leapt out: '... the biggest question of all, what makes us human?' And that was it. Maybe it was a little inhuman of Phil to follow through and schedule a series around the one question we always avoid, but the answers were truly beautiful, every one.

What makes us human is that we never confront that question. If you read on, I hope you'll agree that our dangerous soul-searching has been worth it.

INTRODUCTION

PHIL JONES

Phil Jones, born in 1958 in Wimbledon, is one of the BBC's longest-serving editors. He has worked on *The Jeremy Vine Show* (and its predecessor, *The Jimmy Young Show*) for thirty years, and thought up the 'What Makes Us Human?' feature when he was cycling back from a party while a little drunk. Here, he shares the ideas behind the series and looks at why we ask questions about our existence.

When I was sixteen, my comprehensive school went head-to-head in a debate against the local public school. We relished the chance to do battle. It was our version of class war. I was chosen to oppose the motion 'This house believes Man is no better than a Dog'. My father was the wisest man I knew, so I asked him for guidance. He said, when you want to answer the big questions, take a look at Shakespeare, and in this case Mark Antony's homage to Julius Caesar: 'His life was gentle, and the elements mixed so well in him that Nature might stand up and say to all the world, "This was a man".' In other words, there's no finer accolade than to call someone human.

I was thinking recently about when *The Jeremy Vine Show* team first talked about offering our listeners an insight into what I suspect is the most difficult question anyone can ask: 'What makes us human?'. On the show we don't do philosophy that much. We spend our time making a lot of sound and fury around the subjects that irritate our fellow citizens as we struggle through the second decade of the twenty-first century. The bankers' bonuses, welfare reform, or whether or not you should jump into the sea to save your drowning dog. That sort of thing. Occasionally, though, we like to step back and ponder the deeper questions. Something more profound. Is there a God? Is our planet tumbling towards environmental catastrophe? And now the greatest question anyone can address, 'What makes us human?'

There's a simple beauty to the thought, but does it even have an answer? The idea behind the radio feature – and now this book – is to ask some of our sharpest and most inquisitive minds to grapple with our very existence. We got philosophers and religious leaders on board, but no doubt they wrestle with such thoughts week in, week out. So, we thought, why not spread the net a little wider and challenge others – artists, pop stars, footballers – to compose essays that attempt to find a meaning to our existence.

I'm also rather hoping that our readers and listeners might like to have a stab too. I've made a modest start myself. The obvious place to begin is to compare us with the animal kingdom. There's that statistic that I never quite believe that claims *Homo sapiens* have 99% of the DNA of a chimp or 80% of the DNA of a fruit fly. So it would seem we barely differ from animals at all. But don't we have imagination and consciousness? Sure, but then one day soon a prominent animal behaviourist will no doubt discover that dolphins have imagination and consciousness as well. Do dolphins love, hope and dream?

Maybe comparing us to animals just takes us down a blind alley. I think what really makes us human is that we're cultural beings, capable of creating truly wondrous things. Isn't it incredible that we've created things every bit as beautiful as those found in the natural world? Aren't Van Gogh's sunflowers just as breathtaking as sunflowers blowing in a meadow? If you want awe-inspiring, doesn't the Hoover Dam compare with the Grand Canyon? And can't we marvel at our towering gothic cathedrals as much as the great redwood forests? And who but a philistine would argue that a Cristiano Ronaldo free kick doesn't compare with the flutter of a butterfly wing?

Introduction

But if humankind is capable of such creation and achievement, we are also responsible for great failings, and, of course, for evil almost beyond imagination. Back to Shakespeare. In *The Tempest*, Prospero says of Caliban, 'This thing of darkness, I acknowledge mine'. An acceptance of something dark and bleak in all of us. The human race includes Jesus and Gandhi, but we must also own up to the Holocaust, gulags and the Rwandan massacre. We're capable of great good, but also great evil, which proves I know not what.

Let's leave that to our coming essays. Looking back to that debate when I was just sixteen, I can remember the pleasure I felt when we beat those public-school boys. A small victory in the class war. But now I suspect that the winning wasn't important: just delving into such questions is reward enough – and perhaps our ability to do just that is exactly what makes us human.

Our Past

To understand what makes us human,
these essays explore how we must first consider
our history. By understanding our past, we can
begin to comprehend our place in the
vastness of time.

ALICE ROBERTS

Biologist, broadcaster, author

Dr Alice Roberts' fascinating answer considers how our relationship with time shapes our understanding of what it means to be human, and – through archaeology – how we can find clues to the answer to this question in the records of the past.

We're acutely aware of the passing of time. Not just on a daily basis, but with reference to the deep past and the distant future – even beyond the span of our own lives. The way we appreciate time seems intrinsically linked to our own experience.

I remember being a small kid at primary school and thinking that the eleven-year-olds were impossibly old and unachievably mature, and that teenagers were like beings from another planet. As an eighteen-year-old, thirty seemed old and generally past it. At thirty, I could imagine being forty, fifty, sixty, seventy. And you start to grasp the reality of your own end, of course. Now I'm in my mid-forties, I think I've come to terms with my own mortality, but, at the same time, the concept of not being is impossible to properly apprehend.

Now, many things which we consider to be uniquely human characteristics turn out not to be unique at all. We differ from other animals by degree. Some chimpanzees use thick sticks to make holes in a termite nest, then break a thinner stick down to the right length to fish termites out through the holes. Others use stones to crack nuts. Our technology seems a world away, but it evolved from such humble beginnings.

And yet our understanding of time is, I think, something which is completely distinct. Humans, uniquely, know that they have been born, and that they will end – they will die. I suspect that all of religion is, at its foundations, concerned with providing solace in the face of this unimaginable but unavoidable fact.

We know that there are beginnings and endings – and so we're fascinated with what comes before the beginning, and after the end. Every culture has its own origin myth. The question of origins – who we are, where we come from, not just as individuals, but as humans, seems to be a very ancient one. For thousands of years, questions like these have been explored through philosophy and religion, but now the answers seem to lie firmly within the grasp of a rational, scientific approach to the world and our place within it.

**I know we will keep looking back –
reinterpreting what we've discovered before,
and finding ever more answers, in the ground,
in our bodies, in our genes.**

The clues come from different branches of science: archaeology turns up the material culture of the past, allowing us to see what our ancestors made and to know something of their ways of thinking; we also find physical, fossilised remains of our ancestors' bones. We can interpret brain size from ancient skulls, work out how these ancient people walked and ran, and sometimes even see how they must have cared for those suffering disease or injury. But there are also clues to our origins hidden in living bodies – traces of evolution that we find by studying the fine structure of the human body or its embryonic development. And then, of course, there are genomes: a huge archive of data which we're now mining faster than ever, and uncovering many more answers – and surprises.

And so, I know we will keep looking back – reinterpreting what we've discovered before, and finding ever more answers, in the ground, in our bodies, in our genes. That's what keeps me fascinated by this particular area of science. And then, personally, knowing that I am only here for a short time, and then I will be gone – that keeps me searching for more ways to make this one life meaningful.

MICHAEL ROSEN

Children's novelist and poet

Michael Rosen brings history to life in this stimulating answer about the relationship between the past and the future. Rather than seeing the past as something that's happened and dealt with, this answer encourages you to use it to create a brighter future.

All history is pointless. You can't change it. It's over. It happened.

Yet, we've all got history. Even the person in a coma and the person with Alzheimer's are who they are because of their history. You can see their history in the shape of their bodies, the marks on their hands, the shadings of their skin.

To live with this paradox of history being on the one hand 'gone', yet at the same time 'with us at all times', is what it is to be human. History is all that's not there any more and yet we are nothing without it. Animals don't do history the way we do it. Even if some of them remember stuff, they can't talk about it. This gives us the pain of loss and the pleasure of memory. It gives us a country we can't go to and yet we start every day in the place where it left us. History gives us who we are today by being who we were yesterday.

Today we'll all do history. Maybe we'll talk about what we saw on TV last night. Maybe we'll talk about something from when we were children, or something we saw on the bus. Maybe we'll remember something odd, or strange, or funny. Maybe we'll look in the mirror and notice a line on our faces, a look in our eyes, or that shirt, and remember when we bought it.

I do history for a living. No one calls me a historian, though. People say I write poems, or I broadcast. Or I teach. But, in truth, I'm the bloke going on about things my mum or dad or brother used to say to me, or the places we went. That's history. I'm the bloke scurrying about trying to find out stuff to do with my great-grandparents or great-uncles and aunts. More history. Or I'm the bloke wondering why British people say 'I've got' and Americans say 'I've gotten'. Or wondering how come Joseph Heller came to write *Catch-22*. And where did he get that 'Catch-22' thing from, anyway? And why do so many of us say 'It's a Catch-22 situation'? All history.

History gives us who we are today by being who we were yesterday.

People all around us sing songs, tell stories of what's happened to them, talk about their parents and grandparents, where they used to live. We remember some of this, and somehow it all becomes us. I just happen to be one of those people who mash it up and turn it into writing or telling stories or discussing it in books or on the radio.

Even a joke is history – it's been told over and over again; someone nicked a bit of its shape from one place, someone nicked a bit of the punchline from somewhere else. We are inheritors of all this stuff.

I happen to be someone who spends hours and hours every day on it. Most people aren't quite as into it as that. Even so, everyone does it a bit. Either way, a lot or a little, none of us can escape from what we've inherited – and I don't just mean the genetic things. That gesture you make, your name, the languages you speak, the way you say the words, the food you like and don't like, the work you do, or want to do – all inherited or acquired from people you've known and heard.

But I'll turn all this on its head. If all we are is the stuff we inherit and acquire, we'd just be animals. We wouldn't be able to choose anything or change anything. When I say we're historians,

Our Past

I mean we are creatures who can make something of what we inherit and acquire. We can get to work on it, thinking about it, expressing it, changing it. We work on all the old stuff, to make new stuff.

But how free are we to do that? Can we change anything and everything? We can only find that out if we try things, if we explore what's possible, if we invent things. And here's my last paradox: one of the best ways to find out what's possible is to explore the past. History.

RAY MEARS

Survivalist

For survival expert Ray Mears, the answer to the question lies in the ways we humans have managed to harness the natural world, and how the mastery of fire sent the human story on a different course to that of other animals.

In our lifetime, we share our lives on this incredible planet with many other creatures, each of which has its own special trait or survival skill, a characteristic attribute by which it can be defined. Our special trick gives us the impression that we are in some way elevated from other animals, but of course we are not; I believe it is important to remember that we are mammals, upright-walking creatures, descended from an ancient line of apes, believed to have originated in Africa. With a free thumb, we have the ability to easily fashion tools. Indeed, it is believed that we have been making tools for more than 2.5 million years. But that does not define us; other animals can make tools too. Sea otters, for example, use stones to break open oyster shells, while other primates even fashion weaponry for hunting.

What I believe defines us as human is our mastery of fire. But before we assume that we are the only users of fire in nature, we should think again. Just last year, I watched hawks in Australia picking up burning sticks from a bush fire and dropping them to spread the fire in order to flush out or scorch potential prey. But, to date, no other creature has been found who can make fire at will.

In the world of archaeology, the earliest evidence for the human control of fire is a hotly debated topic, with few definite remains surviving from such antiquity. Tantalising evidence may show fire hearths dating from 1 million years ago. Conjecture is ever present in the early history of fire. It is, however, reasonable to assume that fire was originally obtained from natural sources, such as bush fires, which could then be kept burning. Even today, there are peoples such as the Mbayaka pygmy in the Congo basin that carry fire with them, hardly ever needing to kindle a flame because, as they told me, 'We don't let our fire go out: it is the oldest fire in the world.' I have also worked with Australian aboriginals who historically could not make fire and would have to send runners to bring back fire from distant neighbouring tribes if their own fire was allowed to go out.

Fire altered humankind's potential for ever.

Regardless of how those early fires were kindled, fire altered humankind's potential for ever. Now, wielding a tool powerful enough to keep even the most ferocious early Palaeolithic predators at bay, the fear of nocturnal dangers was dispelled and the fire became a focus for life, around which our forebears could gather in good cheer: a sight still played out on a nightly basis in the villages of the San Bushmen of the Kalahari. In the flames and coals of their fires, our ancestors learned to alter their food, to improve its flavour, to neutralise plant toxins and destroy harmful bacteria. Consequently, our dietary range grew and diversified. It has been well argued that our 'fire-improved' diet may well have been a catalyst for the development of our large brains.

Until fire was harnessed, the length of the day was determined by the sunlight; firelight extended the working day and, along with the improved diet, made time available to communicate, to share ideas and be creative. In the sign language of Native Americans, the concept of meeting for a talk is defined by coming to a fire and the passing of ideas, and even today the footlights of our theatres mimic the flickering light of a fire on the face of an ancestral storyteller.

We don't have to have been there to realise that the question of how to make fire from scratch would have occupied the minds gathered at the campfire. If I could travel back in time, I would hope to witness the first of our ancestors to achieve this remarkable skill. The consequences of that first ember were astonishing. No modern invention comes close in importance to the creation of the first fire.

For more than thirty years, I have been teaching students how to make fire, by every primitive means known. Although we will never know which was the first method of fire lighting, some things never change. Each time a student succeeds in friction fire-lighting, their face lights up with an incredible sense of achievement; like an ancient ritual, the drama of the first fire is relived.

Being able to make fire at will brings confidence. With fire available at will, our ancestors were able to spread out, exploring their landscape in smaller foraging parties, with fire for safety and with smoke to locate each other again. I have witnessed aboriginals in Arnhem Land watching for smoke across flooded swamps to track the movements of distant family members. Now, even colder landscapes posed little obstacle as our ancestors migrated across the planet, perhaps clinging to the unexplored coastline or following seasonal migrations of game inland.

With fire-making mastered, the fireside was to become our most important laboratory. Here, as we stared into the flames, we observed the way fire could transform materials. We learned to harden the points of wooden spears, to soften thermoplastic tree resins and use them as adhesives to haft a stone point. Here, too, we would discover that clay could be hardened into pottery. Along the way, the process of scientific investigation was reinforced: observations, hypotheses and experimentation. Inevitably, we discovered metal and, well, I guess the rest is history; everything flows from here, from the clothes we wear to the incredible devices contained in our pockets and the means by which my words reach you now, all derived from our mastery of fire.

Our Past

You only have to observe the fascination on the face of an infant gazing into a fire to realise how deeply it is rooted in the human mind. Fire has given us power and allowed us, like no other species, to modify the very landscape within which we evolved. Perhaps the question we should be asking is how will humanity be judged to have used its special skill?

MARY BEARD

Professor of classics

Mary Beard compares us ordinary mortals to the lofty Greek gods in this highly original take on the question. Her rare talent for making academic history so engaging shines in this delightful essay.

When we wonder now about what makes us human, we tend to think of the fragile boundary that separates us from the animal kingdom. Are human beings the only creatures in the world to laugh, or do apes and monkeys – and even rats – chortle too? (Don't try the rat experiment at home, by the way: the scientists who have managed to get rats to squeal in delight when tickled admit that the sounds are at such a high frequency as to be inaudible to the naked ear.)

More seriously, is our species really the only one to have a sense of history, to form language or show grief? For – although the most intelligent goldfish may have a memory of only a few seconds – it seems clear enough that we share some of our apparently 'human' talents with many primates, and that even the average Border collie has some very rudimentary grasp of something close to 'language'.

For the ancient Greeks and Romans, it was very different. They were even more concerned with the equally fragile boundary that separated the human race from the *gods*. After all, in their world, human beings could become gods. Hercules was one who started his immortal life as at least half-mortal; so was the god of healing, Aesculapius. And any number of Roman emperors were made gods after their apparent 'death'. So where did the difference lie, except in the simple fact that gods went on to live for ever, whereas ordinary humans did not?

The answer to that question was found in one of the earliest Greek myths. According to this, the first human-like creatures to live on the earth were the Titans, who were actually not humans at all but second-rank gods. To start with, the first-rank gods in heaven and the Titans on earth lived in harmony, but, eventually – and this is to cut a very long story short – they quarrelled, and in the course of these arguments the Titans stole one of the most precious commodities of all, fire, from the gods.

> **The ancient Greeks and Romans were concerned with the fragile boundary that separated the human race from the gods. After all, in their world, human beings could become gods.**

The Titans, of course, couldn't win. And part of the punishment imposed on them was to make the first human being out of mud. These new human beings no longer lived at leisure as the Titans had before, eating food spontaneously produced by the earth. In a way that's a bit reminiscent of the story of Adam and Eve in the Bible, they were forced to work hard at agriculture simply to survive, and to use the fire to cook what they grew. And it was that combination of hard labour and the kitchen that was seen as one of the markers of the human race. No gods ever cooked.

But there was something else that came to mark the sad state of humanity. As an extra punishment, and to the Greek mind worst of all, the first-rank gods created and sent to earth something that had never existed before. It was beautiful, seductive, but a terrible trouble to mankind. I mean woman. Ever after, the human race was also defined by the struggle of men against the bane of women.

Mary Beard

Parts of this story are pretty unpalatable. It certainly reveals the rough edge of ancient Greek misogyny. But you could do worse than think that the defining characteristic of our species is the combination of hard work and cookery. Even if ants keep themselves busy, they certainly don't slave over a hot stove.

NEIL OLIVER

Archaeologist and broadcaster

Our awareness of time and our own mortality is uniquely human. This can often seem like a burden, but Neil Oliver reminds us how it can also be a blessing – it gives us the power to plan, to think in the long term and take active steps to control the time we have on the planet.

Time – our awareness of time. There are many elements to being human – talking, writing, loving, searching for understanding of the cosmos and of our place within it, reaching for the moon and towards the stars: a long list. We are also conscious, and conscious of time. We are finite beings and we know it. The clock is ticking and we hear it.

As far as we know, we human beings of Planet Earth are the first and only animals to have felt the unbearable weight of forever – time before we were alive, time continuing after we are dead. We are the first creatures in the universe that have been bothered by the need to remember and to mourn.

At the moment of our awakening as a species, Earth – even the universe itself – awoke too. The clock started ticking and someone, somewhere, counted one day more, one day less. Time, therefore, starts with us. This is our blessing and our curse.

And so history starts with us as well. Only we have bothered to wonder what came before – and to keep a record of events as they unfold. This urge to keep track is part service to the future and part vanity. In addition to giving our descendants the backstory that will provide a context to their present, we might hope to be remembered there, in the future – to have been noticed and to have mattered.

Memory, remembering, history . . . these are uniquely human too. But they are made of our awareness of time. How much have I had? How much do I have left? We are Earth's youngest apes – feeble, without claws or fangs, with neither speed nor strength, naked of feather or fur – and yet beneath thin caps of bone we are possessed of minds that reach forwards and backwards in time. It is a predicament. In all the universe, we alone are troubled by 'when'?

Without the ticking clock of time, though, we are adrift – in our lives and in the universe. As it is, because of our awareness of time, we are also confronted by the awful (and I use the word 'awful' in its old sense, so that I mean time must give us pause, is worthy of our respect and our fear).

Time, this knowledge we have of time, makes life worth living. However much time I get with my wife, my children, will never be enough and so makes it a gift of incalculable value.

Above all, I think time blesses us with responsibility. Alone among the animals, we might understand our predicament. Our time, however much each of us has, is limited. We know what is coming. In the meantime, it is up to us to decide what to do with the time we have. No matter what must happen, we might choose to pick up and shoulder as much as possible of the blessing and burden of being awake for a moment in an infinite universe.

Time, this knowledge we have of time, makes life worth living. However much time I get with my wife, my children, will never be enough and so makes it a gift of incalculable value. This, if we are lucky enough to know it, is what it is to be alive and human.

JANET ELLIS

TV presenter

Our teenage years are a unique moment when we're not quite children, yet not quite adults, says former *Blue Peter* presenter Janet Ellis. This allows us to explore and experience life to the fullest – and it is this precious time that truly makes us human.

We all share an extraordinary thing that marks us out as different from any other animal in the kingdom. It's a state that is only gifted to human beings and is shared by no other: adolescence. That unique limbo after infancy and before adulthood: a time of experiment, life rehearsal and colossal introspection. And, probably, bad poetry. We are the only species that doesn't require its young to go from wobbly first steps or wriggly larva to full-blown, capable-of-finding-its-own-food adult, with nothing in between.

And what do we do with this gift? Although we tend to remember being a teenager with ease, at first sight we don't seem to use the time especially well. We tend to dismiss it later, not value it, once we're on the other side. Of course, we know it's when we discover love and sex as if we'd just thought of them. We do wild and crazy things in adolescence because we can't imagine danger. We are reckless with time in our youth because we already know there's not much of it until we're old (like, over thirty). But are we actually benefiting from this precious, fleeting state – or just using it to bemoan spots, exams and the stupidity of our elders?

I think we are. I think we do use this time as essential practice in being our more mature selves, taking life to the extreme in preparation for our pared down, more sensible lives. Our growing bodies are strong and flexible. We can stay up late and still appear refreshed if we need to – or, more accurately, if we want to. The teenage body can cope with all sorts of frankly terrible food and drink, and it can usually repel ill-advised 'additives' too. Mostly free from the burden of cooking, let alone shopping, for meals, the teenager is often unconstrained by even eating the right thing at the right time. Mealtimes are for losers, after all. Teenagers are free to just roam the metaphorical plain, waiting for us old lions to kill, then being highly critical of the quality of the meat.

It's the adolescent's right to be annoying and provocative because it reminds us all of the fire inside.

Being an adolescent lets you walk (or, more accurately, hurtle) to the outer limits of your personality and passions, safe in the knowledge you're not actually in charge. Teenagers don't acknowledge the fact that it's a protected state, but of course it is. It's where we learn about relationships; nothing is ever as intense as the technicolour friendships of our youth. We feel emotions more deeply than we think anyone ever has before and fall in love – hard and beautifully – for the first time. But when we hurt, or even when we heal, we are surrounded by people who care for us and who – more importantly – have been there before. Somewhere deep in their animal brain, the necessary information is loaded: stuff happens, it's happened before, you'll be okay.

The process of growing up is not one of changing, I think; it is learning to suppress what's anti-social or self-destructive inside us and enhance our best attributes. Nature allows us, briefly, to be our own work-in-progress. It's the adolescent's right to be annoying and provocative because it reminds us all of the fire inside. If we went straight from cradle to the accounts department or the *corps de ballet*, if there was nothing between teething and teaching or talent-show producer, we'd miss out on the greatest adventures and the privilege of growing up gradually.

Let's celebrate the visible manifestation of this liminal time, when we're held – fragile yet resilient – between two important stages of life. There is still, after all, an adolescent inside each and every one of us.

JULIA DONALDSON

Children's author

For Julia Donaldson, what makes us human is our ability to look backwards and forwards – to brood on the past or look back on happy memories, and to fret about what's to come or look forwards in keen anticipation.

In Robert Burns's 'To a Mouse', the poet pities a little rodent whose home has been destroyed, but then goes on to say:

> *Still, thou art blest, compar'd wi' me!*
> *The present only toucheth thee:*
> *But Och! I backward cast my e'e,*
> *On prospects drear!*
> *An' forward tho' I canna see,*
> *I guess an' fear!*

Burns envies the mouse because it does not possess the human being's awareness of time. It's true that we humans spend much of our lives brooding over the past. Why did I embarrass my children by complaining about that quiche in the café? Why didn't I realise that woman had a tattoo before sounding off about them? Why wasn't I more interested in what my parents did in the war before it was too late to ask them?

Then there is the future to worry about. We lie awake fretting about what we have to do and what might go wrong; we get pre-exam nerves, and stage fright, and although we may try to block out fears of death, we know we are not here for ever.

It's easy to see why Burns regards the ability to look backwards and forwards as a curse, and also why advocates of mindfulness want us to live more in the present (though I can't quite understand why this involves so much colouring in). But of course the curse is also a blessing. Memories, especially shared ones, can bring happiness and often laughter.

Then there are the photograph albums: my daughters-in-law love seeing pictures of my sons when they were toddlers, covered in chocolate ice cream, or teenagers with pillar-box red hair and Goth chains. And we can go back further than our own lives, researching the family tree, finding out about the origins of the words we use every day or the history of the houses around us. We can dig for Roman coins, or watch David Attenborough explaining how dinosaurs evolved into birds.

When I'm at the piano, struggling with a Beethoven bagatelle, however imperfectly I'm playing, I'm somehow with Beethoven, playing the notes he wrote.

For me, one of the amazing feelings, when I'm at the piano, struggling with a Beethoven bagatelle, is that, however imperfectly I'm playing, I'm somehow with Beethoven, playing the notes he wrote – there's a profound sense of contact with a genius of the past.

And then there's the enjoyment of looking forwards, of imagining a holiday, rehearsing a play, wrapping up the Christmas presents. Often anticipation can be more pleasurable than the event itself. And there's nothing like suspense – a nail-biting match between Federer and Djokovic or Dundee and Dundee United, or a gripping episode of *Breaking Bad*.

Which brings me on to my own job as a storyteller – a job I just wouldn't have if we weren't concerned with the past and the future and what happens next. It's hard to imagine a world with no stories, with no 'Once upon a time' beginnings. There doesn't always have to be a 'happily ever after', and not every single wish needs to come true, but to my mind, a good story should leave the reader with a very human feeling – hope.

Our Future

What it means to be human has changed
from our early origins to the present day, and
never more rapidly than in recent centuries.
These essays consider how humanity has
progressed, the benefits and drawbacks
of technological advancement, and the
forces that will shape our future.

JOE SIMPSON

Mountaineer

After his nearly fatal climb of the Siula Grande in the Peruvian Andes, Joe Simpson knows more than most what it is like to take risks. He argues that humans are distinguished by this ability to imagine the future and make decisions based on the promise of a reward.

We own the future. Our ability to conceive of the future and use that knowledge to grow as a species is what distinguishes us from all other living creatures.

A deer with a broken leg will wait to die or be taken by a predator. It can no longer breed, or feed or stay with the herd. It is finished. On an instinctive primordial level, it has always known this and it has no ability to change this inevitability. A human being, however, can imagine a time in the future when, if shelter and food can be found, their broken leg may have healed and life may continue. This perception is an enormously powerful advantage.

Scientists will tell you that one of the signs of true intelligence is the capacity to willingly take risks and benefit from the rewards gained. Risk and reward are symbiotic. Monkeys and primates are innovative creative risk-takers, but humans are truly exceptional chancers. Our ancestors took extraordinarily courageous risks and a great many died doing so, but they saw the risk was worth the reward. They could perceive a time in the future when, if they made the necessary decisions, they could immensely improve their lot.

So, some brave souls built tiny vessels and sailed across vast oceans to settle in new and fertile lands. Others domesticated camels that enabled them to traverse lethal deserts. They scaled great mountain ranges to find new pastures beyond. In so doing, they became the most successful and dominant species on earth, which has not entirely been to the benefit of the planet and the rest of its inhabitants.

We own the future. Our ability to conceive of the future and use that knowledge to grow as a species is what distinguishes us from all other living creatures.

Our ability to conceive of the future is at the core of what it is to be human. Instead of foraging, we realised that collected seeds would grow into many more plants than we could find in any one season. We could see that we no longer needed to follow the food. Making and using tools is all about seeing what they can be used for in the future. The nomadic life became a farming life. Villages became towns.

We educated our children so they, too, could secure their futures. Language enabled us to organise this steady building for the future. Our small nomadic groups became communities bonded by language, cemented by rules, protected by force. These, in turn, became cities and nation states, protected by vast armies forever warring about perceived future threats. Organised warfare, above all else, accelerated the development of our technologies, until now, within the space of a century, we have gone from first flight to exploring the stars.

Humans always look to the future. Animals exist in the present and remain tied to it. It has led to wonders and nightmares in equal measure. It may even be the end of us. No other species has come remotely near humanity in this regard. Only we see the future.

JON CULSHAW

Impressionist and comedian

A vivid and charmingly optimistic look at human history that points towards a brighter future, Jon Culshaw's answer is at once down-to-earth and greatly uplifting.

What makes us human? I'd say curiosity, kindness and potential.

I've always been intrigued to consider the incredible potential and advances that humans may be capable of in the far future. Fascinating because, in so many ways, it's impossible to tell what the amazing potential of the human being is. Some of the most outlandish predictions from the mid-nineteenth century about technology in the twentieth century fell way short of reality. Jules Verne, one of the most inventive minds of his time, when asked to imagine modes of transport in 1950, described a huge Victorian living room with lavish velvet furniture inside a giant gondola suspended from a colossal balloon, which could travel from New York to San Francisco in just a few weeks.

It's our great sense of curiosity that keeps the human race advancing. Thirty-five thousand years ago, Neanderthals were living their harsh lives, making flint tools. That may sound like a hugely long time, but in terms of deep, astronomical time, 35,000 years is less than a micro flicker. Within that time, humans have progressed from being subsistence survivors to walking on the moon, imaging Pluto, populating Mars with robots and landing probes on comets.

Of course, not all advancements bring goodness. Our history and present days are scarred with too many dark, tragic events – by-products of the human condition. But I always choose to be optimistic for the long-term scheme of things.

Our Future

I choose the belief that we possess enough simple kindness, and enough positivity in our survival instinct, to make sure that, eventually, we can evolve past too many turbulent times.

I remember the story of an eight-year-old child watching the news who asked his mother, 'Mum, why do people do such horrible things?' His mum replied, 'I don't know, but look at all the people helping.'

If the 4.6-billion-year-old age of Planet Earth were compressed into twenty-four hours, then the first single-cell organisms would have appeared at around 4 o'clock in the afternoon. The dinosaurs would have appeared at around 10.30 p.m. Modern humans would have appeared as late as fifteen seconds to midnight. When we think about it this way, the human race is a very young species indeed.

**I remember the story of an eight-year-old child
watching the news who asked his mother,
'Mum, why do people do such horrible things?'
His mum replied, 'I don't know, but look at
all the people helping.'**

We can imagine ourselves as the equivalent of a toddler, still having tantrums and throwing our toys out of the pram. Let's hope it follows that our future becomes more matured and peacefully harmonious as our species becomes older. I'm optimistic that it will be, and I think our human curiosity, kindness and intelligence will help us get there.

We need to continue to pursue science. I'm inspired to think of future days when we've reached beyond Earth, into the solar system and the galaxy. When humankind has proudly taken its place as a multi-planetary species. I think this will prove to be a marvellously enlightened chapter in our human future.

We see a snapshot of how this could be by looking at the International Space Station. Astronauts from all over the world, working together in a wonderful spirit of international cooperation. The everyday terrestrial, political squabbles read out by Huw Edwards seem a primitive irrelevance from up there.

So, for me, what makes us human is our curiosity and intelligence. Our kindness and the sheer wonder of our potential. 'We're all made of star stuff.' So said Carl Sagan. That the substance of the universe, elements and matter from long since dead stars should eventually coalesce into sentient beings with consciousness and intelligence. We are a way for the universe to perceive itself.

STEVEN PINKER

Psychologist and Harvard professor

A unique opportunity to read the refined thoughts of a prominent psychologist on the most profound question one can ask. Steven Pinker acknowledges our weaknesses, but also celebrates our mission to constantly better ourselves.

I'm on record as having a jaundiced view of human nature. I agree with Immanuel Kant that out of the crooked timber of humanity, no truly straight thing can be made. At the same time, I'm a champion of human progress. I have presented data showing that we truly are getting better – not all the time, as The Beatles claimed, but on average and over the long run. What makes us human is that these views of the human condition are not contradictory.

As nature made us, human beings got off to an unpromising start. We were shaped by natural selection, a ruthlessly competitive process, which fashioned us for survival and reproduction, not wisdom and happiness. We are vulnerable to cognitive illusions: we reason from anecdotes and stereotypes, and seek evidence that confirms our convictions while blowing off evidence that disconfirms them. We blame misfortune on evil-doers, while placing haloes on our own heads. We confuse goodness with purity, loyalty and conformity, and justice with revenge. Our most intimate relationships are strained by jealousy, rivalry, manipulation. Our appetites can get the better of us: we surrender to fatal attractions, crave pleasures that are bad for us, regret a choice the morning after, and ignore advice to be careful what we wish for.

Yet human nature has also been blessed with resources that open a space for a kind of redemption. We are endowed with the

46

power to combine ideas recursively, to have thoughts about our thoughts. We have an instinct for language, allowing us to share the fruits of our experience and ingenuity. We are deepened with the capacity for sympathy – for pity, imagination, compassion, commiseration. Our outsize frontal lobes can exert self-control, allowing us to hold our horses, count to ten, save for a rainy day.

These gifts have found ways to magnify their own power. The scope of language has been augmented by the written, printed and electronic word. Our circle of sympathy has been expanded by history, journalism and the narrative arts. Our puny rational faculties have been multiplied by the rules and institutions of reason: intellectual curiosity, open debate, scepticism of authority and dogma, and the burden of proof to verify ideas by confronting them against reality. We evolve norms of acceptable behaviour: what a decent person just doesn't do.

We will never have a perfect world, and it would be dangerous to seek one.

As the spiral of recursive improvement gathers momentum, we have eked out victories against the forces that grind us down, not least the darker parts of our own nature. We penetrate the mysteries of the cosmos, including life and mind. We live longer, suffer less, learn more, get smarter, and enjoy more small pleasures and rich experiences. Fewer of us are killed, assaulted, enslaved, oppressed or exploited by the others.

From a few oases, the territories with peace and prosperity are growing, and could someday encompass the globe. Much suffering remains, and tremendous peril. But ideas on how to reduce them have been voiced, and an infinite number of others are yet to be conceived. We will never have a perfect world, and it would be dangerous to seek one. But there is no limit to the betterments we can attain if we continue to apply knowledge to enhance human flourishing.

Yes, you can be realistic about human folly and hopeful about human progress. They both come from an appreciation of the same thing: that infuriating, endearing, mysterious, predictable and eternally fascinating thing we call human nature.

BONNIE GREER

Author, playwright and critic

We must listen to the younger generations, as they will be the ones to drive the world, Bonnie Greer argues in this passionate essay.

Disruption and intervention, flexibility and the ability to change, are what make us human.

What will be the biggest challenge of the twenty-first century? Not global warming, terrorism, the economy, the human population explosion, super bugs or an ageing society. The biggest challenge will be our capacity to expand our brains and our minds; and to be flexible.

Multi-linguality, transnationality, multi-culturalism, transgender, cross-border multi-nationality: these will be the factors and quality of the world by the end of this century. It cannot be halted. Rigid, by-rote curricula that do not allow for intervention and disruption (by that I mean the ability to change) from both students and teachers – and parents, up to a point – will be as useful to the digital natives, who will be increasingly creating things, as a horse and buggy is to Lewis Hamilton.

It is the Millennials – that generation born between 1980 and 1995 – who will drive this world, for good and evil. They are the digital natives who we *must* listen to, and be flexible enough to allow at the top tables of industry, commerce, government, the arts. Now.

Why? Because our very humanity, our being human, will be challenged by VR – virtual reality – and by AI – artificial intelligence. They will cook our food, drive our cars, take care of us when we're sick, be us: a state of being that I wrote about in my 2009 novel *Entropy*, in which I talked about robots who create empathy by recreating little gestures that their masters do, like the tilt of a head, a vocal inflection. They already talk to each other and are getting smarter (as is our cousin, the chimpanzee, by the way).

We can only be smarter than them by cultivating our flexibility; our inconsistency; our nuance. VR games are starting to appear, but there is a shortage of content. This is an area of job growth – of job boom – but we can't take advantage of it without flexibility. Which, by the way, is the lament re: the Chinese economy. Chinese kids tend to be great at tests, etc, but aren't always particularly flexible: able to think out of the box.

**The biggest challenge will be our capacity
to expand our brains and our minds;
and to be flexible.**

But we have to be flexible, if we are to thrive and survive. The fact is that, by 2027, 75% of the S&P 500 firms today will be replaced by new ones – eleven years from now. It is said that design-led products will win in the future. Design is creativity. Creativity is the natural state of a flexible mind with a multitude of experiences to stimulate it. We can no longer remain siloed.

To be human is to expand, not contract; to try; to fail and to go forward. Humankind is on one of its great migratory arcs – we are a migratory species, after all – and cannot be stopped. Variety, variety, variety and making way for the young are important for our survival, our happiness and our delight – some of the gifts of a flexible, expansive, forward-facing future.

NICK CLEGG

Former leader of the Liberal Democrats

In a world where it is often easier to be cynical than sincere, Nick Clegg argues that we need to take feeling seriously. Our lives are shaped by emotion as much as they are by cold, hard facts, and if the robots are poised to take over, this is something we need to keep a hold on now more than ever!

Imagine we lived in a world run by robots. It isn't hard. They can already assemble computers, play chess and drive cars. So, imagine a world in which they can also talk, clean your house and make a nice cup of tea. This world is only – technologically speaking – a heartbeat away. What will, then, set us humans apart? If they can do the handiwork of humans, what is there left for those of us made of flesh and blood?

Film-makers have grappled with this unsettling prospect – a world in which machines and humans become interchangeable – for years. *Blade Runner, A.I., WALL-E, I, Robot, Oblivion, Chappie*: all of them, in different ways, depict a future in which the boundaries between biology and technology begin to blur.

As my children roam the streets glued to *Pokémon Go* and Miriam and I book holidays, meals, gifts and the weekly shop online, I like to think I'm pretty comfortable with the dizzying pace of technological change. But even I find myself muttering grumpy, middle-aged platitudes about how technology will not change our world as much as people claim. I listen to all the hype about the 'internet of things', where inanimate objects – from our fridges to our toilets – will, we are told, be able to babble to each other like animals in a zoo and I think to myself, 'I bet it won't really turn out like that.'

Our Future

Elon Musk, the swashbuckling founder of Tesla, waxes lyrical about a new age in which technology will generate a parallel consciousness, a doppelgänger world in which the truth and an all-encompassing CGI universe feel just as real as each other. I shake my head incredulously. Maybe that's how it feels in the high tech, android nirvana of California, but a rainy day in Putney or Sheffield still feels like . . . well, a rainy day in Putney or Sheffield.

But what if my middle-aged scepticism is wrong? What if the machines are really poised to take over? What, then, can I hold on to as uniquely, inalienably human?

What if the machines are really poised to take over? What, then, can I hold on to as uniquely, inalienably human?

Well, here's my challenge to our robotic cousins: listen to a piece of music and tell me what you feel. You poor, poor robots: you will feel nothing. A painful, heart-wrenching song will leave you cold.

So maybe that's what really makes us human: we can feel. Love, hate, revenge, pity, sorrow, guilt, fear, pride, joy, jealousy, shame, compassion – and so, so many more emotions that flicker, rage and fade within all of us, all of the time, every day, every night and everywhere across the globe. Maybe, in the end, that is what sets us humans apart.

Of course, the one breed of humans who are widely held to be bereft of much emotion – indeed, some would say are barely human at all – are politicians. Along with journalists, bankers and estate agents, politicians are generally depicted as venal, amoral, unprincipled creatures incapable of empathising with real people in the real world.

So here's a dramatic revelation: politicians are human too. Indeed, politics is an intensely emotional vocation. Hope versus fear is the oldest contest in politics. It is a contest of competing emotions, not policies. People tend to vote with their hearts, not their heads. That's why the emotionally compelling – if deeply misleading – refrain to 'take back control' in the EU referendum campaign was bound to trump George Osborne's bloodless statistics about the impact of Brexit on household finances.

Descartes said, 'I think, therefore I am.' Maybe, what actually sets us humans apart – politicians included – is really this: 'I feel, therefore I am.'

PAUL McKENNA

Psychotherapist

What separates us from robots are our imperfections, according to Paul McKenna. Although he champions people becoming the best version of themselves, he also values imperfection, and says we should ultimately focus on being authentic.

I have been in the trenches for thirty years as a psychotherapist, working both with people who are severely challenged and also helping those who are high achievers. This is what I have learned about being human.

We all have certain qualities that make us human. On a purely biological level, humans are electrical impulses and chemicals. We are an amazing ecosystem of thoughts, emotions, choices and actions, which build themselves into the lives that we live. We are each a set of multi-sensory experiences of successive moments of now.

However, there are some things about our humanity we all know but can't prove. If you ask a neuroscientist and a poet what love is, although both may be correct in what they say, you'll get two very different answers. We all know what love feels like, but you can't put love under a microscope. If you use the Null Set Hypothesis, which is the gateway to scientific proof, you could prove that, when people are in love, there are electrical and chemical changes in a person, but that wouldn't fully explain what love is. I love science, but science is only useful if it has a date on it. Light is either particle or wave, depending upon the century you were born in. It happens to be both.

I also like the Buddhist philosophy. The Buddha was not a god, he was a man who perfected himself, and I am drawn to anything that involves human evolution and perfection. My job, essentially, is to give people hope and help people change. Sometimes, it's to help change a behaviour, but rather than bolt on a new personality or help them to become something they're not, I do my best to help people to become better versions of themselves – to be more authentic – and, in very simple terms, I believe that authenticity is at the heart of being human.

However, that doesn't mean we all have to be perfect – I think that perfectionism is something that can work for us or against us. Indeed, I would say that, very often, some of the biggest learning experiences that I've ever had, or I've noticed other people have, have been when mistakes have been made in our lives. Often, it's our imperfections that give us our humanity.

For example, if you were to put in the Albert Hall an orchestra of robots, the robots would be able to play every instrument perfectly. Every note would be perfect, the timing would be perfect, but it wouldn't be human. It's the imperfections and, if you like, the soul and the passion that we put into the playing of the instruments, rather than just a series of perfect zeros and ones, that make us human.

> **In the next few years, we are going to see a marriage between human physiology and cyber technology, which will mean that human beings and computers will merge.**

So, I believe being human is living a life that is filled with curiosity, purpose, making mistakes (or, if you like, having 'learning experiences'), but also wondrous creativity, because, once upon a time, there was nothing in the world – it was just Planet Earth – but look how much we have created, look how much there is now! All the art, all the science, all the genius creativity, all the amazing inventions – many of them positive, some of them negative – that human beings have made.

The human race is about to experience a profound change as human beings, because according to the great American scientist and philosopher Ray Kurzweil, who has written about this extensively, in the next few years we are going to see a marriage between human physiology and cyber technology, in different forms, such as artificial intelligence, which will mean that human beings and computers will merge. In a sense, we will go through a massive evolutionary jump, from which we can never return. So, being human is something that perhaps we understand to some extent now, but will be very different in the future.

GARRY KASPAROV

Chess grandmaster

Since being the first chess world champion to lose to a computer in 1997, Garry Kasparov has devoted much of his time to thinking about how we work with and against machines. Kasparov's highly thoughtful answer argues that it is through this relationship that we realise our fullest human potential.

The nature of our humanity is defined by how we use our bodies and minds, but also by how we use the technology we create to enhance and eventually substitute those physical and mental efforts. We can follow our evolutionary path from the trees and caves to villages and cities, and we can put our inventions on a parallel timeline. Hunter-gatherers made weapons and farmers built tools. Towns and trade led to longer lifespans and gradually lifted the burden of dedicating every waking moment – and every mental process – to survival.

When and wherever this occurred, civilisation progressed in every way. Science and medicine flourished, as did art and literature. Philosophy, mathematics, every field of human knowledge leapt forward. Throughout history, the societies we look back at as the most successful are those that nourished this life of the mind. We recall with contempt the hordes that sacked cities and burned libraries.

There is no way to separate ourselves from our inventions, nor should we try to do so. Our technology is an intrinsic part of this process, a process of distillation of what makes us unique, of what makes us human: our restless minds. We become attached to our labours and routines and romanticise them even as we discard them for new ones that are far safer, more efficient, and economically beneficial. We often preserve them as art forms or pastimes, kneading bread and knitting baby blankets by choice instead of by necessity. It's ironic, of course, that the developed world does for relaxation things that the developing world strives to leave behind. Nostalgia, too, is a powerful human force.

It is also generally a harmless one. It only becomes a problem when it inhibits us from continuing our civilisational quest to innovate, to push ourselves, and to find new ways to pass our tasks on to our technology. When we seek to maintain the status quo instead of taking risks and moving forward, we undermine another fundamental element of our humanity: our sense of purpose.

We are the product of stardust and alchemy, imbued with a consciousness that forces us to ask why we are here – and each of us has our own answer, or no answer at all. This uncertainty fuels us, and also separates man from beast. We are more than our cognitive abilities, a cauldron of emotions and needs and desires. These most human factors can lead us astray, cause unpredictable results, and yet they are responsible for all that we are and what we have achieved.

I have found that nearly every discussion of human and machine cognition inevitably trends away from science into philosophy. What is intelligence – artificial or not? What is consciousness? What makes us human?

Our machines are steady precisely where we are fallible. They can tame the uncertainty, enabling us to take greater risks and rise to greater heights. We must trust them, and teach them. We are fantastic at training our machines how to do our tasks, and we will only get better at it. The only solution is to keep creating new tasks that even we don't know how to do ourselves. We need new frontiers and the will to explore them. Our technology excels at removing the difficulty and unpredictability from our lives, and so we must seek out ever more difficult and uncertain challenges.

I have found that nearly every discussion of human and machine cognition inevitably trends away from science into philosophy. What is intelligence, artificial or not? What is consciousness? What makes us human? In the end, being human means being able to ask these questions, to need to ask these questions, knowing all the while that we may never know the answers.

The Human Animal

These essays consider our origins as
intelligent primates and ask what separates
humankind from the rest of the animal world.
While there is much we have in common with
other creatures, a few key traits stand out
as uniquely, definitively 'human'.

RICHARD DAWKINS

Scientist

We know Richard Dawkins doesn't shy away from pointing out what he sees as humanity's foibles. But in this uplifting answer, he takes us on a journey through all the reasons science gives us to be optimistic.

Human beings are animals. We aren't plants and we aren't bacteria, we are animals.

Among animals we are apes, specifically African apes. The other African apes – chimpanzees, bonobos and gorillas – are closer cousins to us than they are to the Asian apes: orangutans and gibbons.

So, one way to understand what makes us human is to ask: 'What makes us different from the other apes, and from the rest of the animal kingdom? What makes us special?' For instance, unlike all the other apes, we walk on two legs, and this frees our hands to do all kinds of things that other apes can't do. And (perhaps the two are connected) we have much bigger brains than the other apes.

There's another way to interpret the question 'What makes us human?', which I won't be dealing with, although it is important. What makes us humane? What are the qualities that we admire and aspire to: qualities that make us human as opposed to brutish?

We have big brains. Other species are marked out by other qualities. Swifts and albatrosses are spectacularly good at flying, dogs and rhinoceroses at smelling, bats at hearing, moles, aardvarks and wombats at digging. Human beings are not good at any of those things. But we do have very big brains; we are good at thinking, remembering, calculating, imagining, speaking. Other species can communicate, but no other species has true language

63

with open-ended grammar. No other species has literature, music, art, mathematics or science. No other species makes books, or complicated machines such as cars, computers and combine harvesters. No other species devotes substantial lengths of time to pursuits that don't contribute directly to survival or reproduction.

Our uniquely big brains evolved after our habit of walking on two legs. We can now trace our ancestry through a pretty continuous series of fossils, and are confident that our ancestors of three million years ago were members of the genus *Australopithecus*. The best-known australopithecine is Lucy – so called because the camp record player in Ethiopia was blaring out The Beatles' 'Lucy in the Sky with Diamonds' when the fossil hunters returned to camp with the momentous news of her discovery. Lucy had a chimp-sized brain but she walked on her hind legs. It is probably no accident that our brains started swelling like evolutionary balloons after our hands were freed from the burden of walking and could concentrate on carrying food or manipulating tools.

One way to understand what makes us human is to ask: 'What makes us different from the other apes, and from the rest of the animal kingdom? What makes us special?'

But human beings have only recently shown how very special they are. Fifty thousand years ago, we had the same bodies and brains as today and we probably had language. But we didn't have much by way of art, and our artefacts were limited to the functional – stone tools for hunting and butchering, for instance.

That changed around 40,000 years ago, when the archaeological record shows a sudden magnificent flowering of art and even musical instruments. Cultural evolution – which outpaces by orders of magnitude the superficially similar genetic evolution that had given rise to our big brains in the first place – went into overdrive.

Next came the transition from the hunter-gatherer to the settled agriculture way of life, soon to be followed by cities, markets, governments, religion and war. The Industrial Revolution expanded cities to megalopolises, propelling our species to worldwide (and potentially disastrous) domination, and even seeing us reach out to the moon and planets.

Simultaneously, the human mind has reached out to the wider universe, and far beyond the time constraints of a human lifespan. We now know that the world limiting our ancestors' brief lives is a tiny speck orbiting a small star among some hundred billion stars, in an average galaxy among some hundred billion galaxies. We know that the world began 4.6 billion years ago, and the universe 13.8 billion. We understand the evolutionary process that generated us and all DNA-based life.

There's plenty that we still don't understand, but we are working on it. And the urge to do so is perhaps the most inspiring of all the unique qualities that make us human.

BRIAN BLESSED

Actor, writer, presenter

Delivered in his inimitable style, Brian Blessed's wide-ranging essay is full of fascinating facts about how the unique qualities of our brains fundamentally shape our vivid and complex existence.

What makes us human? It is a terribly difficult question, and one that I find almost impossible to answer. I mean, it would be easy to gloss over the subject and pontificate about love, compassion, self-sacrifice, and all the staggering achievements of mankind. But I feel that would be copping out. So, where to begin?

Forgive me if I take you on a short history lesson. It is understood the earth is 4 billion, 600 million years old. Six hundred million years after its birth, the vast oceans appeared. Six hundred million years ago, the miraculous Cambrian Explosion took place. Suddenly, the oceans throbbed with many different life forms and the first vertebrates appeared. In that dramatic geological landscape there were winged insects, amphibians, reptiles and the first trees. After the magnificent dinosaurs, the primates arose: our great ancestors.

Less than 10 million years ago, the first creatures that resembled humans evolved, accompanied by a spectacular increase in brain size. It is the past that is the clue to the complex nature of man. Man: an impressive being that made his entrance on to the world stage with formidable effect. It is the brain of this creature that intrigues me the most. Deep inside is the brain stem, and capping the brain stem is the R-complex. This is the seat of aggression, ritual and territoriality, which evolved hundreds of millions of years ago in our reptilian ancestors. Deep inside the skull of every one of us, there is the brain of a crocodile – 'never make friends with a crocodile'.

Surrounding the R-complex is the limbic system, or mammalian brain. This is the part of the brain that is associated with moods and emotions. Living an uneasy truce with these primitive brains is a cerebral cortex, where matter is formed into consciousness. It is here that we have ideas and inspirations. Here we read and write, compose music, form the sciences and meditate on all things sacred. This is a distinction of our species. The root of our humanity. It is what makes us human. Each of us has over one hundred billion cells in our brain, comparable to the number of stars in a giant galaxy. The cerebral cortex is liberation. No longer are we at the mercy of the reptilian brain.

I experienced the cortex in all its glory when I reached 28,400 feet on Mount Everest in 1993 without oxygen. It was a stunning sensation. A sparkling field of rhythmic, flashing points. When I closed my eyes coming down the mountain, I could see the cortex and observe millions of flashing lights, dissolving and emerging in a sea of cosmic delight. I couldn't stop laughing. But you can see that the cortex has to deal with the ancient R-complex, the seat of aggression. It is here that anger, greed, war and strife is nurtured. This is our problem.

An old Dervish in Armenia informed me that the term human means tiger-man. We need to quieten the tiger. Will we succeed? I believe so. But we cannot afford to sit on our backsides. Our wonderful Earth is taking a terrible beating. She is being wounded from all sides. However, I have to say that thousands of people are making a colossal effort to save Planet Earth. I am convinced they will win.

Our intelligence has provided us with awesome powers. It is not yet clear whether we have the wisdom to avoid our own self-destruction. Yet, we have so much to be proud of. In our insatiable quest for knowledge, we are revealed as fine, brave explorers who are heaven-bent on seeking limitless horizons. Science works. It is not perfect and it can be misused. I find myself huffing and puffing trying to keep up with it all. Exploratory spacecraft are being launched to study seventy worlds. Twelve human beings have been on the moon. We are the children of stardust.

My biggest love in life is space. We are venturing into it. It is our destiny. I long to journey to the planets and the distant stars. They feel almost like a race memory. Just imagine climbing Mount Olympus on Mars, three times higher than Mount Everest. Yet there are moments when I am chilled when I think what some humans would do to these new worlds.

We are the children of stardust.

When Pandora opened the box, she let out all the dark furies. When she tried to close it, a sweet, small creature flew out and said: 'I am hope, I am hope!' Ladies and Gentlemen, we have hope, which embraces the heart and is the essence of the soul. We have begun to seek our origins. We are stardust yearning for the stars. I speak for Planet Earth. As long as we love and protect it, we will survive and prosper.

P. D. JAMES

Crime novelist

P. D. James (1920–2014) explores the history of human evolution to show us how asking big questions is uniquely human. But then she pushes this conclusion further, encouraging us to think about how this makes us responsible for our fellow human beings and the planet.

What makes us human is the brain which enables us to ask just this question.

Increasingly we are aware of how much we share with the animal kingdom and how close indeed is our DNA to that of the higher mammals. We are increasingly hearing how much we all have in common with the animals. Animals often show at least an equal concern with looking after their young. We know that elephants can grieve, that chimpanzees and other apes learn to use tools and even to share them, so there is the beginning of what we think of as unselfish sharing for mutual benefit.

But animals, even those whose DNA is closest to ours, cannot make or control fire. One wonders how this powerful tool was first discovered: perhaps by primitive man constantly rubbing two dry sticks together in a moment of boredom and producing a spark which lighted a pile of dry leaves. With this apparent miracle, a significant step in the long rise to humanity was taken. Fire could be used to frighten away predators and provide the warmth which enabled early man to survive extreme cold. It also gave him the ability to cook meat and render it more digestible and life-sustaining. The making of fire was one of the most important discoveries which set human beings on the path to domination.

But most people, when faced with the question of what makes us human, give thought to a wider dimension than the difference between *Homo sapiens* and the animal kingdom: a dimension which includes ethics and morality and the recognition of responsibility for other than the immediate family or species. An animal has no concept of reality outside its own life and that of its young, and its place in the herd. Because we have the capacity to imagine and sympathise with the emotions of others, including their pain, surely that implies a responsibility to alleviate suffering and promote well-being among all sentient creatures, including the animals of which we make use for our sustenance, convenience and pleasure.

To describe a person as acting like an animal is an insult, while the expression 'crime against humanity' implies that there is some behaviour regarded as so appalling that the perpetrator is offending against a recognised code of what is acceptable from human beings. If the offence is committed by a single individual, he is commonly labelled a psychopath, a diagnosis which it is seldom possible to follow with effective treatment. If the outrage is committed by a country, as with genocide, international opprobrium and a system of reparation, where this is possible, usually follow. We have the ability, both internationally and at home, to militate against behaviour we view as unacceptable and make it illegal and punishable by law.

We set up complicated legal and social contrivances designed to enable us to live together in peace and safety which, in all civilised societies, are accepted and incorporated in words. The extent and richness of a country's language is among the most important measures of its civilisation, and it is primarily language which makes us human.

When we think about what it means to be human, we are often considering what personal preoccupations, ambitions and conduct to others make us unique creatures on the planet. Unlike animals, humans occupy their minds with concerns outside the compulsions of sex, food, shelter and the herd: the creation of our universe, and the possibilities that other planets might sustain life and that eventually we shall make contact with other intelligent beings and communicate with them. We create gods, ranging from tribal images in wood and stone to complicated theological arguments, and set up organisations to accommodate these deities and define the obligations of belief and worship.

Unlike animals, we have the means to destroy Planet Earth by our greed, or to make it a safer place in which all living creatures can exist.

But in the end, the simple difference remains. Over millions of years, the Darwinian process of evolution, which has given us a Newton, a Shakespeare and a Mozart, has resulted in the human capacity to think, to wonder, to create and to invent.

The capacity which enables us to use science to destroy each other in wars is also used to conquer disease, with the risk that we reproduce in numbers which inevitably outstrip the natural resources on which we depend. Unlike animals, we have the means to destroy Planet Earth by our greed, or to make it a safer place in which all living creatures can exist.

How should we relate to each other? How do we deal with those aggressive impulses which seem to be in our nature? How do we tolerate people who are different, especially when they come to live among us? How should we educate our young? Is the nuclear family the only right pattern for marriage and parenthood? How can we save the planet which we alone among living creatures have the power to destroy? This is the ultimate question which faces us as humans and it is one to which the animal kingdom is oblivious. It is our responsibility, and it is this responsibility that makes us human.

BILL ODDIE

Naturalist and broadcaster

With his trademark warmth and wry humour, Bill Oddie speaks with wonder about the originality and variety uniquely inherent in human nature.

I sometimes feel that people expect me to say that I prefer animals and birds to people, but I don't. At their best, humans are simply fantastic, but what I do believe is that contact with and caring for animals brings out the best in humanity.

Unfortunately, it also brings out the worst. There is nothing more obnoxious than pointless, mindless destruction and vandalism, be it a bunch of inebriated hooligans on the rampage; a lout of a father (again, probably drunk) abusing a child, a wife or a pet; a crowd baying for blood at an illegal dog fight; or a shooting party blasting the life out of birds purely for 'sport'.

There is a lot of it about, but the fact that there are also many people who are outraged, compassionate and dedicated enough to go into battle for the cause of protecting species other than ourselves is surely a fine example of altruism. By and large, non-humans don't do that. Wildlife tends to be totally self-centred. Mind you, I might have to exempt dogs, who are generally so caring they should perhaps qualify as honorary humans. (Of course there are some pretty nasty dogs around too.)

If I ask myself 'What can humans do that members of the animal kingdom can't?', the answer has to be 'be creative', in the widest possible sense. Okay, animals and birds can build remarkable structures – spiderwebs, bird nests, etc – but there is very little variety within a species. All swallows make mud cups, all termites build mounds. What is wondrous about human creations is that there is an infinite variety.

What's more, this is something we value. Artists, musicians, writers all strive for originality. A recognisable style, a unique voice, a brand-new concept. I know they say that 'there is nothing new', but we still keep on looking, and we constantly contradict the cliché by developing new technology, holding more spectacular events, breaking new athletics records and so on. So, if I had to choose two quintessentially human characteristics, they would be creativity and variety.

Rather than flounder around in more philosophical waters than I am used to, I have just jotted down a few of the human experiences that have delighted me in recent times, and made insidious comparisons with non-human equivalents.

You don't get migrant birds congratulating one another on crossing the Sahara, or gibbons applauding a particularly mellifluous song.

Great sporting performances. The Stanley Mathews Cup final. England winning the World Cup. Murray winning Wimbledon, Linford Christie winning the Olympic 100 metres, Cristiano Ronaldo on song. The London Olympics with Jess Ennis, Mo Farah, our lovely rowers shrieking, 'We're going to be on a stamp!'

It can't be denied that animals achieve all sorts of extraordinary physical feats that are comparatively way beyond what humans can do, but they don't show their appreciation. You don't get migrant birds congratulating one another on crossing the Sahara, or gibbons applauding a particularly mellifluous song. Be honest: with them it's all food, sex and fighting.

If I had to nominate humanity's most deep and delightful creative achievement, it would have to be music. Yes, birds – and some animals and insects – 'sing', the melody or rhythm depending on the species. And there is little doubt that human singers and musicians were originally – and still are – inspired by nature, but boy, have we built on it, over the centuries and round the world. The most uplifting musical experience, for me, is being part of a mixed-race and mixed-age audience at a gig where the mood is one of joy, appreciation and gratitude. The artist often asks, 'Are you having a good time?' and the answer is 'Yeaaaah!' (You may have guessed from that example that, for me, it won't be a classical concert, but there are equivalents, I am sure. I suppose the Proms would qualify, even though they remind me more of the Nuremberg Rally.)

There are human traits that can be good, not so good, or downright evil. For example, principles, beliefs, convictions, religions. They may represent the best in people, or the worst. And what about 'memories?' They say elephants never forget. Incidents and faces, perhaps. But do elephants – or any animals – reminisce, or keep a mental or literal scrapbook the way humans do? And another ability that, we presume, animals don't have – imagination. At best a wonderful aspect of being human, but at worst potentially terrifyingly stressful.

Talking of stress, I know this mindfulness business is meant to restrict our awareness to the present, 'cos the future only exists in our imagination. Yes, but doesn't that preclude enjoyable anticipation – looking forward to something – and having the foresight to avoid disaster? Or is it just that I couldn't meditate on a hazelnut for ten minutes without giggling? That's another thing that makes us human – a sense of humour.

SUSAN GREENFIELD

Scientist, writer and broadcaster

Susan Greenfield's answer is a masterful journey through the science behind this question, exploring the traits that separate humans from animals.

'Human nature' is often invoked but rarely defined. In itself, the term is a paradox: 'human' clearly and immediately disenfranchises the rest of the animal kingdom, whilst 'nature' suggests a quality completely divorced from 'nurture', from the environment. So what is it that every single human being does exclusively, irrespective of historical era or geographical location, that no other animal on the planet ever does at all?

Clearly we need to rule out all the behaviours common to all animals: feeding, reproduction, movement. So, 'human nature' is obviously something more cognitively subtle and sophisticated, but still exclusively human, and not even seen in our nearest evolutionary relatives, the chimps. Some time ago, the archaeologist Steven Mithen suggested that a clue could come from a clear discrepancy between us and them. Chimps are highly sociable animals, living in complex hierarchies with sophisticated inter-relationships. They are also highly dextrous creatures, as witnessed by their well-documented ability to use sticks to 'fish' for termites. So, Mithen asks, how come you never see a chimp wearing a crude necklace, say, or any other symbol of tribal status? Not just *Homo sapiens*, but even our Neanderthal ancestors – apparently – did use such artificial trappings in their lives, from cave art to flowers at burials.

Mithen's idea was that the crucial difference is that humans, unlike chimps, can think metaphorically. Although chimps can solve problems, use objects around them, communicate with each other in sophisticated ways – and, above all, learn – they still lack our ability to see one thing in terms of something else. So could it be this particular ability, seemingly exclusive to our species, which is the clue to the essence of 'human nature'?

Certainly we have the best possible neuronal machinery to make connections. The wonderful thing about being born a human being is that, although we are born with pretty much a full complement of brain cells, it is the development of connections between those cells that accounts for the growth of the brain after birth.

We have the superlative talent to adapt to whatever environment in which we are placed.

We human beings don't run particularly fast, nor see particularly well, and we're not particularly strong compared to others in the animal kingdom: but we have the superlative talent to adapt to whatever environment in which we are placed. Hence, although different species can 'learn' to varying extents, we occupy more ecological niches than any other species on the planet.

How can this quantitative difference in our brains translate into the qualitative difference that we call 'human nature'? We often invoke the term 'human nature' as an excuse for bad behaviour: eating too much, say, or showing off. Interestingly enough, such 'bad behaviour' is summarised well in the Seven Deadly Sins, which have endured over the centuries – and are instantly recognisable, irrespective of the religion – in all human cultures, history and literature. Why are these sins so universal, and considered so bad?

I'd like to suggest that it's because they are exaggerations of normal animal behaviours, but taken out of a normal biological context in an exclusively human tradition, and made to stand for something else – to 'say something about you'.

The sin of greed, for example, comes from the most essential biological activity of feeding, but taken to an excess as a symbol of conspicuous wealth, or perhaps as signifying compensation for perceived personal inadequacies. The size you are will 'say something about you', although the message it sends out is different in different cultures. The sin of sloth is excessive sleep, but exaggerated out of biological context to symbolise a high status that can afford substantial leisure, or the opposite, an underclass that is feckless and lazy. Meanwhile, the tendency towards excessive degrees of copulation, the sin of lust, could reflect your status in terms of the quantity and quality of lovers you are seen to attract, and therefore how wonderful you are. The sin of anger is an exaggeration of the biological behaviour of aggression that could be indicative of status being threatened, for example when someone disagrees with you or doesn't pay appropriate deference to you and your views, your importance.

The sin of envy goes beyond the biological territorial imperative and would be the awareness of the obvious disparity in possessions, health, youth and beauty, and hence in status. In contrast, the sin of vanity would be an exaggeration of biological grooming behaviours, where possessions, health, youth or beauty signify that you have a higher status than others. Finally, the sin of avarice is the ultimate in metaphorical thinking that is based on money, itself a symbol for symbolising greater power.

What makes us human is not so much a need for status, but the expression of that status through symbols dependent on a cultural context, in turn dependent on a personalised, individual brain.

HENRY MARSH

Neurosurgeon

Leading surgeon Henry Marsh's answer considers how our propensity for abstract thought and our knowledge of our own mortality separate us from other primates. He speaks movingly about the delicate tightrope doctors walk between having too little empathy for their patients, and not enough.

What makes us human, compared to a rock? That we consist of countless billions of living cells, all derived from a single cell, that work together, constantly changing in an infinitely complex dance, all striving to preserve the genes contained in that original first cell.

What makes us human compared to a tree or plant? That we move independently. There are good reasons for thinking that brains developed in evolution to permit movement. The famous sea squirt has a primitive brain, called a notochord, in its larval stage when it swims in the sea. In its adult stage, it fastens limpet-like to a rock. It no longer moves and no longer needs its brain, so it reabsorbs it.

What makes us human compared to other animals? Here it gets more difficult. Whales and elephants have larger brains than us (but larger bodies as well); chimpanzees and New Caledonian crows can use tools; bonobos – our closest evolutionary relatives – show empathy and have a sense of fairness; many animals have (admittedly limited) language. Some species of birds can even count.

It is only in the last 11,000 years or so that we started living in large groups as opposed to small hunter-gatherer tribes, and that technological civilisation developed. Our brains now are the same brains as those of our hunting and gathering ancestors. A visitor from outer space visiting Planet Earth 200,000 years ago would not have seen our ancestors as being so very different from the other primates – bonobos, chimpanzees, gorillas, orangutans – with whom we shared the world, and whom we are now driving to extinction.

Perhaps there are two qualities which distinguish us most profoundly from other animals. First is the ability for abstract thought. It is this that enables us to extend the natural love for our kith and kin, which we share with other primates, to other people and creatures to whom we are not related, as a matter of principle and not of feeling. Modern society, technology, huge cities – all depend on co-operation, on understanding that we will benefit from working with people for whom we have no instinctive feelings or affection. Second, is the knowledge of our mortality.

> **Modern society, technology, huge cities –
> all depend on co-operation, on understanding
> that we will benefit from working with people
> for whom we have no instinctive feelings
> or affection.**

This means that the practice of medicine is a very human undertaking. We must try to care for all our patients equally, but we must also find a balance between clinical detachment and compassion, between abstract duty and our feelings. If we actually felt empathy for our patients – meaning that we felt their pain and anxiety as though it was our own – we would not be able to work. And yet, at the same time, we need some kind of empathic understanding of what our patients are going through if we are to be good doctors.

In the past, our ancestors had no choice as to when they died. One of the great problems of modern medicine is over-treatment – of not knowing when to stop, when it is time to tell patients nothing more can be done. Our fear of death is such that this is very difficult indeed. Modern medicine always holds out the hope that the latest, maybe experimental, treatment may yet allow us to live a little longer. But treatment always comes with the risk of complications and side effects – how can we, as doctors, find a balance between giving hope and being realistic? Between our innate feelings of empathy and fear of death, and our rational understanding of the limits of life?

SUE MACGREGOR

Neurosurgeon

Our attempts to distinguish man from beast aren't quite as straightforward as we might think, says Sue MacGregor, who considers not only the differences between us but also the many similarities we share.

Man – that's to say human beings – and of course I hasten to say I include women in that definition before someone rings up to complain. Oh, all right then – mankind. Mankind, almost as far back as written records can tell us, has always been fascinated by what separates us from the animal world. Fascinated by what makes us human.

King Solomon, three thousand years ago, according to the Book of Proverbs, thought long and hard about it; so did Sophocles, the Greek philosopher, quite a few centuries later. And so, most memorably, did Shakespeare. Remember Hamlet's musing?

> *What a piece of work is a man, how noble in reason,*
> *How infinite in faculties, in form and moving,*
> *How express and admirable; in action, how like an angel;*
> > *in apprehension,*
> *How like a god!*

When I first came to live in London, in 1968, *Hair*, the musical, was the must-see musical theatre experience – and if you saw it then, or in a revival, you'll remember the creators of the show used precisely that bit of Shakespeare at one point. Classy lyrics, classy cast, including Elaine Paige, Marsha Hunt and Tim Curry.

*

81

But what exactly is it that makes us human? A unique ability to communicate? No, it can't be that. Animals, birds and fish can communicate with each other in a sometimes extraordinary and often, to us, mysterious way.

Is it an aptitude for empathy? Well, some animals – and I'm thinking especially of elephants – show an impressive amount of empathy with their fellow elephants, protecting their young and those that are sick or disabled. And some animals, birds and even insects have an intensely mutually beneficial relationship with other species.

We shouldn't think that animals are all that different from us.

Is it the ability to think things through and work things out? Watch a squirrel, a chimp or a crow work out a puzzle, man-made or created by nature, to achieve their aims – especially if food is part of the reward. Chimps can fashion their own tools.

We shouldn't think that animals are all that different from us, then. But certainly there are human traits which animals don't possess – like our capacity for deceitfulness, for murderous intent, for unreasonable jealousy and for deliberate cruelty.

The ways in which animals and humans differ in their biological make-up is a matter of constant new discovery. Only recently, the magazine *Nature* published its account of the work of Dr Ajit Varki of the University of California in San Diego, who is a glycobiologist – he studies the sugars in biology. He has discovered a sugary molecule in the covering of cells which only human beings possess – it protects us from a certain strain of malaria.

So it could be just a tiny difference in a single molecule on the outside of a single cell which makes us uniquely human.

That – and the human ability to worship a higher being, human spirituality, if you like; the ability to create beauty in words, and in pictures, and music; the ability to love and cherish and care for another human being, the ability to do good deeds in a nasty world – that's what makes us human. It also makes us do evil, selfish and terrible things, too, which animals don't do. But I'm an optimist – and I believe the good that humans do outweighs the bad.

At least, I very much hope it does.

ESTHER RANTZEN

Journalist and TV presenter

As the founder of the counselling charity ChildLine, Esther Rantzen certainly knows something about human values, and she speaks movingly about the power and generosity of volunteering as something that makes us human.

There are times when you do feel like giving up on the human race. Listening to the atrocities – pointless, merciless atrocities – daily perpetrated in Syria, or the Central African Republic: rapes, tortures, the deliberate killing of children . . . I won't go on. When I went to a preview of the hideously violent film by Ridley Scott, *The Counselor*, I sat in the cinema with my eyes shut, unable to believe that my fellow humans, some highly talented humans, would simulate torture and murder for fun. Is that what makes us human? Pointless killing and maiming of our own species for territory, or power, or just for fun?

And then I thought about cats. One reason I don't like cats is the way they, too, torture their helpless prey, a mouse or a baby bird. Some of the monkeys form hunting groups to tear other monkeys to pieces. They won't eat them; they're not threatened by them. There's no other motive. So maybe our ferocity is just part of our animal DNA, not uniquely human?

Maybe there's something about our absurdity that makes us human? The way, for instance, that we dig up bits of stone and crystal, and believe they are hugely valuable; why do it? Diamonds, for example, are just bits of coal that have been squeezed a bit, for a few million years. Why didn't Elizabeth Taylor put a lump of coal in her favourite ring, instead of the diamond she liked to polish to prove how domesticated she was? Surely no other animal would treasure a bit of pressurised coal so much?

Except the bower bird. You may have seen the glorious film of a male bower bird carefully selecting dozens of pretty pieces of stone to seduce his mate. The Richard Burton of the bower birds. So that human daftness isn't unique in the animal kingdom.

**I looked more closely at the word 'humanity'.
That's not just the collective noun for us
humans; it means much, much more than that.
It means giving. Offering love, support,
care to others.**

What is? We laugh, but so did my Labrador when he managed to trip us up with a stick he was carrying. We cry, but so do elephants when a baby elephant dies. We use tools, but I've seen a clever crow use a twig to get at a specially succulent ant, and elephants use branches as fly-swatters. We fall in love, and marry, but swans pair for life, rather more faithfully than we do. We use language, but then so do dolphins.

So I then looked more closely at the word 'humanity'. That's not just the collective noun for us humans; it means much, much more than that. It means giving. Offering love, support, care to others. Don't all pack animals do that? Wolves, for instance, or buffaloes, for their own survival? Yes, they do – to members of their own pack, or herd, or family. But we help strangers, foreigners, people with no link to us; we travel across the world to try to save them when a tsunami or a typhoon hits. In one week we raised over £30 million for the Philippines, and another £30 million for Children in Need. Not tax. Not extracted from us, but willingly, voluntarily given. And that, I suggest, is uniquely human. We volunteer.

Look at the Lifeboat men and women. It may be crazy, but it's wonderful that they are all volunteers. That they risk their own lives, taking their little boats out in the fiercest storms, and they are paid for by the RNLI, a voluntary charity. Look at Samaritans, another enormous army of more than 22,000 volunteers, donating their time to listen, and, by listening, saving lives. I know from my work with ChildLine that our volunteer counsellors really value the time they spend listening to and supporting desperate children; one paediatrician told me it was the most valuable time she ever spent. Why? Because the people they help say it matters that the work they do is donated. Volunteers do it because they care. They do it because they are humans, offering their precious time and skill to other humans.

Obviously there is a real reward. Volunteering lifts the heart, feeds the soul, so when you give, you get so much more back in return. And, for me, that impulse far outweighs our cruelty, our greed, our absurdity. We humans are the only animals who volunteer.

Science

From a renowned physicist on how humans are made of stardust to a geneticist on how our DNA unites and divides us – these essays take a scientific approach to the question of what makes us human.

CARLO ROVELLI

Physicist

A spellbinding tour of the galaxy from the pre-eminent physicist. It will make you think again about our place in the world, and fill you with wonder.

I work as a physicist. My job is to study the elementary ingredients of the world, whatever they are, and the way in which they behave. Physics is a rather successful science: it still has many holes, where we are in the dark, but overall it has reached a pretty neat understanding of the building blocks that make up the stuff we see: stones, light, oceans, stars, clouds, perfumes, sounds, and the rest. In spite of much searching, nothing has been found so far to indicate convincingly that there is anything else in the universe besides what physics has unveiled: flickering elementary particles, quantum fields, and all that.

If so, what are we – humans – then? Where are our joys and fears, thoughts and anguishes, love and hate, values and hopes, in the minimalistic texture of the world of contemporary physics? Are we made of the same stuff as the rest? Or of something else? As a human being, I have been wondering about this over and over and over again, all my life. Here is what I now think.

I have got increasingly convinced that we are an integral part of the physical world; we are not external to it, in any sense. We are a part of it. A tiny part, indeed. There is an immense ocean of galaxies: millions of billions, and hundreds of billions of stars in each galaxy, with a phantasmagoric variety, of all sorts and all colours, and we are in a remote corner of this immensity; amidst the infinite arabesques of forms which constitute reality, we are an irrelevant flourish among innumerable other such flourishes.

Science

We are made up of the same stuff as atoms, stars' dust; we are made of the same light signals as those exchanged between stars in the galaxies, and pine trees in the mountains.

What confuses us, and makes it hard to understand how this is possible, is the fact that reality is unbelievably complex. It is our imaginations which are limited. Thus, it is hard for us to conceive of the stratospheric variety of what nature is able to produce, just by combining a few ingredients. But our lack of understanding does not count as evidence that we are of a different realm.

We are made up of the same stuff as atoms, stars' dust; we are made of the same light signals as those exchanged between stars in the galaxies, and pine trees in the mountains.

We believed we were at the centre of the universe – we are not. We thought we were a race apart from the family of animals and plants – we discovered we have ancestors in common with butterflies and larches. We are like an only child who, on growing up, realises that he is not as special as he'd thought. Mirrored by others, and other things, we learn who we are.

What makes us human is not what distinguishes us from nature. It is by nature that we love and hate, that we are saints and poets. It is part of our nature to long to know. What we are is a tiny natural part of an immense combination of things. I feel this is so very reassuring – we are not strangers in nature: we are home.

STEVE JONES

Geneticist

What makes us human, genetically? This beautifully inquisitive answer, written by one of the leading geneticists in the UK, explores why the answer lies in our DNA.

To a geneticist like myself, we are not just another ape – we are unique. Uniquely boring, that is. All chimps may look much the same, but beneath their skins, a chimp can boast of around twice as many inherited differences at the DNA level as can anyone reading this essay.

We are dull not just as individuals, but as groups, for the average genetic difference between, for example, Australian Aboriginals and the British is far less than the difference between two populations of chimpanzees a few hundred kilometres apart in Africa. That tells us that humans were an endangered species and chimps were common, but now the boot is on the other foot. Today there are 6 billion humans and 200,000 wild chimps.

Genetic diversity gives us a way of asking how large populations used to be over history; on an island with twenty people, nineteen with blue eyes and one with brown, if the brown-eyed person has no children, the brown gene is lost for ever. If the population were 100 times bigger, it's very unlikely that all forty such people would remain childless; and the gene would survive down the generations, as would many more.

If we map the levels of diversity across the world, every human group outside Africa is only about half as variable as those who stayed in their native continent, and the further away they are, the more genes they lose. The least variable of all are in the south of

91

South America, about as far as you can get if you walk overland from Africa. All this comes from bottlenecks, sometimes of only a dozen people, as small groups moved on to fill the world. Evolution by accident is a powerful force.

But what about the differences in appearance between, say, Africans, Europeans and Chinese? Surely these must be genetic – and they are; and in the early days of my science, everyone assumed that skin-colour patterns showed that there must also be big differences at a deeper level – but they were wrong.

In the early days of my science, everyone assumed that skin-colour patterns showed that there must also be big differences at a deeper level – but they were wrong.

Why did the world outside Africa go pale? It has to do with sunshine and vitamins, vitamin D most of all. We can make that in the skin – if the light can get in. Africa has plenty of sunshine and its inhabitants have been able to keep their dark skins. Without vitamin D, we face all kinds of problems – most people know about rickets, the soft bone disease, but plenty of other conditions, such as multiple sclerosis and even some cancers, are much commoner in cloudy places. Nowhere in Europe can we make enough of the vitamin to stay healthy in every month of the year, and north of a line drawn through Birmingham, nobody can ever make enough through sunlight alone to stay healthy.

Natural selection – inherited differences in the chances of having children – noticed at once, and the dark skin genes were quickly replaced by light ones. Cheddar Man, who lived 10,000 years ago, had, fossil DNA tells us, very dark skin, so his pallid descendants – and the Scots are among the palest people in the world – must have evolved at breakneck speed.

Even so, only around a dozen genes among the many thousands are involved in skin colour, so that, at the biological level, we remain the most tedious primate of all; but as chimpanzees cannot do genetics, they will never find out.

ANNE HEGERTY

Champion quizzer best known as 'The Governess' on *The Chase*

Anne Hegerty writes that it is our DNA, and only our DNA, that makes us human. As someone with Asperger's Syndrome, an autism spectrum disorder, she argues that people who experience the world differently must not be considered any less human if they do not share the same traits as others.

What makes us human is that a DNA analysis shows us to be of the species *Homo sapiens*. There may be some admixture of Neanderthal DNA, especially if we're European, or Denisovan DNA, if we're from the Pacific. But we will be discernibly different from our closest hominid relatives, such as bonobos, chimpanzees or *Homo naledi*.

That's it. That's literally what makes us human. And it is all that makes us human. We don't need any other shared traits to be human.

We do not have to be sociable, co-operative or at all altruistic. Plenty of people aren't. Many autistic people are none of these things and will never be any of these things. There are people to whom humans are essentially opaque objects, incomprehensible, simply things that you go round or get out of the way of. Terry Pratchett said that evil began with treating people as things, but if you are to be a brilliant surgeon, for example, you pretty much have to do exactly that; you can't be weepingly empathetic over an open-heart surgery. Alternatively, you could be a psychopath. You could be Ted Bundy. But you would still be human.

You don't have to communicate. You don't have to want to, or be able to. You can have locked-in syndrome, or be in a persistent vegetative state, and still be human. You can even undergo brain-stem death and remain human: there's a young woman who had a massive stroke that destroyed her brain stem, but electrical activity demonstrates that her brain is still functional. Whatever she is experiencing in that brain remains uncommunicable to the rest of her body or to anyone else, but she is still human.

> **When you start pointing to some human traits and claiming that they are fundamental to anyone claiming to be human, you begin cleaving off some humans from the main tree.**

The inhabitants of North Sentinel Island in the Indian Ocean fire a volley of arrows at anyone who approaches them. It is impossible for strangers to relate to them safely. They are still human. When Colin Turnbull wrote *The Mountain People* about the Ik of East Africa, he may have exaggerated, misunderstood or made things up. But insofar as he was accurate – about a group of people who feel no affection towards each other and take no care of each other, even babies – he was most definitely talking about humans.

Am I a biological essentialist? You bet I am. Because it is the only safe option. When you start pointing to some human traits and claiming that they are fundamental to anyone claiming to be human, you begin cleaving off some humans from the main tree.

At a Catholic mass on Good Friday, the gospel is read communally. The shouts of 'Crucify him!' and 'We have no king but Caesar!' are delivered by the congregation. Because the answer to the question 'Who killed Christ?' always has to be 'We did. We, us, the humans.' I once heard a rather dim priest observe, 'It wasn't the poor who killed Christ.' I don't know how he presumed to know so much about the relative income levels of the Jerusalem mob, but any time someone says, 'We didn't kill Christ, that lot over there did', you know civilisation is about to take a dive.

Science

Some humans are happier than others, or make others happier, and that may be to do with certain cultural choices made by them or by others. But nothing, none of that, makes them any more or less human. The Ancient Roman playwright Terence said, 'I am human; nothing human seems alien to me.' In fact, a great many things people do may seem alien to many. But they are never anything other than human.

PETER PIOT

Microbiologist

Peter Piot recalls discovering the world through medicine, as a doctor and policymaker specialising in infectious diseases, and how this has shown him both humanity's complexity and also our flexibility in coping with what life throws at us.

Think about how often we say 'It's only human nature' or 'Sure, I'm only human'. In general, we mean that we are not perfect, that we make mistakes, that we are not behaving as rationally as we sometimes believe. It is truly remarkable what we have achieved as a human species. We have never been healthier, and science has made life so much easier. Yet, at the same time, we are destroying our planet, as well as our fellow human beings, through war, discrimination and poverty.

Being human is about living with complexity, and about managing our own internal contradictions. These contradictions go well beyond the commonly accepted paradigms such as yin/yang, rational/emotional, or genes/education – and the age-old nature versus nurture question. The tension generated by these contradictions can result in great creativity, love, generosity, caring for others we don't even know, but also in following totalitarian ideologies, hate, destruction, apathy, suicide and the rejection of dialogue. The numerous combinations and influences on our own contradictions make each of us totally unique.

I grew up in a small village in Flanders where everybody was white and Catholic. I was a very curious child, and discovered the world through books, while slowly discovering the contradictions in my community and myself. It made me question much of the prevailing 'conventional wisdom', and led to my main goal at the age of ten: get out of here and discover the world.

And so I did. I studied medicine because I wanted to make a difference for others, but also because it would give me a passport to the world. I was hungry for discovery, and went into research in infectious diseases. This shows how such tension can also be a major driver for humans to push boundaries, and imagine what can be possible – be it going to the moon, developing a new vaccine or composing original music.

As a physician and as a policymaker working on Ebola and AIDS across the world, I have seen the worst and best of human nature. At the beginning of the AIDS epidemic, the disease elicited widespread stigma, discrimination, homophobia. Similarly, some reactions to the recent West African Ebola epidemic varied from rejection to racism. One of my proudest moments was in 2014, when hundreds of colleagues at the London School of Hygiene and Tropical Medicine volunteered to join local front-line workers to care for patients with Ebola, often at the risk of their own lives.

As a physician and as a policymaker working on Ebola and AIDS across the world, I have seen the worst and best of human nature.

Even though living with our contradictions can be a challenge, it provides the human species with a major evolutionary advantage, because we may be better equipped than other animals to confront the ever-present uncertainty in an ever-changing world.

Being honest about our own contradictions and those of others should make us less judgemental of those who are different from us, and help us to avoid oversimplifying what is complicated – as seems now to be the norm on social media. So let us enjoy our lives in all our dimensions.

COLIN PILLINGER

Planetary scientist

Colin Pillinger (1943–2014) gives a personal perspective on how science exemplifies many of the qualities that make us human, through his own unlikely journey from reluctant school student to principal investigator for the Beagle 2 Mars lander project.

What makes us human? In my case 'us' means scientists. Scientists, like all humans, are curious, but we're real nosey-parkers. And like the lady in the corner house on the street where I was a kid, who hid behind her aspidistra to watch the comings and goings of everyone in the neighbourhood, we like to tell people what we've found out.

But what made me a scientist? I can't claim it was school. I only went there because there were other boys to play football with. I planned to leave as soon as I could. I ended up at university because the maths teacher called my parents in and persuaded them I should become a sixth-former. My mother would have been easily convinced – when she passed an exam to go to grammar school during World War I, her 'Dickensian' stepmother threw the offer letter on the fire and my mother worked in a factory making boots for soldiers.

I didn't enjoy being an undergraduate much better than school. Again, I was hoping to pack it in when I discovered research – the chance to find out things that nobody else knew. And you were expected to tell people about your discoveries by writing them up and publishing the results.

Not that I was any good at writing essays, but the first paper I submitted was an instant success. I had more than a hundred letters asking for a copy. I had devised a set of rules to allow other scientists to understand the spectra they measured for unknown organic chemical compounds which they had extracted from plants and things.

It was the method used to make new drugs, but as I was about to find out, it was also a way to determine when life began on Earth. When applied to certain ancient rocks, the instrument I was expert with, a mass spectrometer, can search for 'chemical fossils'. You can't see a chemical fossil: they are compounds made of carbon. Mass specs detect them and, by measuring the abundance of different forms of the element (isotopes), demonstrate biology was involved in creating these molecules billions of years ago.

My next lucky break was that, in 1969, NASA needed people like me to see if there had ever been life on the Moon. My first job, after getting a PhD, was to analyse the lunar samples collected during the Apollo missions, looking for evidence of extraterrestrial life. I say lucky because somebody else had turned the job down, saying he couldn't see a long-term future in the space programme.

I was being paid to answer a question everyone was interested in: are we alone in the universe?

Me, I would have done it for nothing; instead, I was being paid in order to answer a question everyone was interested in: are we alone in the universe? And, believe me, I mean everyone. If I went into the local pub with my father, who was out and out working class, I was bombarded with questions from his mate, wanting to know what I was doing.

When, years afterwards, I was trying to raise funds for Beagle 2, in order to land on Mars and prove myself and my colleagues had discovered Martian life by studying meteorites which had fallen to Earth from the 'red planet', I knew I had 'the man in the street' on my side. While I was involved with Beagle 2, I never met a taxi driver who didn't want to spread the message about what Britain was doing to the next person he had in his cab.

I don't know who said 'The only thing that increases in value if you share it is knowledge', but if no one else claims it, I will. The grants we get for our work these days require us to communicate what we find out to the public. Many scientists do it to audiences that already have some knowledge. I prefer talking to people who would never have believed they had any interest in science – preaching to the unconverted.

This brings me back to where I came from: Kingswood – a place where, 200 years ago, as a child I would have been crawling underground dragging a truck overloaded with coal. I would probably have ended my days, if I survived, in 'the workhouse'. The man who changed all that was the local evangelist, George Whitefield. He was destined to become a missionary until a friend suggested there was no need to travel to far-off countries, asking, 'Are there not savages enough for you in Kingswood?' It was a rough place.

I guess I must have picked something up in the Kingswood schoolroom that bears Whitefield's name, where he provided free teaching for the poor miners' children. By talking to ordinary people about the excitement of space exploration, I hope to make a few converts. Any typically nosey human can become a scientist and share the fun I've had from science.

Nature

Human beings are inseparable from
the planet that we call home. These essays
consider our connection to the land around us
and the joys to be found in nature, but also our
responsibilities in a world increasingly
shaped by climate change.

TERRY WALTON

Gardener

From *The Jeremy Vine Show*'s own beloved gardening correspondent comes the heart-warming story of how he has grown up and grown old with his allotment – the one true constant in his life, and the thing that has made him human.

Life has many tricks and turns; some make us laugh, some make us sad. I feel that we should all look for something constant in our lives which brings us back to a start point and renews our basic needs. My constant has always been my allotment: it's always been there throughout my life to bring me a place where little changes. It is my grasp on life.

I was born about 500 yards from the allotment, and I swear that the first time I opened my eyes I saw the allotment and that made a lifetime impression on me. My first recollection of visiting the allotment was at the age of four, grasping my father's hand tightly he led me through the large gates into the place that has always remained my paradise. He gave me a small piece of ground alongside his shed and a few packets of seed to sow. Whilst other children played sport or indulged in other occupations of childhood, I went most days to this piece of heaven and enjoyed myself immensely in the simple pleasures of growing things.

At the age of eleven, I was pretty grown up and applied for and got my own allotments. For those of you who have no idea of the size of a normal allotment, it is approximately the size of a lawn tennis court. This was my first adventure into growing my own. The older people there took me under their wings and taught me hundreds of years of gardening knowledge, which my sponge-like brain could take in readily. As my teen years progressed, so did the number of plots.

To me, an allotment provides all of my life requirements. It is an outdoor gym that tones and keeps my body fit. It is my tanning parlour, which gives my complexion that rosy, healthy look. In times of trouble, it becomes my counsellor to relieve my tensions and troubles, and bring my life into perspective. It brings me into an environment that is sharing and caring, and is a model from which true life can learn a great deal. Finally, it provides much of my daily need of food – which tastes so much better, having been grown in the way that I determine and free of all chemicals and pesticides. I am at one with nature!

> **My first recollection of visiting the allotment was at the age of four, grasping my father's hand tightly he led me through the large gates into the place that has always remained my paradise.**

Throughout life there are many changing moments – when you meet and marry that special person; when you are blessed with children. Then, as years roll along, grandchildren become so special in your life. These all have a strong influence on my daily life, but I still feel that need to spend some of my time with my constant, the allotment. This is never to the detriment of family life, but I need it to make me a total human.

When I lived a busy life in industry, with all the modern-day technologies and noise, the first thing I usually did when I got home was to spend an hour at the allotment to make me a whole human again. This meant I was calm, approachable and fully relaxed, ready to spend time with those I care about most.

Then, after a successful career, I had another life-changing experience. *The Jeremy Vine Show* hit the airwaves and did a programme on allotments. The show was enthralled by the enthusiasm and 'niceness' of allotmenteers. They decided to adopt an allotment, and I was fortunate enough to be the one chosen to spread the gospel of gardening and the outdoor life. It was exciting for me, on a Friday afternoon, to be given the chance to extol the 'good life' to millions of listeners, whether they are ardent gardeners or not. This changed my life in so many ways and yet still, at heart, the allotment was the constant.

It has made me human all of my memorable life, and I hope that my input changes the lives of others. I am so grateful for the life I have led and would not change it, as it has made me a rounded person and, most of all, a human.

PETER HERMON

Computer pioneer and hill-walker

In his evocative answer, Peter Hermon describes the magic of the Welsh hills that illuminate the most transcendent aspects of being human. A glowing account of a life spent in love with hill-walking.

I must have been born with hill-walking in my genes. Ever since I was taken to climb Thorpe Cloud near Dovedale as a nine-year-old, it has beguiled me. Soon I was cycling to the Peak District in school holidays and youth hostelling in the Lake District and Wales. I caught the bug early and it has never left me.

I have trekked in Nepal, climbed Ayres Rock, hiked across Corsica, traversed Majorca's rocky spine, greeted the sunrise on Mount Sinai and crossed the Grand Canyon more times than I can remember. Even so, it is the Lakeland and Welsh Hills that hold pride of place in my affections and I have claimed one of their 300-odd 2,000-foot tops nearly 2,500 times. They are just the right scale for day hikes, with a variety of scenery that has to be experienced to be believed. I am at home on the hills in fine weather and foul: on sunny days when clouds throw shadows on distant fells but equally on squally days when the wind seems determined to blow you off your feet.

There have been moments of magic, like the day I climbed through mist to see the Snowdonia peaks thrusting through a blanket of wool and, with the sun behind me, my own shadow eerily hovering like some giant on the mist below. Then there was a day in winter when, at dusk, Moel Hebog's rounded top became girdled in an arc of mist that momentarily turned pink in the setting sun. And then was gone.

In the Song of Solomon in the Bible, the poet likens the tresses of his lover's hair to 'a flock of goats surging down the slopes of Gilead'. Today, in autumn, you can likewise see columns of sheep descending the hills as they are shepherded down to their winter quarters.

After studying mathematics at Oxford, an academic career beckoned. It would have been ideal in giving me lots of time to enjoy the hills. But I wanted more: a nice home, travel, some of the good things of life. Unfortunately, that would mean taking a job with, at most, three weeks' holiday a year. So I was torn. Eventually, I squared the circle (but that is another story). Staying with J. Lyons in computers, I quickly climbed the corporate hierarchy and ended up on the board of British Airways. But though I sampled the 'high life' – first-class travel, top hotels, wheeling and dealing – I headed for the hills at every opportunity.

There have been moments of magic, like the day I climbed through mist to see the Snowdonia peaks thrusting through a blanket of wool and, with the sun behind me, my own shadow eerily hovering like some giant on the mist below.

Few things can compare with the sense of well-being a day in the hills provides, or the satisfaction that comes from successfully navigating your way by compass in impenetrable mist. The hills combine quietness and freedom with a purity, a simplicity and timelessness that reveals the hurly-burly of our consumer lifestyles, with their striving for instant gratification, as the superficial charades they are. Like great music, the hills bring repose and contentment and rekindle the soul. There was one holiday when I followed up glorious days on the Lakeland fells with evenings enchanted by the sublimity of Beethoven's late quartets.

There is a spiritual element too. I do not think it is a coincidence that God's bestowal of the Ten Commandments to Moses, or Jesus' transfiguration before His disciples, both occurred on a mountain. To me, the loveliness of creation is nowhere more amply revealed than in the hills. And I do not mean just the grand vistas, but also the dance of burbling streams and tumbling falls, rock-girdled tarns, gentle breezes and the baaing of lambs, the silence of lost cwms, glimpses of valleys far below cradled in holes in the cloud as rain and mist abate, thickets of heather, glowing autumn colours.

In such glorious company, one is soon led to the most fundamental question of all. What is life all about? Have the manifold wonders of creation all come about by chance, the result of blind, mindless, evolution? Hardly.

AMANDA OWEN

The Yorkshire shepherdess

Amanda Owen encourages us to re-evaluate our relationship with our surroundings; we must make time to notice the little things and find a sense of belonging and community where we can.

As I write this, life as we know it has changed drastically – and not in a good way. The global coronavirus pandemic has made us all take stock and ask questions about what it is that makes us human. My conclusion is simple: it is our need to feel a sense of belonging within society.

My vocation as a hill shepherdess is, throughout the winter months, one of mostly isolation; time spent in the main part alone or with just my sheepdog, tending to my flock on one of the highest, remotest hill farms in England. Social distancing has been practised by generations of hill shepherds. In fact, two metres seems awfully close when on an everyday basis I can be at least two miles away from the nearest living soul.

Lockdown has gifted many of us with time at home when we would otherwise be in the office and on the daily commute. Even my routines have changed: not just because I have nine children at home and not in school or university, but because summertime for me is usually about the social aspect of serving afternoon teas to tourists, looking after guests or travelling to speaking engagements. Wearing one of the many other hats that I don in order to make a living nowadays.

During this time, I have re-evaluated my relationship with the land and my surroundings and I do feel more of an affinity to my home and workplace than ever before. I have watched lizards bask in the sunshine, seen curlew chicks hatch from their eggs, discovered new constellations and spotted shooting stars at night. All things that previously I did not have time to fully notice and appreciate.

I know that I am extremely fortunate to have such an extraordinary amount of space and freedom.

Therefore, just like my sheep are heafed to their moor and have a natural inbred homing instinct that keeps them settled and safe, I, too, am at ease with in this pastoral scene. So it came as a huge shock to me how acutely I have felt the sense of disconnection from the community and society during lockdown.

Social distancing has been practised by generations of hill shepherds. In fact, two metres seems awfully close when on an everyday basis I can be at least two miles away from the nearest living soul.

Just as my sheep are part of a flock, so we as humans need kinship and to form friendships and bonds. We need a framework, a structure to our lives, to be appreciated, valued and to feel that we are a part of a bigger picture. That sense of belonging comes through a connection with other people.

What elevates us above the realms of a flock of sheep, though, is that we are a society that is inclusive, tolerant and can embrace difference.

Being human is not about a ubiquitous conformity, but about sharing common values and social responsibilities and accepting and celebrating our own and each other's individual characteristics. For although we are all biological humans and therefore one of a kind, and although we all have our own unique personalities and dispositions, it is our inherent need for an all-inclusive societal belonging that makes us human.

MICHAEL FISH

Meteorologist

This answer is a thoughtful reflection on our place as humans on the planet, from the perspective of a meteorologist who has witnessed how much our climate has changed in recent decades.

I'm sure my family would argue that often it's hard to tell if I actually am human! But I believe that, with what seems to be an increasing number of life-taking extreme weather events hitting the planet each year, what makes us human is surely understanding the respect we must pay to Mother Nature. Only a fool would believe that we are the masters of the planet.

There have been two major influences on my life and career. First, the North Sea floods of 1953 that killed 1,800 people and cemented my interest in the weather and a determination to join the Met Office. Second, of course, was the Great Storm of 1987, which started off as the lowest point of my career, but, since the clip became famous, even being part of the Olympic Games Opening Ceremony in 2012, my feelings have changed. Who would believe that it would still be doing the rounds thirty years later?

As humans we have caused global warming, and as humans we can do something about it. Although it is too late to reverse it all, what we can do is to slow it down and make it manageable, but we are rapidly running out of time. If we don't act, the amount of energy in the atmosphere will continue to increase, giving us more viscious storms. The amount of water vapour will continue to increase, producing more flooding. More heat will continue to melt the ice, further raising the sea level and flooding our major cities. Eventually, we won't be able to feed the vastly increasing population, potentially leading to mass migration and civil unrest. In the distant future, Earth could be uninhabitable and we'll have to go to Mars!

Extremely worryingly, concentrations of atmospheric CO_2 have reached a record high and are now at a level last seen some 3–5 million years ago (even before my time!), when the climate was 2–3 degrees Celsius warmer and the sea level 10–20 metres higher. There has also been a very worrying mysterious rise in methane levels – an even more powerful greenhouse gas than CO_2.

With what seems to be an increasing number of life-taking extreme weather events hitting the planet each year, what makes us human is surely understanding the respect we must pay to Mother Nature.

Already climate change is hitting hard, with hurricanes, floods, drought and fires across the world.

So, what makes us human? Yes, we have discovered, to our huge detriment and shame, that we can influence our climate and ruin this planet. But we can't control it . . . well, not yet. As humans, we are still very much at the mercy of Mother Nature.

CHRIS PACKHAM

Wildlife expert

These are the hard-hitting words of a man who has devoted his life to nature only to observe our species destroying it. In one of the most powerful and passionate responses to the question, Chris Packham argues starkly that to be human is to contribute to the destruction of this world.

In a defining act of our arrogance, we have recently named a new geological epoch after ourselves – the Anthropocene – the age of human. Sadly, this epithet is justified, because of our species' terrifying assault on the world – an assault which will be indelible for hundreds of thousands of years. Whilst our structures, our machines, will rust and crumble, our plutonium footprint will only slowly fade, and the strata of the earth's crust will be studded with plastic fossils that will for ever tell a tale of toxicity.

And now, at this point at which we're crawling beneath the creeping violence of climate change, we are wilfully indulging increases in carbon emissions, alongside mass species extinction and the uncontrolled explosion of our all-consuming population.

We are presiding – worse, consciously presiding – over a great dying, an extermination of life. And our wilful subversion of nature shows not only a wholesale disregard for other species but also for our own. Who cares about the humans of tomorrow? We burn, pollute and destroy their ground, ruin the air they won't be able to breathe.

But who are the humans that are actually manufacturing this Anthropocene? Well, the blame is not shared equally – the world's poor are suffering our crimes more than the world's wealthy: the landscape of inequality is obvious. It's our materialism, our technologies, our excessive inventions, the combustion engine, those plastics, those nuclear weapons which are creating the new 'Geology of Capitalism'.

Can't we see what we are doing? Is no shock sharp enough to shake us from our lazy stupor? We have become death, the destroyer of worlds: *the* world – very likely the only world in the known universe – and still we breed, spew carbon into the air, massacre other species, annihilate ecosystems and ravage our precious planet.

No, we actually seem to revel in it – our perverse obsession with global collapse is boundless: zombies, post-apocalyptic tribes, last men standing, future legends of survival, escape into space . . . these might be the movie fads of the moment, but this is all just a grotesque vanity. The happy endings are just plain silly, stupid, fabricated to bolster our anaesthetised securities.

I'm sorry, but if we don't stop and actually think, and actually act, really act, now; if we don't listen to ecologists rather than economists; if we don't stop voting for ignorant short-termists, then we are very probably doomed. Doomed in that our civilisations will collapse amid the horrors of starvation, disease and war. But ironically as a species, as a population of organisms, I'm sure we are secure. We're too smart, too adaptable, too clever to vanish: we will survive . . . but life, Jim, will not be as we know it.

We are presiding – worse, consciously presiding – over a great dying, an extermination of life.

So there, sounds glum, doesn't it? What it is to be Chris's human. But I'm afraid that all the things that sparkle as examples of human good – consciousness, art, science – maybe they are no more than tiny trinkets in the filthy pocket of the rampaging giant that is me, that is we, that is us, *Homo sapiens*.

PS Misanthrope might be the word critics will use. Reality is the one they really need. R. E. A. L. I. T. Y. And to paraphrase *Crimewatch*, do have nightmares . . . they might just save us.

MICHAEL MORPURGO

Author

A striking lament for the ways in which our exploitation of nature has, in fact, made us lose touch with our humanity, and how we need to rediscover care and respect for the earth.

For one reason or another, religious or tradition, hubris or simply prolonged self-delusion, we have long been persuaded that we humans are superior to all other life on earth, to our fellow creatures and plants on this planet; that they have been put here merely to serve humanity, that we have the right to exploit them as we wish.

Societies and tribes that live close to nature feel part of this earth, that the belonging is mutual. Hunter-gatherers, as we all once were, understood and understand well enough that our survival depends on this harmony, that we all, wombat to whale, wallaby to wasp to weasel, willow tree to watercress, have a right to be here, that we are interdependent, an integral part of the same whole.

This relationship between us and nature is and always has been delicate. It has to be handled with care. We have to rely on it, lean on it, but never take it for granted. When we lived close to nature, as we all once did, when we felt part of this creation, we knew instinctively that nature needed to be nurtured, respected, known and understood. From the bounty of land and sea about us came the food to feed us, the plants to heal us, our clothes and shoes, our warmth in the winter, our shade in the summer. We were thankful for sun and rain, needed both, were thankful for water and salt. To conserve was to survive. All nature knows this.

But our ingenuity as a species, our ability to use language, to think and discover, gave us supremacy. We were, we imagined, the gifted species, God's chosen. It was our world. Hubris grew in us like a cancer, became a madness. Now we no longer took what we needed from this earth, we took what we wanted. And the more we took from this earth, the more we cut it down and killed it, to satisfy our new needs. The more successful we were, the more we grew in numbers, the more our needs became insatiable, and the more we detached ourselves from the earth. The very genius we believed had made us unique was destroying nature around us, poisoning the air, fouling the water, melting our ice caps.

We were, we imagined, the gifted species, God's chosen. It was our world. Hubris grew in us like a cancer, became a madness.

Our self-delusion, our hubris, our madness – call it what you will – still does not allow us to believe this is really happening. We are entrenched in toxic greed, addicted to a way of being certainly no longer sustainable, no longer connected to the natural world about us. We have forgotten how to be friends of the earth. We imagine we don't need the earth any more.

Those who the gods would destroy, they first make mad. We have to learn again, fast, to handle one another with care, to handle the earth with care. Humans were once like this. We must rediscover our humanity. Fast.

Culture

The many ways in which people can express and define their humanity is evident in our culture. These essays explore how art, music, food, travel and sport define our culture, bind us together, and are proof of our humanity.

MAUREEN LIPMAN

Actress

Maureen Lipman's poetic answer is a vibrant celebration of creativity, in all its forms. Humans are unique, she writes, because we think of posterity, of leaving a legacy. From her own personal tragedies, she writes an elegiac portrait of the creations that matter to us.

What makes us human? The beautiful enigma of empathy is the first human quality that comes to mind. We grit our teeth when we're told 'walk a mile in my shoes', 'try to put yourself in his place', 'eat your chard, they're starving in Africa', but the prompt is always necessary. Empathy is a rare quality, as we find when life makes us look for a shoulder to whine on. And, unlike generalised kindness, which most people possess, it involves a subtle shift of priorities that only come, like perfect pitch, as a gift.

Surprisingly, perhaps, actors and writers tend to have it in spades – it comes with diamond hearts and reaches into Ivy clubs – possibly because artists need immediate access to the emotions of others. Maybe the membrane between the character we play/ write and our own selves is sometimes so wafer-thin that identification bleeds in by osmosis. Empathising can become obsessive, and those politicians and philanthropists who devote their lives to it often seem unable to feel it for their own families.

'I don't feel terribly grandfatherly towards my grandchildren,' said a friend of mine. 'Well, learn to,' I replied tartly. 'Because they're the ones who'll decide which home you're going in to.'

But, as a species, are we alone in feeling empathy? I watch David Attenborough with the reverence I'd give to God. The elephants who return to the scene of the poacher's crime each year to grieve for their murdered; the nursing cat, high on hormones, suckling orphaned ducklings; the Labrador who waits daily by the bay to swim with a lonely dolphin. Are they not displaying instinctive, shared compassion?

No, I need to look further to find the quality that marks us out and makes us human. Could it be the awareness of our own mortality? A moment stands out in my own life, during my husband's decline from Multiple Myeloma. A crisp April day, and I'm wheeling him through a North London park after laboriously springing him from the hospice. Bundled up in an oversized overcoat, an unlikely tweed cap on the vulnerable head where soft black hair once sprang, he surveys the silver birches fringed by blue croci, the flying frisbees and the shuffling spaniels and turns radiantly to me:

'Look at it all . . . it's all just . . . wonderful, darling . . . isn't it?' and I feel, empathise with the nostalgia, pain and joy behind his words . . . and his jolting realisation that his time is up. With this memory comes the reminder that he left a legacy. Not just a family, who will leave their own, but a body of work of over 250 television and screenplays, written, perhaps unconsciously, against the ticking of the clock. With, as Andrew Marvell said, 'Time's wingéd chariot hurrying near'.

**The need is so strong within us to say:
I made this. I was here. This is my mark.
Think of me.**

Which brings me to our next, and possibly most important human quality: creativity. Touring a play around England recently, I filled my days exploring the Pitt Rivers Museum in Oxford, the Millennium in Sheffield, the Holburne in Bath, marvelling again at the human need to paint, pot, sculpt, stitch, decorate, pin to a wall, use in war, use in worship, steal, acquire, display. Back in town, the Colombian exhibition at the British Museum is a catwalk, fashioned from pure gold, back to the Incas. To them, a trove of everyday, decorative artefacts and, to ambitious Spanish warlords, a coveted stash, worth killing for, to bankroll Europe.

One doesn't need to be a creative genius, of course, to create. The letters written from a trench, a boarding school or a far-flung land, the crocheted baby bonnet, the antimacassar destined to sit invisibly beneath an aspidistra all its life – all these sprang from the same spark of creativity. So did the crystal radio, the scratchy voice of Sir Arthur Conan Doyle on a disc collated by an owlish BBC boffin, and the delicately coloured-in bird-watching book. I have a treasured Florence Greenberg recipe book, pages stained with onion tears, which transports me back to the thousand gracelessly-received meals my mother cooked for us. I have the nineteen scrapbooks she kept of my career; every role I played, from Dr Faustus at Newland High School to *Oklahoma!* at the National; every small triumph and every puffed-up interview I ever gave.

The need is so strong within us, to say: I made this. I was here. This is my mark. Think of me.

The dictionary says: 'Creation; To bring into being or form out of nothing. To bring into being by force of imagination.' I don't entirely discount the Bower bird's need to build an elaborate shrine of beads, glass and twigs – but that, like Jane Russell's hydraulic bra, is for procreation not posterity.

Yes, I think what most defines us as human and distinguishes us from other species is our creativity. And that's what ultimately makes us divine – Darling!

NB: I haven't even started on the human sense of humour, because, to me, it's there in all of the above. In a theatre, laughter indicates an audience's understanding (empathy); humour flashes unexpectedly like sun through our awareness of mortality; it powers some of the most serious creativity – and to explore it in full, I'd need 700 more words and as many jokes.

A. C. GRAYLING

Philosopher

In his wide-ranging essay, renowned philosopher A. C. Grayling explores the distinctive power of human culture. Taking us on a whistle-stop tour through scientific innovations and artistic achievements, his upbeat answer reminds us of all the reasons there are to be optimistic.

According to genetics, there is not *much* that makes us human. Depending on how you count, we share 98.5% of our genes with chimpanzees. Perhaps this is not such a significant matter, given that we also share about 60% of our genes with tomatoes. As this shows, human beings are fully part of nature, and the elements that make us also make not just the rest of the animal and vegetable kingdoms, but the rocks beneath our feet and the stars in the sky above us.

So what *does* make us human? It is not that we live in social groups: ants, antelopes and sparrows do the same. It is not that we have nuanced emotional lives: so do dogs and baboons. It is not even the fact, by itself, that we have language, for other things – including trees, as it happens – have communication systems too, and it might be that some of those systems are quite complex – as appears to be the case with dolphins, for example.

But, in the human case, the system of communication – language – is particularly complex and flexible, with great expressive power, and this makes possible the phenomenon of culture. If I were to pick one thing that separates humanity from the rest of the living world, culture is it.

There are two senses to the word 'culture'. It is used by anthropologists to talk about the traditions, practices and beliefs of a society in general. But it is also used to mean the art, literature and intellectual life of a society – and it is this that most spectacularly differentiates humans from all other animals.

Think of history and literature, think of philosophy, politics and economics, think of schools, theatres, museums, art galleries, concert halls, libraries. Think, above all, of science, that wonderful achievement of the human intellect, which explores the structure and properties of the physical world, the minuscule strangeness of the quantum level, the immensities of space and time, and the intricacies of living organisms – and then, through the applications of this knowledge via technology, enables us to fly through the air, communicate around the globe at the speed of light, cure diseases, and transform the world around us so that we can live in all climes at all altitudes, even in space and under the sea.

Think of history and literature, think of philosophy, politics and economics, think of schools, theatres, museums, art galleries, concert halls, libraries.

The effect of culture in this sense is not always benign: we might think of damage to the environment and the existence of weapons of war – these too are, alas, the results of human ingenuity. But serious as they are, the many positive aspects of what humans make and do are a cause for celebration. It is only if we read and travel – the two best sources of the best kind of education – that we see the extent of this achievement.

One part of this achievement is the development of law. Only think: if there were no laws and no institutions that administer law, life would be very insecure. The strong would prey on the weak, might would be right, we would have to be on constant guard against the depredations of others. But civilisation flourishes where laws provide protection against the excesses of a situation where 'everyone has to look out for himself', for the existence of law presupposes forethought, discussion, negotiation, compromise, agreement, mutual responsibility and acceptance of the rights and interests of others. These things are the basis of community, and make it possible for most people to live together most of the time in harmony.

When we think of culture, we naturally think of the arts and education, along with science, and these are all the true marks of humanity at its best. Both science and the arts express the invent-iveness of the human mind, but the arts captures its playfulness too, and its desire to take the one great step that leads us even beyond knowledge: the step to understanding – understanding ourselves, our world, and our place in it.

This is the self-reflexiveness of the human mind, the ability to look at itself and to put itself into the context of everything it interacts with. Chimps and dolphins can recognise themselves in mirrors, and therefore have a degree of self-reflexive awareness too – but it is hard to find anywhere else in nature the sheer scale and elaboration of the human mind's response to things. The expres-sion of that response is culture, and as the distinguishing mark of humanity, culture exemplifies what other animals lack – adaptive-ness, progression, change and diversity, in behaviour and activity.

I'll admit that I have given an optimistic and upbeat account of human nature; cynics will wish me to remember how horrible we can be to each other too, and, alas, history provides too much support for that fact. But it is not the violent, tribal, greedy side of humanity that is distinctive; animals are territorial and can be aggressive and violent in ways wholly untempered by the occasional pangs of conscience that humans can muster. I focus on the good side of culture because that is what differentiates us, and gives us our best reasons for being hopeful that we can master the destruc-tive sides of our nature, and make life and the world something that is ever-closer to Utopia.

PAM AYRES

Poet

The magic of creativity is the way it can communicate feelings and messages across vast distances of space and time. Through personal anecdotes of her own formative encounters with books, art and music, Pam Ayres's inimitable voice, warm and bright, shines through.

What makes us human? In my opinion, it is creativity. Creativity, the great, powerful force that compels humans, unlike any other species, to make things. They may be things of beauty, might, poignancy or destruction, but they send out their message to everyone who sees them, and they deliver specific emotions to the soul.

Creativity is harnessed by one human and felt by another. It is the silent language, the conveying of intense feeling from a thing, and it is everywhere.

For example, our home was happy and chaotic. If we even noticed that we had few books, we certainly didn't mind. But when I was in my early teens, I found a beaten-up paperback copy of *A Stone for Danny Fisher* on the windowsill. I idly started reading it and was transported, by the creativity of Harold Robbins, from the lushness of rural Berkshire to the mean streets of Manhattan's Lower East Side, to anti-Semitism, to the squalid life of a bribed boxer. I was enthralled.

Books just turned up in our house, and another paperback appeared on the windowsill. This one was entitled *Death of a Man*, about a person with cancer. I read the book, but it was the cover photograph which absolutely gripped me: a sculpture of a man kneeling, arched back, arms stretched out in a gesture of pleading. It was forceful and astounding. I couldn't take my eyes off it.

Culture

Inside the cover it said: 'The Prodigal Son by Rodin'. Never heard of him. Yet that silent figure spoke to me so strongly that, reading about a Rodin exhibition, I did an unheard of and brave thing: I got on a train and went to London, a foreign land to me. I found the Hayward Gallery and wandered round the exhibits all day. I was affected by it all, especially *The Gates of Hell* and the anguished *Burghers of Calais*. When I found the actual sculpture of *The Prodigal Son*, that work gave me such an indescribable feeling, the pathos in it, the yearning of it for forgiveness. From Rodin to me. That extraordinary two-way flow, down a century, the silent language even more powerful than words.

Endearing, horrifying, transporting, inspiring, heartbreaking, hilarious. Human creativity is sophisticated and varied. We make things.

Let's look at something lighter. In my twenties, I was a bored shorthand-typist and my friends at the Witney factory where I worked invited me to go to Oxford with them to see The D'Oyly Carte Opera Company in *The Pirates of Penzance*. I didn't think I'd like opera, having never seen any, but I was as uplifted and delighted by the deft delivery of 'I am the Very Model of a Modern Major-General' as any of the audience there that night. Such great songs spring from the human brain. 'Do You Hear the People Sing?' from *Les Misérables*: how stirring is that? How the blood rises up, the love and admiration for those doomed young men on the barricades.

It's in architecture, of course. I saw it in the cathedral of Notre-Dame before the disastrous fire, viewed from a rip-off boat ride along the Seine, but still, soaring up beside the black, late-night river, artfully lit, it was awesome and enchanting.

Let's look at something less spiritual. The potency of film. Remember *Jaws*? Remember the bit when Hooper found Ben Gardner's boat, and dived down into the gloom to examine it?

That jagged hole smashed below the waterline, which we were all studying with growing dread when what should float gently into view, but somebody's head, minus the body. I screamed out loud in the cinema. Spielberg used his creativity to inspire terror, and he succeeded. Boy, did he succeed.

Humans create images that we love. Look at Sir Edward Landseer's painting *The Connoisseurs*, where the artist is painting with a dog looking thoughtfully over each shoulder. Look at the face of the dog on his right, at the eye, at the nose. It is magical. With his simple materials and his creativity, he gave us an utterly endearing image.

Endearing, horrifying, transporting, inspiring, heartbreaking, hilarious. Human creativity is sophisticated and varied. We make things. Things which bring about a silent, potent flow from one person to another. Creativity: it is what sets us apart.

TOM PIPER

Theatre designer

Tom Piper, the theatre designer known for his commemorative art installation of ceramic poppies at the Tower of London, has written an essay about play, imagination, and childlike freedom. He says that theatre illustrates the best things about being human: it's creative, social, and everyone plays their part.

I work in theatre, where a group of people come together, make a play and then share this piece of storytelling with another group of people who've come to watch.

'Play' is an apt name for what we do – in that the best work is created with a spirit of open enquiry and a playful use of the imagination.

As children, we happily create fantasy worlds and narratives; we are alive to the possibilities of imaginative transformation. We can turn mud and leaves into pizza or a motley arrangement of random toys into a whole army.

Actors are able to recapture that childlike freedom – without fear of the kind of embarrassment that would cripple most of us – exploring and improvising imaginary scenarios in the rehearsal room and on stage.

Working on a large number of Shakespeare plays over the years has taught me how, through the poetic power of the language of a gifted storyteller, words alone can be used to conjure up locations in the mind's eye. And the simplest of props can suggest a whole world. Words create pictures, as Shakespeare beautifully suggested in *A Midsummer Night's Dream*: 'And as imagination bodies forth the forms of things unknown, the poet's pen turns them to shapes and gives to airy nothing a local habitation and a name.'

We all have our own mental, internal CGI, and we seem to have an innate appreciation of beauty. But what fascinates me is how different people see the visual world in such different ways. We are all open to visual metaphor, but we bring our own life experience – and individual imaginative forces – to bear. Sometimes that metaphor is very clear, as in the transformation of scarlet flowers into a sea of blood. Part of the power of the poppies installation was the shared appreciation of that transformation. At other times, people interpret what is in front of them in a variety of very different ways, often depending on their own state of mind. I, for one, delight in the textures of urban decay which to many might seem ugly!

Telling stories is one of our most basic human needs. Through them, we share ideas and create situations which can inspire, move, educate, entertain and engage our listeners. We're also able to suspend our disbelief that the person in front of us is only pretending; we enter into their fictional emotional life and empathise with their situation. This is, ultimately, what allows us to be moved by the performance: that we can make that imaginative shift and see the world through another's eyes.

Telling stories is one of our basic human needs. Through them, we share ideas and create situations which can inspire, move, educate, entertain and engage our listeners.

Audiences feed off each other: your laughter can infect your neighbour. Or you are all silenced in a shared, profound stillness in the face of human tragedy. I believe that to be there as part of that two-way communication between stage and audience taps into our deep-rooted desire for shared communal ceremony and celebration. Even though I am not religious, it seems clear to me that we need occasions to gather together and share experiences, to help us understand each other and find shared meaning and purpose in our lives.

Theatre, for me, illustrates what is best about being human: it is a creative, highly social endeavour in which lots of skilled individuals bring a range of different talents to bear on a shared vision. Each person's skill and experience is essential to the success of the piece. And when it works, the sum of the separate parts adds up to something far greater than the individual contributions. There is always a tussle of opinion and debate, but in the end the human need to create and collaborate wins out.

The quality of mischief – so often ironed out of our children – is also vital for our creativity; and we should remember to value society's rule-breakers and inventors, in both the arts and sciences. I am a Humanist, who believes that humans are best when they share, learn and collaborate with each other, and that together we can improve what it means to be human.

GILLIAN REYNOLDS

Radio critic, journalist and broadcaster

Gillian Reynolds argues that what makes us human is the ability to fantasise. From her own experiences as a wartime child, her discussion of fantasy as an escape is fascinating, and makes for an insightful and touching answer.

When cats sit purring by the window, are they fantasising about the birds outside? When the spider in the bathtub scurries as you approach, was it because its mother told it scary tales of giants? I doubt it.

What humans do, from very early on, is take reality and play with it. Turn it inside out. Make up stories with it. Fantasise. Think about the songs we learn in childhood. That faraway little star, twinkling, mysterious, wonderful. Hush-a-bye baby, on the treetop. A baby on a treetop? Fantasy lets us manage the unknown, the fearful.

I grew up in the war. I remember looking up at the sky as my dad carried me out to the air-raid shelter. I saw the searchlights, the barrage balloons. I heard the planes. I wasn't scared. My dad was holding me and my mother was already down in the shelter with my brother. And the people who lived in the houses all along our street were going into their shelters too. It was what happened.

In the shelter we'd sing, 'Twinkle Twinkle' and 'Incy Wincy Spider' and songs off the radio. It was years before I could actually grasp the reality of then, the danger. The grown-ups must have known there was a good chance we wouldn't be there next day. *We* didn't. We went into the world of the songs – 'Run Rabbit, Run Rabbit' – and the stories – 'Jack and the Beanstalk', 'Sleeping Beauty'.

Culture

I was an early reader. But there weren't a lot of new books in the war. So I grew up with old books, second-hand books with battered bindings and mottling on the pages. The *Lang's Fairy Books*, Andrew Lang's collections of folk and traditional stories, were my treasures. To this day, I can't look at the sea without thinking of the salt mill at the bottom of it, grinding away. I can't see a tree without imagining a door in its trunk. And behind the door? Another world. I knew such things weren't real. But they coexisted alongside the everyday. Just for me.

Think about the songs we learn in childhood. That faraway little star, twinkling, mysterious, wonderful. Hush-a-bye baby, on the treetop. A baby on a treetop? Fantasy lets us manage the unknown, the fearful.

I fantasise endlessly still. I pass empty shops and imagine what they could be. I look through windows of houses and wonder who I would be if I lived there. I sit opposite strangers in trains and, silently, invent their life stories. I go to sleep imagining my duvet is a cloak of invisibility.

I don't have horrible fantasies, of pain and torture. Maybe I've been through enough not to need them.

And when the person you marry turns out not to be the person you thought, and your children reach teenagerhood and turn into strangers, how could we manage if it weren't for being able (occasionally) to escape (safely) from sudden harsh realities? Birds can't do it, bees can't; even educated fleas don't fantasise. *We* do.

NEIL BRAND

Silent film and radio drama composer

A remarkable portrait of the power of the human imagination, from the creative mind of Neil Brand. Offering both a sweeping tour of human history and a touching personal insight, he suggests that our imaginations are responsible for both the very best and the very worst of who we are as human beings.

What makes us human is the power of the human imagination. As far as we know, we're the only species on the planet that can create ideas in our heads of things that don't exist until we have imagined them. These can be works of art, inventions, technological leaps, stories, political ideas, designs or even just thoughts about something we'd like to eat.

The human imagination is what drives our development. It's what's given us our modern society, for better or worse. Our imagination is capable of creating the finest possible achievements and of enacting the worst excesses of human cruelty. Without imagination, we are not proactive beings but reactive ones, able only to respond to events we undergo without the power of imagining alternatives or planning ahead.

One explanation of the cave paintings of Lascaux was that, by representing the animals they hunted in picture form, early man could somehow gain control over them – if they lived in his mind, or on his wall, they could be overcome in reality. Now, it seems to me, the imagination is undervalued in education and in daily life, in our cultural make-up and in the workplace, despite being responsible for most things that give our lives meaning, quality and piquancy. Individual imagination is powerful and very hard to control.

Culture

In the two main areas in which I have worked, silent films and radio drama, there is a gap that needs to be filled by the storyteller. With silent film, it's music, hence my fascination with film music, the most powerful inspiration I knew as a child. Before my teens, I would leave the cinema with the music still roaring in my head and race home to try to pick the tune out on the piano. I bathed in the sound-world of films because the music seemed to contain so much information.

With radio drama, it's pictures, the best pictures possible, because we make them ourselves in our heads. When I write about Groucho Marx or Dickens's Scrooge, they leap out of my mind into the listeners' as they would recognise them, fully formed and alive. Ghost stories on the radio are more terrifying because we can't see anything – yet we can 'see' everything. And, in radio drama, a character can go from a beach in Barbados to a prison cell in a medieval castle in the blink of an eye. I fell in love with radio drama when I was writing a play set in 1930s Hollywood and realised that this was the only medium in which I could afford, within the budget, to send my characters out on to a balcony to look at the view.

Our imagination is capable of creating the finest possible achievements and of enacting the worst excesses of human cruelty.

Of course, there's a down side. The imagination can create demons that could destroy us, fears and imaginings that can harm. But even that darkness can be of value in creating something new. The first story I ever wrote was the result of a nightmare.

I have been very lucky: I haven't had real pain in my life as many have, and my work comes from a place of curiosity and human nature, not the pain of personal experience that needs to be worked through. Yet the losses that have come my way, and the depression that has sometimes afflicted me, has made me speak more directly as a composer and, I hope, as a writer.

In working with pianists, improvising to film, I have tried to teach them to, as it were, 'read' a film and then to find the authentic music, 'their' music, which serves to make the scene come alive. It has to be their idea of sadness, happiness, joy, desire, whatever – it can't be mine. It's an actors' technique of getting to the heart of a character; it's also called empathy. That, too, is a product of the imagination, and is particularly valid now when we are asked on a daily basis to imagine the plight of others and react to it. It is, after all, what makes us human.

AKALA

Musician and writer

A deeply felt, profound and poetic answer about how art makes us human – and none more so than music. As humans, we are united by our innate desire and need to express ourselves.

Art. Art makes us human. Even though art itself is intangible and subjective, it is somehow also universal and concrete. The impulse to create, to express a deep truth or imagine an alternative reality, to distil a thought, to tell a story – to shock, to please, to provoke, to protest – all of this we do through the medium of art.

The powerful in human societies have always understood the fundamental power of art and thus of the artist. And art is, in many ways, an alternative system of power because the artist can provide or encourage a different way of seeing and being from the one that is currently in fashion.

And if art makes us human, music – of course I am not biased at *all* as a musician – is the most central and fundamental part of that artistic expression. It is not that musicians are better or more talented or more important than other artists, it is simply that music is the most universal aspect of this universal thing – as far as we know, pretty much every culture that has ever existed had or has music.

And the reason that music is universal is perhaps very simple: all we need to create it is our bodies – our voices, hand-claps, stamps, shouts and hollers alone can often create sounds that are as moving as any of the wonders of modern recorded music.

I was extremely lucky growing up. Though my family was far from 'well-off' in monetary terms, my exposure to art from as early as I can remember was incredibly rich and very much shaped the lens through which I viewed the world. Whether it was the reggae and soul music that my parents and their friends played at their countless 'blues dance' parties, or the scores of productions that I saw at the Hackney Empire theatre because my stepdad was the stage manager there; I was lucky enough to have a rich and varied introduction to this most fundamental of human expressions. I helped do the lights for Slava Polunin's famous *Snowshow*; I saw the legendary South African play *Sarafina!*, featuring Hugh Masekela, more times than I could possibly remember; I emceed on my dad's sound-system, recorded in the studio for the first time with my uncle aged just four and created dance routines with my cousins.

Art is our way of dealing with love and death and war and sex and happiness and hurt and the entire range of our experiences.

My secondary school took us to Barcelona and Rome and, even as a rowdy angsty teenager who was not religious in an Abrahamic sense, I could not deny the effect that Gaudí's church and the Sistine Chapel had on me. Along with Dalí's museum, they provoked me to think differently about the boundaries of what an artist could create and, looking back, it was mad, because all of my school friends also understood this, even though we obviously did not express it in those terms at the time.

Art is our way of dealing with love and death and war and sex and happiness and hurt and the entire range of our experiences. A communion with the ancestors, a prayer to whichever gods you worship, a doubting if such a being exists, the soundtrack to our morning exercise, the solace we seek in times of desperation, the pure joy of dancing – really, really dancing.

Art is what makes us human, and music even more so.

JULIAN LLOYD WEBBER

Musician

Julian Lloyd Webber's answer celebrates music as a universal language. He advocates for musical education as not just a luxury but a central human experience: one that has immense power to combat society's ills through the skills and values it teaches.

What distinguishes human beings from animals? Composing, playing and appreciating music is certainly one thing which humans do and animals don't, although I do remember reading an article which claimed that cows produced more milk when they were played piped muzak (or should that be piped MOOzak?). But, seriously, music can and does portray every human emotion – from anger, fear and sorrow to happiness, joy and love.

Music speaks directly from one human being to another, with no barriers of language, background or race. This is one of the reasons I loved playing the cello – I felt I could communicate directly with each and every member of the audience through the instrument which most closely resembles a sonorous human voice.

Along with countless millions, my life has been immeasurably enriched by music and I can't imagine existing without it. Music has an incredible knack for conjuring up memories. In an instant, a tune can transport you back in time to that romantic trattoria where you first heard it with your partner, or to that football stadium where your team won that epic cup game you went to with your dad.

But music is not only a joy to play and to listen to – it's not simply 'leisure', as many see it. Music also teaches skills which can be useful in many other areas of life, including teamwork, discipline, motivation and self-awareness, as well as social skills. Not only that, music has the power to literally transform lives.

Julian Lloyd Webber

As Chair of the charity Sistema England, I have witnessed the incredible changes that music has brought not only to children's lives but to the lives of entire families. Sistema England is based on Venezuela's visionary El Sistema programme, which is a social programme with music at its heart. It was founded nearly forty years ago by José Abreu – an economist and classical music-lover who believed that every poverty-stricken child should have free access to music and that their lives would be transformed as a result. And he's been proved 100% right, as more than 500,000 Venezuelan children are currently clamouring to be part of the system.

Music is the great leveller. When the conductor gives his or her downbeat, every player in the orchestra is equal and the music itself is greater than any single individual.

Music is the great leveller. When the conductor gives his or her downbeat, every player in the orchestra is equal and the music itself is greater than any single individual. But can music really play a part in reducing knife crime, drug addiction and many more of society's ills? Yes, it can – it already has in Venezuela and, after only a few years, it has already produced extraordinary changes in some of England's most disadvantaged communities. Teachers are reporting hugely increased levels of concentration, discipline, motivation and attendance. 'It's been a miracle,' says the headteacher of Faith Primary School, West Everton. And on Lambeth's Landsdowne Green Estate, the headteacher observes that: 'The change in the pupils has been unbelievable – we cannot afford to let this go.'

As the philosopher Nietzsche said, 'Without music, life would be a mistake.' Try telling that to the animals.

SEBASTIAN, LORD COE

Conservative life peer and former Olympic track athlete

As a former athlete and the man who led London's bid to host the 2012 Olympics, you might expect Lord Coe to discuss sport in response to the question. But, instead, he writes about his love of jazz. His essay is an ode to trumpets, basslines, jazz clubs and the wonders of the music that makes up the soundtrack to his life.

'Jazz music objectifies America; it's an art form that can give us a painless way of understanding ourselves.' These are the opening words in Ken Burns's ground-breaking documentary on the history of jazz. He could have added it also makes us human.

But it's American all the same and, in my layman's opinion, the unique American art form. Roots in the Mississippi Delta and then making its way, by river and rail, into the stomping grounds of Kansas City and Chicago, and on to New York. Jazz has been my companion since I can't remember when.

Looking back, it was inevitable. It was a recurring soundtrack from the moment I began to audibly absorb. My parents' best man was Jamaican bass player Coleridge Goode. It was on in the house much of the time. And from the moment I heard it, I was hooked.

Humphrey Littleton's *Best of Jazz*, originally a Saturday lunch-time broadcast on BBC Radio 2, and Steve Race's *Jazz Record Request* only hours later on Radio 3, were weekend fixtures. The first jazz to make its impact on my young years, probably before my sixth birthday, was Dave Brubeck's recording, 'History of a Boy Scout'. I also found the driving rhythm section of the Basie Band spine-tingling when pumped through my father's handmade speakers, complete with beautifully crafted cabinets, which dwarfed the sitting room.

Although my tastes since those early years have broadened, these recordings are still my old haunts, to be dipped into rather like a favourite book. Has there ever been a band with the raw blowing power of Count Basie in his pomp? My collection of his work alone runs into three figures. So much of it on vinyl, which has a magic all its own. Records look so much better on a shelf than ubiquitous plastic cases. And the accompanying sleeve notes, crafted by some of the most discerning writers, are themselves as collectable.

Jazz has been my companion since I can't remember when. Looking back, it was inevitable. It was a recurring soundtrack from the moment I began to audibly absorb.

The late, great Benny Green's prose is as good, arguably better, than any. The big recording studios also tapped into some of the best creative talents to decorate their sleeves. Best in class has to be Blue Note Records – that has become iconic. Verve Records gets close.

Jazz has been my permanent fellow traveller. Sidney Bechet's recording of 'Just A Closer Walk With Thee' was still playing in my head as I made the lonely walk from the warm-up track at the Moscow Games forty years ago, minutes before the Olympic 1,500-metres final. Four years later, the night before setting out to the Los Angeles Games to defend the title was spent in a Chicago jazz club until the early hours of the morning. And another quarter of a century later, on the morning of the final presentation in Singapore that saw London cross the line in the race to stage the 2012 Olympics, I lay on my hotel bed listening to the mellifluous piano of Jimmy Rowles, which I know mightily unsettled the other bid members.

My favourite pieces? That's a tough one, and so dependent on mood and surroundings. Louis Armstrong's 1928 recording of

'West End Blues', opening with the hauntingly beautiful twelve-second unaccompanied trumpet cadenza. Lester Young's 'Lady Be Good', eight years later. Coleman Hawkins's incomparable recording of 'Body and Soul' too. All these are emotionally overpowering. Each giants of their art. Others legitimately cite the talents of so many who have dignified and distinguished its history. And most would press the case for the geniuses Charlie Parker and Art Tatum.

Not long ago, I was on World Athletics duties – island hopping in the Caribbean. On descent into one of those small land masses that boasts a mammoth athletics pedigree, I was prompted by a member of the cabin crew to remove my earphones in preparation for landing: 'You wouldn't be able to hear the emergency instructions,' she politely explained. After momentary reflection, I thought it better not to tell her I'd much rather go to the pumping left hand of pianist Erroll Garner when my time comes.

PRUE LEITH

Great British Bake-Off judge

Prue brings together a reflection on history, an appreciation of culture and a concern for the future. This is a fascinating read that creates nostalgia for the power of communal meals as well as a stark warning about our changing habits.

You'll not be surprised to hear that I think what makes us human is food. Not just eating it – all creatures do that – but making it into a ceremony that embodies our national and personal culture. The way we eat and what we eat defines us. Americans eat burgers, Zulus eat flying insects, the French eat frogs, the Dutch are addicted to eels, the Bhutanese live on blow-your-head-off chilli. And we eat pudding. And cake. And the roast beef of old England.

So our diets are as different as our varied national cultures. What we have in common with other races, but with no other species, is that we prepare and eat it in community. Some animals hunt in packs and share the spoils, but we take trouble with our food. We flavour it, cook it, assemble a complex meal and eat it together. We have added the concept of pleasure, and leisure, to mere feeding.

Food, everywhere, in any culture, accompanies all important occasions. We have special food at Christmas; we put a tiny bride and groom on top of a wedding cake; eastern religions make food offerings to gods; Christians symbolically consume the body and blood of Christ. (That is a bit weird, I agree, but the ceremony is called 'Communion', and as the devout troop up together to be handed a flake of bread and a sip of wine, they are brought closer to the divine.) The Jews bring bread and salt to new householders – the bread to sustain life and the salt to spice it up a bit.

Culture

Until very recently, all this was common for nearly everyone, but we are losing our traditions. I think we lose the habit of communal eating at our peril. It's the eating together and the talking that helps the world go round. Whether it was family meals, or school dinners, or grand banquets, the knees-under, knife-and-fork, two-or-three-times-a-day event was an opportunity to make friends, understand each other, relax, enjoy. I believe our modern habit of a sandwich alone at a desk, a TV dinner eaten alone in a bedroom while playing games on a phone, a chocolate bar and a Coke consumed by way of breakfast on the way to school, all erode the structures that stick us together, and make for more stress and anxiety. And more obesity and unhappiness.

> **We lose the habit of communal eating at our peril. It's the eating together and the talking that helps the world go round.**

Just as mobile phones and screens are changing our brains, modern eating is changing our bodies. It is almost impossible to eat a healthy diet if you are dependent on vending machines and takeaways.

We think we have a choice, but manufacturers are brilliant at designing irresistible hand-held snacks out of sugar, fat and salt, and psychologists and behavioural scientists exploit our instincts to make sure we buy them. We are buying into, and eating our way to, a global, anodyne, unhealthy and, above all, inhuman culture.

HUGH FEARNLEY-WHITTINGSTALL

Chef and restaurateur

Hugh Fearnley-Whittingstall's richly emotional answer is about how food transcends mere necessity to become an important ritual, one that sits at the heart of families and friendships.

Nothing makes us human more than cooking – the act of turning raw ingredients into something delicious. Or at least more delicious than the raw ingredients on their own!

Arguably, this is a scientific truth – it's now widely recognised that the application of fire to fish, meat and vegetables has played a vital role in the evolution of our brains and intelligence. It does this by making food more digestible and helping us to take up the most important nutrients.

But, just as importantly, it's a cultural truth – and a profound one.

All living creatures eat, of course, but humanity is alone in making the act of eating about far more than essential nutrition for survival. And I'd argue that we *need* it to be about more than that.

Food is at the heart of families and of friendship. It is a vital shared experience that bonds human beings together, playing a part in all the most important moments of our lives: births, marriages and deaths.

One of the most memorable meals of my life was the one I knocked together at two in the morning for my wife, and the midwife who had just delivered our first child at home. Sausages with creamed spinach. Not a combination I'd put together before, or since. But somehow just right for that moment.

Culture

Most of us still choose to mark those moments of high family emotion with the sharing of great food – often very specific dishes, carefully selected to suit the occasion, to continue a tradition or to honour a particular person. In our family, the birthday boy or girl is always allowed to choose the menu for their birthday tea or supper. Chloe will have fried plantains, Oscar a fish, if he can catch one, Freddie his lasagne, and if Louisa wants sausages and mash with unlimited ketchup, followed by ice cream, well, she can have that too. On these occasions, food is just as important a way for us to express our love as a hug, a kiss or a cuddle.

Food is a vital shared experience that bonds human beings together, playing a part in all the most important moments of our lives: births, marriages and deaths.

And great meals don't just take place on milestone birthdays and festive holidays, either. The best kind of contact with the most special kind of food can be informal: the Sunday lunch when the kids who have flown the nest turn up in the hope of a hearty roast . . . the cake baked in a bit of a rush when a friend says they're going to drop by.

Sometimes, however, it seems to me that we are in danger of losing this relationship with food that is so fundamental to our nature. Many of us are moving away from a sense of occasion around food, as we navigate through our days via takeaway coffees, desk-bound sandwiches and microwaved ready meals, simply fuelling up while on the go, gratifying only our own immediate appetites.

At the same time, some of us obsess over food, employing it as a badge of identity, looking to it as the answer to all our problems, investing it with transformative powers that are just not realistic. We ask food to paper over the cracks in our lives, or to fill a void that we are too frightened to confront.

You might argue that this imbalance is part of what makes us human, too. Whether by losing touch with something that is such a simple source of health and happiness, or by freighting it with far too much angst and anxiety, we humans are pretty good at messing ourselves up around food.

Fortunately, we are also pretty good at learning, growing, trying something new, making amends. I'd like everybody to discover, or rediscover, the simple but profound satisfaction of putting together an uncomplicated but tasty meal and sharing it with somebody they care about.

So, if it's a while since you made time to cook, don't be daunted by the prospect. Pull out a few of the cookbooks gathering dust on your shelf. Or get online and browse until you find something that looks delicious and achievable. Then send a text to a friend, a sibling, a parent, a grandparent – someone whose happiness makes you happy too. It only takes five words: 'Fancy popping round for supper?'

SIMON REEVE

Geographer and broadcaster

Travelling off the beaten track offers an opportunity to explore new cultures, and, as Simon Reeve reveals, it is not just a modern invention: humans have been travelling long distances for thousands of years.

A thousand abilities and emotions help to make our species unique, but near the top of any list of what makes us human, I'm going to put in a bid for one close to my heart: the powerful desire to travel and explore.

Our journeys can be epic quests to distant lands, or local ramblings around unknown hills near home. But humans have always been on the move. In 1991, Ötzi the Iceman was found frozen on a high ridge in the Alps. Perfect needlework on his preserved clothes meant the authorities initially believed he was a lost hiker from the early 1900s. Only after carbon-dating did scientists realise Ötzi was truly ancient. Older than Stonehenge, he was travelling through the Alps more than 5,000 years ago. His discovery was a revelation.

Ötzi's sophisticated travel equipment contained at least fifteen types of wood, each for a specific purpose. His clothing included leggings, insulated shoes made from deer hide, an axe from central Italy and a bearskin hat. He carried a backpack, embers for lighting fires, a medicine kit and drills. Ötzi was better equipped than many modern hikers. He is clear evidence of long hikes and ancient trade at a time when Europe was sparsely populated, and most of the Egyptian pyramids were just being built. Clearly 'travel' is not a recent invention.

Centuries after Ötzi, pilgrimages became great adventures for our ancestors, involving epic journeys across the country and around the world. During the golden age of European pilgrimage, from the eleventh to the early sixteenth century, it's thought up to a fifth of the population of the continent were either on pilgrimage or directly involved in the industry of inns, churches and hostels that sprung up around the routes. Pilgrimage was a chance for long-suffering peasants to see what was over the hill, and find romance and adventure by travelling and exploring. The journey was key.

Our journeys can be epic quests to distant lands, or local ramblings around unknown hills near home. But humans have always been on the move.

Today I think too many associate travel just with flying and flopping by a pool. But that will never gift the experiences and memories offered by exploring a little further off the beaten track, meeting locals, pushing ourselves out of our comfort zones.

Personally, I don't come from a travel-y family, and I didn't get on a plane until I was an adult. My first adventures were as a young child, when my grandma took my brother James and I on magical mystery tours in her little car. We'd explore exotic places . . . like Hounslow. Discovering what was around a corner was exciting (!).

Now I make and present documentaries that combine travel and adventure with stories of conservation, history, wildlife, culture and conflict. I've travelled extensively in more than 120 countries, to some of the most beautiful, dangerous and remote regions of the world. Perhaps what's slightly different about my TV journeys is that we set out to combine adventures with issues – light with shade. We don't shy away from problems. I'm not there to film a holiday brochure. Which is why I've found myself in war zones and drug dens.

Culture

I believe learning more about the places we visit – both the light *and* the shade – makes for a more interesting experience. It ensures there are still incredible adventures to be had – and that modern travel can still thrill.

Over the centuries, our desire to travel and explore has had profound consequences: innovation, brutal conquest, trade, settlement and love all flow from our fundamental drive to journey. Travellers have helped to create our culture and civilisation, and to forge the modern world. Our endless adventures are evidence of something fundamental: going on a journey is the essence of our species. Our desire to travel and explore helps to make us human.

HENRY BLOFELD

Cricket commentator

The legendary cricket commentator show how the sport that has brought him fame has also shaped his values and personal philosophies.

I was lucky. Of course I did not know it at the time. What has, I think, made me human was presented to me on a plate when I was still only seven years old. In April 1947, I arrived at my prep school in Sunningdale and found myself thrust into what was known as the third game of cricket – a form of raggedly disciplined exercise for seven-, eight- and nine-year-olds, firmly presided over by Miss Paterson. It was bumble puppy cricket, but, even so, I found I was rather good at it.

Over the following year, cricket became an obsession with me, and not just as a player. I read everything about the game I could lay my hands on. I cut cricket photographs out of the newspapers and stuck them into huge scrapbooks, and I watched the game, no matter who was playing, whenever I could. This is how it all began, and I have never deviated since.

I was taken over, too, by the ethos of cricket. Cricket, above all, is a game which demands high standards: of behaviour, of sportsmanship, of selflessness and honesty. It was drummed into me by my parents, and those who taught me to play, that the phrase 'It isn't cricket' is as important to the game on the field as it is to life off it – perhaps even more so.

Taken only in a cricketing context, these words were important. When you are out, you walk off the ground without protest; when given out by the umpire, you do not dispute his decision. If you were unlucky and were given out unjustly, you left the crease without a murmur of resentment if the umpire sent you on your way. Good manners were a crucially important part of the game.

I carried with me into life beyond cricket these and many other by-products of the game. I found that these qualities were a huge help to me in later life too. In the outside world they enabled me to enjoy life, to get on with my fellow human beings, and to communicate with them.

**Cricket, above all, is a game which demands
high standards: of behaviour, of sportsmanship,
of selflessness and honesty.**

I think, above all, my experiences as a player taught me the two most important things in my life. They taught me not to take myself too seriously, although I am afraid there have been times when I have let myself down here with rather a bump. They also taught me the importance of a sense of humour, the need to laugh and also the great value of being able to make other people laugh. Cricket, like life, is a competitive game. The modern world seems to object strongly to competition, but let us be honest: life is, from first to last, strongly competitive.

Those who get on in life are the best equipped to cope with this competition: to try hard to win and to not make a fuss if they don't. Cricket has taught me all these things and one other, probably the most important of all. Always be yourself; never try to be someone you are not. It has certainly given me a huge helping hand in this direction. For me, all of this has been a direct legacy of the game of cricket and, of course, the commentary box with *Test Match Special*.

JUDY MURRAY

Tennis coach

It's not hard to see how Judy Murray has become a national treasure; it is clear from her answer how much of her heart and soul is invested in bringing joy and purpose to children's lives through coaching.

What makes me human is teaching tennis at grass-roots level. I've been a tennis coach for over thirty years, and I started out as a volunteer at our local club in Dunblane when my kids were in nappies. There were no tennis coaches in our area back then and I went over to help out, really just to give myself a break from two demanding toddlers for a couple of hours, but also to get some exercise. I wasn't a coach, but I had been a decent player and I discovered I loved teaching the game as much as I enjoyed playing.

Things started to snowball as more and more parents asked if their kids could join in. Before I knew it, I was trading tennis sessions for childcare. We had no money and I was working for free, so the parents had to look after Jamie and Andy in the clubhouse or in the park across the road. As player numbers grew, I started to set up recreational competitions and school teams, because the fun of sport is the competition and I've always understood the importance of being part of a team and having that sense of belonging. I also built up a parent workforce – mostly mums – to help me to deliver more activity within the club. It was a real community effort, very much focused on families, and it became a wonderfully fun, stimulating and safe environment in which kids could thrive.

I took a few coaching qualifications over the first few years and, although it gave me more information on how to hit the ball, it didn't really give me any clues about how to put it all into practice. There were never any practical examples of how to apply the theory, especially to kids. So I learned for myself. Mostly by experimenting with lots of homemade games and activities and applying common sense.

One thing I never lost sight of was the importance of making the sessions and the club environment fun, because you want kids to come back. And the other thing was all about making kids feel good about themselves, regardless of age, stage or ability level. I learned a lot about the art and psychology of teaching just by being in amongst it and observing how kids reacted.

I'm a huge believer in investing in people and sharing what I've learned and experienced.

I'm lucky to have worked at every level of tennis, from club volunteer to GB Fed Cup captain, and I've learned loads along the way, but in the last five years I've gone back to grass roots. It's much more fun and hugely rewarding. I figure I can have much more long-term impact on growing tennis in Scotland if I build a bigger and stronger tennis workforce, so I started my own Judy Murray Foundation, and I travel around the country in a van full of equipment, taking tennis to places you wouldn't normally expect to find it. I focus mainly on rural and deprived areas and build workforces from within the local communities. Teachers, students, parents, youth workers, sports coaches, club members, high-school pupils. I show them how to get others started using whatever space and equipment they have available. It's not what you have, it's what you do with what you have. That's my mantra!

I'm a huge believer in investing in people and sharing what I've learned and experienced. It's what I learned way back when I started as a volunteer. It's adults who will make things happen for others. It's all about creating opportunities in tennis. To play, to teach, to organise, to inspire. Because everyone should have the chance to play.

And that's what makes me human!

Language and Literature

These essays reflect on how language and literature are at the heart of what makes us human: as the building blocks of civilisation, a means of bonding with others, a way of creating art – and, ultimately, the means by which we articulate the human experience.

GYLES BRANDRETH

Former MP, author

Gyles Brandreth's answer is a captivating, playful and personal story of a lifelong love affair with words. Beyond his own experience, he shows how important words are to a flourishing society.

I know exactly what makes us human. Words. Language. Speech. Talking. Oral communication.

Language is what defines us as human beings. As the philosopher Bertrand Russell observed, 'No matter how eloquently a dog may bark, he cannot tell another dog that his parents were poor but honest.' Only words can do that. Words are magic.

In fact, with just one word – *abracadabra* – you can conjure up a whole world of magic. With three words – *I love you* – you can change somebody's life. And with six, you can ruin it: *I don't love you any more.*

Language is power. Many people reckon that Barack Obama became 44th President of the United States because of his way with words. And language defines you. I only remember the 43rd President of the United States because of his way with words. George W. Bush was the guy who is said to have announced: 'The trouble with the French is they don't have a word for entrepreneur.'

In fact, we're luckier than the French because our language is so much richer than theirs. English is the richest of the world's 2,000 languages. *The Oxford English Dictionary* lists some 500,000 English words, and there are at least half a million English-language technical terms you can add on top of that. The Germans, by contrast, have a vocabulary of 185,000 words. The French have fewer than

100,000 words in their vocabulary – and that includes *le week-end,* *le snacque-barre* and *le feel-good factor.*

I was born in a British Forces Hospital in Germany. The first school I went to was the French Lycée in London. I speak a bit of German and a bit more French, but the English language is the love of my life. I like music; I quite like the ballet; I enjoy painting; but words, to me, are *everything.* And they are everything to all of us, whether we realise it or not. The way you use words will have an impact on the friends you make, the job you get. They're the building blocks of every relationship.

Yes, you can get by with grunts, gestures and occasional expletives – but to get the best out of life, you need words.

I love words. I love playing with words. I love thinking about words. Why do people recite at a play and play at a recital? A slim chance and a fat chance are the same thing, really, but a wise man and a wise guy are opposites. When the stars are out, they are visible. When the lights are out, they are invisible. I love all that. And, happily, I'm not alone.

I'm told that Her Majesty sometimes watches the TV word game *Countdown* – she prefers the racing, but she watches *Countdown.* And she likes 'doing the crossword'. So Her Majesty enjoys word play and, of course, she speaks the Queen's English. I'm the proud patron of The Queen's English Society. We're a group of word enthusiasts who think good English matters.

Why? Because, yes, you can get by with grunts, gestures and occasional expletives – but to get the best out of life, you need words. All the research shows that the more effectively people use language, the more successful and the happier they are.

A great English actress, Dame Sybil Thorndike (who lived to be ninety-three), kept her mind agile by learning a poem by heart every day. If you can't find the time to learn a poem a day, try learning a word a day instead. Playing with words will increase your vocabulary, willy-nilly. And will help you live longer, while keeping your wits about you – like Sybil Thorndike and the Queen.

Willy-nilly, by the way, comes from the Old English phrase *Will ye or will ye not*? Did you know that? You didn't? Well, now you do. Yolo.

STEPHEN FRY

Writer, comedian and broadcaster

Exuberant and quintessentially Stephen Fry. Arguing against linguistic pedantry, he says that words are the ultimate creative resource with which we are all equipped, and should be empowered to enjoy. *This text was adapted from Stephen Fry's blog.*

Language. Language, language, language. In the end it all comes down to language. My language (as the sum of my discourses, as linguistic strata that betray my history, as geology or archaeology betrays history) is my language and it is a piece of who I am, perhaps even the defining piece.

For me, it is a cause of some upset that more Anglophones don't enjoy language. Music is enjoyable, it seems; so are dance and other athletic forms of movement. People seem to be able to find sensual and sensuous pleasure in almost anything but words these days. Sadly, desperately sadly, the only people who seem to bother with language in public today bother with it in quite the wrong way. They write letters to broadcasters and newspapers in which they are rude and haughty about other people's usage and in which they show off their own superior 'knowledge' of how language should be. I hate that, and I particularly hate the fact that so many of these pedants assume that I'm on their side. When asked to join in a 'let's persuade this supermarket chain to get rid of their "five items or less" sign', I never join in.

Yes, I am aware of the technical distinction between 'less' and 'fewer', and between 'uninterested' and 'disinterested' and 'infer' and 'imply', but none of these are of importance to me. 'None of these are of importance,' I wrote there, you'll notice – the old pedantic me would have insisted on 'none of them is of importance'. Well, I'm glad to say I've outgrown that silly approach to language.

There are all kinds of pedants around with more time to read and imitate Lynne Truss and John Humphrys than to write poems, love letters, novels and stories, it seems. They whip out their Sharpies and take away and add apostrophes from public signs, shake their heads at prepositions which end sentences and mutter at split infinitives and misspellings.

But do they bubble and froth and slobber and cream with joy at language? Do they ever let the tripping of the tips of their tongues against the tops of their teeth transport them to giddy euphoric bliss? Do they ever yoke impossible words together for the sound-sex of it? Do they use language to seduce, charm, excite, please, affirm and tickle those they talk to? Do they? I doubt it. They're too farting busy sneering at a greengrocer's less than perfect use of the apostrophe.

Well sod them to Hades. They think they're guardians of language. They're no more guardians of language than the Kennel Club is the guardian of dogkind. If you are the kind of person who insists on this and that 'correct use', I hope I can convince you to abandon your pedantry. Dive into the open flowing waters and leave the stagnant canals be.

My language – as the sum of my discourses,
as linguistic strata that betray my history,
as geology or archaeology betrays history –
is my language and it is a piece of who I am,
perhaps even the defining piece.

But, above all, let there be pleasure. Let there be textural delight, let there be silken words and flinty words and sodden speeches and soaking speeches and crackling utterance and utterance that quivers and wobbles like rennet. Let there be rapid firecracker phrases and language that oozes like a lake of lava.

Words are your birthright. Unlike music, painting, dance and raffia work, you don't have to be taught any part of language or buy any equipment to use it; all the power of it was in you from the moment the head of Daddy's little wiggler fused with the wall of Mummy's little bubble. So if you've got it, use it. Don't be afraid of it, don't believe it belongs to anyone else, don't let anyone bully you into believing that there are rules and secrets of grammar and verbal deployment that you are not privy to. Don't be humiliated by dinosaurs into thinking yourself inferior because you can't spell broccoli or moccasins.

Just let the words fly from your lips and your pen. Give them rhythm and depth and height and silliness. Give them filth and form and noble stupidity. Words are free and all words, light and frothy, firm and sculpted as they may be, bear the history of their passage from lip to lip over thousands of years. How they feel to us now tells us whole stories of our ancestors. It is language that makes me, you and every single one of us human.

CHARLES MOORE

Journalist

Charles Moore reflects on how words belong to nearly all human beings, and the many ways in which they are powerful – as a currency, a tool to uphold democracy, or a call to action.

I'm a writer, so my trade is words, and here are 500 of them. But words don't belong just to those paid to use them. They belong to virtually all human beings. You could almost say they define what makes us human. St John starts his Gospel by saying, 'In the beginning was the Word.' He goes on to explain that Jesus is the word made flesh. The word 'infant' literally means 'wordless': the mature human being is full of words.

True, a word is something you can say to yourself, all alone, but it is essentially a social thing. Like money, words are a currency we recognise. They are powerful because they are an exchange between people. Also like money, they can be devalued. They can be worn down by over-use or by lying.

But – luckily – words are incredibly resilient. The writer Kingsley Amis once said to me, 'You can't beat "A shot rang out", as the first sentence in a novel, even though it's a cliché': you cannot avoid wanting to read on to know what happened. In the same way, if someone you care about says 'I love you', it's pretty hard to ignore it, even if you strongly suspect it isn't true.

The English language has roughly twice as many words as French. I suspect this is because, in France, they try to define by law what is and isn't a word. That is a mistake. Words make us human because they express our infinite possibilities. There is, therefore, no end to them. Governments can't control them, though they often try to. Words are the most important tools of human freedom.

So being paid to carry the toolbox is my pleasure and my privilege. This is equally true when one composes the half-dozen words needed for a newspaper headline and when writing hundreds of thousands of words in a book. When I was an editor, I loved trying to sift a story for its nugget of gold to lead the front page. As the biographer of Margaret Thatcher, I sift thousands of documents and hundreds of interviews to try to put her true story into words. All of us – not only the great – have stories. It is really only in words that they can be fully told.

> **Words make us human because they express our infinite possibilities. There is, therefore, no end to them. Governments can't control them, though they often try to. Words are the most important tools of human freedom.**

Mrs Thatcher herself liked to proclaim: 'If you want something said, get a man. If you want something done, get a woman.' But there is a paradox in that, since her piece of advice is itself something said. In reality, words and deeds are not always opposites. Words can get things done. Who won the Battle of Britain – hundreds of fighter pilots, or Winston Churchill speaking of our 'finest hour'? The right answer is: both.

I prefer the radio to television, because it is the medium which lets words speak. If what I've just said means something to you, we have established the bond unique to human beings. We can understand one another, even though we may never meet.

CHARLIE HIGSON

Writer, actor and comedian

Language is the cornerstone of human civilisation, says Charlie Higson, and the ability to write words down is an even more unique human trait.

I think what makes us human is language. The ability to talk, to read and to write – which are all aspects of the same thing. It's our ability to use language that makes it possible for me to be here, communicating with you. We're the only creatures that can use language, and it's what's made us the most successful creatures on the planet.

Language enables us to cooperate with each other, to share knowledge and skills. Yes, other animals have basic communication systems that allow them to send signals to each other, but this isn't really language as we know it and use it. So a bird might tweet to attract a mate, but after they've settled down and built a nest, they're never going to have a conversation like: 'You know what, if we built some proper walls and put in double glazing and central heating and an insulated roof, we wouldn't have to waste our lives flying south every winter . . .' It's never going to happen.

Just as the ability to fly is something birds are born with, the ability to use language is something humans are born with. Way back in prehistory, we developed the language instinct, which meant that we could join together in sophisticated groups, build shelters, cultivate crops, domesticate animals, make clothing, tools and weapons, make wheels and vehicles . . .

We have invented cars and computers, televisions and radios, all because we could talk to each other. In an extraordinarily short space of time, we've gone from cave-dwelling brutes to Armani-wearing sophisticates living in vast cities and looking to the stars.

But there's one drawback to using speech as a means of communication – you can only beam your thoughts into the heads of someone nearby who can actually hear you. Obviously, the invention of radio changed that – but, before the invention of radio, human beings invented something far more powerful.

I've always thought that writing was a form of magic.

Being able to talk is an innate ability that we can't take any credit for, but writing is different. Writing is entirely our invention. The idea of depicting sound – speech – graphically was an incredible one, and an incredibly powerful one. It meant that you could write something down and that knowledge could be held for ever. And you could send it to someone else, who could add their own knowledge to it and correct your mistakes. Once we had the written word, human civilisation advanced at an incredible rate.

I've always thought that writing was a form of magic. Look at a page of writing. It's just a load of mad black squiggles. But run your eyes across those squiggles and something awesome happens. A book will come alive in your hands. Writers – and we are all writers: if you can talk, you can write – can create characters that can make us laugh or cry; we can fall in love with them or hate them. And it's not just people – towns, cities, a whole universe can be contained within a book. Coded into those weird black squiggles.

Most of the things that give us pleasure today would not be possible without language. The very core of our humanity.

BERNARDINE EVARISTO

Author

Bernardine Evaristo's answer is about creativity and individual artistic expression as the way in which we assert our humanity and provide others with original ways of seeing the world. For Bernardine, her own creativity provides not only a career but also a platform through which she can address inequality in society.

In the context of my own life, individualism with community responsibility is paramount, essential – the two are conjoined. By this, I mean that there are many ways in which we humans manifest our differences as human beings, and I'm talking beyond the markers of race, class, gender and so forth, and it's important that each one of us nurtures our individualism as people, because who doesn't want to be and feel unique?

We are not clones of each other, robots, machines, and even though some of us are more conventional in our thinking, choices and lifestyles than others, we still need to satisfy our natural urge to be seen as individuals. Further, in the arts, individualism is the key to creativity. Creative people want to find original ways of seeing the world through multiple art forms and from multiple standpoints. We admire creatives because of the ways in which they offer unique perspectives on our societies.

As a writer of fiction, a novelist, I cherish my unique thumbprint and the means through which I create narratives and manipulate language into new and unusual literary forms. I want people to acknowledge the individualistic nature of my writing, which is experimental in form and unusual in subject matter, and which uproots characters from invisibility and the periphery and places them in the centre of human experience. Through expressing their individualism, as opposed to a perceived homogeneity, we also see their humanity.

Commensurately, I'm also someone who has long believed in the concept of community responsibility, which is clearly in direct relationship with my creative imperative. While I am ambitious and foreground my own career as my number-one priority, I am deeply committed to using my platforms to address some of the iniquities and injustices in our society.

As a black woman writer who is keenly interested in seeing people like myself have access to the arts and as many opportunities as others, I see my role as one of enabling this to happen in whatever way I can. I belong to many communities and I see the term as quite fluid, but the main one of which I speak now is the black British community, because I know that, by and large, if we do not speak up for ourselves, who will speak up for us? This community has been peripheralised in the arts, and most relevantly in my field, literature, and I have taken a personal responsibility to help improve this situation in whatever way I can.

**Writing is my greatest pleasure, but being
an agent for social change also brings
huge rewards.**

As such, I have long been an activist who has set up arts inclusion projects, because I believe in taking people with me, people who are otherwise on the margins. It's not that I'm selfless, because my ego is as healthy as anybody's, but I try to fight the spirit of selfishness while simultaneously pursuing my own ambition. Nurturing my sense of community responsibility certainly makes me feel better able to enjoy the good things that have come my way since winning the Booker Prize. In the age of social media, there are multiple ways in which we can look out for our communities, shout out our support, lobby for change and help create a critical mass in order to be heard beyond our silos.

Writing is my greatest pleasure, but being an agent for social change also brings huge rewards. When we are heard, when change happens, when you realise you can make a difference, from both my artistry and my activism.

JOAN BAKEWELL

Author, journalist and broadcaster

Joan Bakewell describes how the art of poetry elevates language to a new level. From nursery rhymes to the markers of key life events, we turn to poetry as a way of capturing what it means to be human.

What makes us human is poetry.

Language has so many uses: it instructs, commands, explains; delivers messages, endearments, shopping lists. Together with intonation, it expresses anger, curiosity, bewilderment, eagerness and joy. In narrative form, it tells stories, perpetuates myths and legends, records and reinterprets history, describes birds, flowers, hills, rivers. It helps us mourn, love, regret. But shaped into poetry, it does all these with something more. Poetry answers the needs of our emotional and intellectual lives with an intensity and focus that makes it stand alone on the page and in our hearts and memories.

I learned nursery rhymes when I was small: I loved the sing-song way the words sounded clear and bright: 'rock-a-bye baby', 'I had a little nutmeg'. It caught the rhythm of my pulse, my beating heart. At school we learned poems by heart too: the expression 'by heart' rather than 'by brain' is indicative. I came to know all the popular favourites: 'Season of mists and mellow fruitfulness'; 'I met a traveller from an antique land'; 'It little profits that an idle king'; 'Much have I travelled in the realms of gold'; 'I must go down to the sea again' . . . all these phrases – lyrical, evocative – are bedded in my memory.

The intensity and focus of a poem can bring a random event to life and give it a unique resonance: Philip Larkin sharing a

Whitsun train with newlyweds; the ailing Clive James enjoying the maple tree. T. S. Eliot captures his protagonist's precise fussiness: Do I dare to eat a peach? There is no impulse of the emotions, no response, however visceral, to the body and its behaviours that cannot be caught most acutely within the words of a poem. And our responses are correspondingly acute.

This happens most evidently at times of crisis: birth, death, love and loss command the high ground of poetic aspirations. Letters from World War I trenches are full of poems; older people whose thoughts turn to loss more readily than the rest are, I'm aware, compiling anthologies of poems about ageing.

Poetry answers the needs of our emotional and intellectual lives with an intensity and focus that makes it stand alone on the page and in our hearts and memories.

But living as we do in a golden age of poetry and its pleasures, the impulse can come from anywhere. The tiniest incident can prompt an idea, can start a train of thought, can tease out phrases and words, can illuminate, where before there was indifference. In the corners of newspapers and magazines, in small dedicated publications, in slender volumes, we can find, for a fleeting moment, the contact with another sensibility that can lift our day and possibly our life. And the scope stretches across continents and languages. Humanity has within its reach the chance to share with others what it is to be alive.

ROGER McGOUGH

Poet

From one of the nation's best-loved poets comes a beautiful message of connectedness. Roger McGough shows us, through the magic of his own poetry, that what makes us human is nothing to do with our qualities as isolated individuals – it is the understanding that we are part of a bigger story of human history.

I took the title of my new book from an early poem called 'joinedup-writing', which goes: *From the first tentative scratch on the wall/ to the final, unfinished hurried scrawl/ One poem.* In other words, artists often believe they are original, have a unique view of the world – whereas, in an attempt to explain existence, there is just one poem, one canvas, one piece of music, created by billions down the ages.

What makes us human is the awareness that we *are* human. A part of humanity, that continuum of the dead, the living and the yet to be born. Not to feel isolated, unloved and untouchable, we need to verify our existence by reaching out and making contact with others. We do this through language, touch, and the comfort we can give each other on the journey.

> **Not to feel isolated, unloved and untouchable, we need to verify our existence by reaching out and making contact with others.**

To the puzzlement, and it must be said, mild amusement of many friends, I still go to Mass on a Sunday. Religion helps me keep my head in the air and my feet on the ground. I mean, be good, be kind, love your neighbour as yourself: the basics are faultless.

Through prayer and meditation, I get a sense of otherness, of a life beyond this one. But, for heaven's sake, don't ask me to describe God.

However, ask me to describe, for instance, old age, and I'm off . . .

> It's a joy to be old/ Kids through school/
>   The dog dead and the car sold.
> Worth their weight in gold, bus passes/ Let asses rule/
>   It's a joy to be old.
> The library when it's cold/ Immune from ridicule/
>   The dog dead and the car sold.
> Time now to be bold/ Skinny-dipping in the pool/
>   It's a joy to be old.
> Death cannot be cajoled/ No rewinding the spool/
>   The dog dead and the car sold.
> Don't have your fortune told/ Have fun playing the fool/
>   It's a joy to be old,
> The dog dead and the car sold.

Or, for instance, that hot potato, global warming. This is 'Recycling' . . .

> I care about the environment/ And try to do what is right
> So I cycle to work every morning/ And recycle home every night.

Ba bum! And I'm back to language and touch. Trying to reach out and touch people through poetry. Arranging little squiggles on the page, or making words walk the walk on stage. Bringing a smile, hopefully, perhaps even a tear? Guiding the reader or the listener towards a thought they didn't know they had. Above all else, writing poetry is what makes me feel human: vulnerable, and yet powerful. Yin and yang, male and female, transhuman, and above all, alive.

So, when all is said and done, and there's nothing left to say or do, no more *diem* to be *carpe*-ed, and it's time for me to leave . . .

Finally, as in when I'm sliding towards no longer being human, I might be thinking about all the people in my life, and the places, and the things. And I'd want to thank them and give them all, each and every one, a big hug. This poem is called 'Big Hugs'.

> *Before I go, who do I give a hug to?*
> *Family, obviously, big soppy hugs all round,*
> *and relatives, including those I've never met.*
> *Exes. Lovers and girlfriends, especially the ones*
> *who'd rather I didn't. Classmates? Most.*
> *Teachers? Some. Friends who have passed away,*
> *and parents long gone? Big, big hugs.*
> *Places. How do I give Liverpool a hug?*
> *High-five a Liver Bird? Edinburgh?*
> *Each Fringe a playful tug? Hull*
> *University? A pat on the back?*
> *Gigs and dressing rooms? Holidays*
> *and hangovers? File them under memories.*
> *Memories? Give them all a hug,*
> *even the bad ones, it wasn't their fault.*
> *Failures, embarrassments, anxiety and fear,*
> *sickness and pain, you all are forgiven.*
> *Come here. Time for a group hug.*
> *When it's time to go, who do I give a hug to?*
> *(Or should it be, to whom do I give a hug?)*
> *Language, of course. A big hug for words,*
> *which have been good company throughout.*
> *And who gets the final hug, that fretful,*
> *lingering embrace? Unable to let go,*
> *clinging, clinging until, fighting for breath,*
> *something dark closes in and hugs, hugs, hugs me to death.*

CERYS MATTHEWS

Musician and broadcaster

Come on a journey with Cerys Matthews, through a kaleidoscope of images that convey in breathtaking fashion the beautiful, overwhelming, sometimes terrifying experience of being alive.

What makes us human?
When you see the finish line and run as fast as you can. The rest of the field passes you by, but you don't mind.

> And you dial on high,
> Paint the skyline, clear the wings, the ifs now lived.
> Words skip and sing like parables: naranja, bahar, melocoton,
> Chinkerpin, gwanwyn, chitterling,
> jackaranda,
> Rumbledthumps,
> Possum, ginkgo, chirashi,
> sua, gin que ya,
> parfait.

Traded words, traded spice, shared poems, stories cracked open under pomegranate skies, an innocent spared. A cog somewhere, somehow . . . small increments of change.
Sweet songs, wild rovers, days yawning ahead, cold beer in hand, Reinheitsgebot law, an acorn, a grain,
The warmth of the sun, my son's hand in mine and home-roasted bread, clean sheets, a candle, a book in hand, ideas born, machine full and humming, Tweedy the clown,

Eyes crinkled at corners, unanimous votes, olive oil, flakes of salt, roasted artichokes.

Local music: sounds freewheeling from bars wrap around holiday-wide-eyed revellers, arms open, feet light.

No detail, but forms, inadequate laws, skewing for profit, the clothes that you stand in, and hands to the wall.

The spray of that paint: we were all here once, and we will all pass and go, all colours, shapes, sizes, class, creed, for that sense of belonging, a purpose, a voice. Do not want what you do not need.

Lichen moss and honeysuckle nectar, hear the call of the wild. As good as you'll get now, go, swim with the tide.

Everest spindrift, trust the rope, the buzzing of bees, butterfly sighs and vultures in flight, the clapping of pigeon wings, jasmine full breeze,

Clocks ever ticking, those layers of grief.

Play in the shadows.

Confess to your daughter, it never makes sense, it just is, and that's it and that's that, so live while you have it, love while you breathe.

Say goodbye to your father, Mr Tambourine Man in every Parkinson tremor, once, always your sideman. You grow old only once, you do what you can.

Mind wanders and wonders, cromlechs and tombs, but the train leaves the platform and rides out of view; you walk back into town.

**Confess to your daughter, it never makes sense,
it just is, and that's it and that's that, so live
while you have it, love while you breathe.**

Cerys Matthews

The sun always rises, and no one can tell, and bells/boys won't stop/will keep swinging, there's no use in shame.

And click goes the camera (Llorona), the bags will be packed, dreams will be dreamed. And that's what makes us human, an unstoppable march.

So read a new story, lay some more plans,
Live while you're living, and die when you're gone.

Emotions

These essays show that our emotions

are at the heart of what makes us human.

They demonstrate the fragile barrier between

laughter and tears, and how both joy and

sadness shape the human experience

in their own ways.

NOREENA HERTZ

Economist and broadcaster

Packed full of mind-boggling examples from the world of economics, this answer from global thought leader Noreena Hertz is an unconventional look at humanity that demonstrates how recognising our irrational nature can point us towards a host of advantages.

I am fourteen years old, sitting in my first economics class. We are taught that we make decisions as rational men, *Homo economicus*. That we objectively weigh up pros and cons and coolly evaluate information. Rational men. Hmmm. Not only does economics, in one swoop, ignore my entire sex, it also assumes that we are robotic, dispassionate creatures.

We are not.

What makes us human is our *irrationality* – the way we are drawn to some types of information over others, the way our past experiences shape our present-day judgements, the way our emotional and physical states affect the choices we make.

Take colour. It turns out it plays a surprisingly significant role in the way we evaluate situations. Men rate women as more attractive if they see their photographs set against red backgrounds rather than white, grey, blue or green ones. Waitresses are tipped more when they wear red. Football referees are more likely to give penalties to teams wearing black strips than to those in other colours.

Language – the choice of words, images and metaphors used – also has a huge impact on the judgement calls we make. I may not fall for politicians' fear-mongering, but beauty companies have at times caught me out. In my bathroom cabinet are products that 'correct' dark spots, 'fight' aging and can infuse my eyes with 'youth'. Really, though!?

And how about the British study which revealed that when two groups of psychiatrists were told the same story of a young man who had attacked a train conductor – the only difference being the attacker's name – they provided different diagnoses depending on what they believed him to be called. When the psychiatrists thought the attacker was called 'Matthew', they were more likely to diagnose him with schizophrenia. When they thought he was called 'Wayne', they were more likely to diagnose him with a drug problem.

Time and time again, we are affected by factors we are not even aware of.

Time and time again, we behave irrationally.

**What makes us human is our *irrationality* –
the way we are drawn to some types of
information over others, the way our past
experiences shape our present-day judgements,
the way our emotional and physical states
affect the choices we make.**

It's not just the way information is presented to us that we need to be mindful of. We need to be aware, too, of the impact of our physiological and psychological state on the choices we make.

If we're anxious, we're more risk averse. Stress makes us prone to tunnel-vision, less likely to take in all the information we need. When we're happy, we take more risks, are more trusting, more generous. It's why a country's stock market tends to rise off the back of a national team's win at football.

If we're tired, that messes with our decision-making. If you've ever pulled an all-nighter, you'll know the symptoms of sleep deprivation all too well: difficulty concentrating, brain like cotton wool, memory lapses. But did you know that if you go twenty-four hours without sleep or spend a week sleeping only four or five hours a night, it's as if you're making decisions drunk?

Are you the type who skips breakfast? If so, you might want to rethink that. Fascinating research in Israel on why judges decided to grant prisoners parole revealed that the main determinant wasn't the applicant's gender, ethnicity, or even the type of crime, but whether the judge had recently eaten! If you went before the judge just before their mid-morning snack, disaster. Zero per cent chance of getting parole. Immediately after, 65%. Just before lunch, disaster again. Only a 10% chance of getting parole. Immediately after, 65%.

And if you're feeling horny, well, you probably want to wait before you make that important call. When Canadian male undergraduates were given one of two images to look at – either a Victoria's Secret model or a neutral object, a rock – and then asked to make a financial decision, the guys who'd been looking at the Victoria's Secret model made significantly worse financial decisions than those who'd been looking at a rock.

What makes us human is our *irrationality*. The fact that the choices we make are influenced by a whole host of factors that have nothing to do with the decision at hand. What makes us smart is our ability to acknowledge this, and then actively challenge ourselves and our immediate impulses.

MATTHEW PARRIS

Journalist

Matthew writes vividly about an expedition to the Sahara that showed him the unique human quality of playfulness. It's an original and surprising perspective, full of spirit and joy.

Playfulness is what makes us human. Doing pointless, purposeless things, just for fun. Doing things for the sheer devilment of it. Being silly for the sake of being silly. Larking around. Taking pleasure in activities that do not advantage us and have nothing to do with our survival. These are the highest signs of intelligence. It is when a creature, having met and surmounted all the practical needs that face him, decides to dance that we know we're in the presence of a human. It is when a creature, having successfully performed all necessary functions, starts to play the fool, just for the hell of it, that we know he is not a robot.

> **It is when a creature, having met and surmounted all the practical needs that face him, decides to dance that we know we're in the presence of a human.**

I was once in the south-eastern Sahara, in Algeria close to the border with Libya, near a settlement called Djanet. There's a range of mountains there called the Tassili n'Ajjer: bone-dry, a thousand square miles of treeless rock. A few millennia ago, before the climate changed, this was a fertile region where big game roamed and African bush people lived and hunted. They lived in caves and beneath big overhangs of rock. At night, they painted scenes from their lives and their fantasies, daubed in black and ochre on the walls and ceilings. There are literally hundreds of such sites, many more still doubtless undiscovered, scattered through these mountains.

With my fellow expeditionaries, I stood beneath one of these overhangs, admiring the fine artwork, the beautiful lines of giraffes, buffalo, gazelles and bird-men . . . you could usually recognise at once what was being depicted.

But one set of paintings – if you could call them that – defeated us. Across part of the rock ceiling was a series of five-dot clusters. The dots were of red ochre and were simply crude blobs, varying in size, but mostly a bit smaller than a penny piece. There were usually five, some blobs firmer than others, in nothing that looked like the shape of anything. We puzzled and puzzled.

Then: 'Of course!' one of my comrades exclaimed. 'Look!' And he jumped from the earth floor as high as he could, one hand above his head. His fingers stretched up, could just touch the rock above. And we saw at once that, if he'd daubed them in paint, the fingers and thumb would have left five blobs, just like the ones we had been puzzling over.

All at once, it was clear. The bush people, hunting over, well fed, and lounging about after dark in their family shelter, perhaps around a fire – basically just hanging out – had been amusing themselves doing a bit of rock art. And, perhaps with some leftover red paste, a few of the younger ones had had a competition to see who could jump highest, and leave their finger marks on the overhang.

This was not even art. It called for no particular skill. It was just mucking about. And yet, for all the careful beauty of their pictures, for all the recognition of their lives from the vantage point of my life that was sparked in me by the appreciation of their artwork, it was not what was skilful that brought me closest to them. It was what was playful. It was their jumping and daubing finger-blobs competition that brought them to me, suddenly, as fellow humans across all those thousands of years. It tingled my spine.

Emotions

Caprice. Frolic. Joke. Jest. Dance. This is the word-cloud that takes me to what makes us human. The great German philosopher, Frederich Nietzsche, said this: 'One must still have chaos in oneself to be able to give birth to a dancing star.' It is the chaos in ourselves that is divine. We can be trained to do almost anything, harnessed to almost any purpose. But there remains a wayward spark whose unpredictability lies in the fact that it is pointless. That is humanity.

An age is coming when machines will be able to do everything. 'Ah,' you say, 'but they will not be conscious.'

But how will we know a machine is not conscious – how do we know another being *is* conscious? There is only one way. When it starts to play. In playfulness lies the highest expression of the human spirit.

CAITLIN MORAN

Journalist, author and broadcaster

Many essays in this book will make you think, but this essay will make you feel. Caitlin Moran celebrates joy as the triumphant quality that defines us as human. She provides a personal insight into her experiences with joy, but it's one that many readers will connect with.

What makes us human? God, it's such a long list. The ways in which we are – and no offence to any animals reading – totally superior to the beasts are manifold: let's just open with mixer taps, beat-boxing, Manhattan and trifle, then pause for a minute, to give them a chance to cede immediately.

It's not like I don't respect the fauna. I really do. But we are the species that invented a machine that vends crisps to drunken, hungry, heartbroken people at deserted coach stations at 2 a.m. in the morning, *PLUS* we made *Ghostbusters,* and it's hard to argue with that level of imagination and excellence. In your *face,* the things on the Ark that didn't use a toilet.

However, of all the things I love about humanity, there is one that triumphs above all others: joy. Whilst some animals can undoubtedly experience joy – anyone who has seen a newly washed dog roll in fox poo in a field cannot doubt that – humans are the only creatures on Earth that can actively, persistently *create* joy. Construct whole days and industries and relationships dedicated to nothing more pressing – i.e. amazing – than being gleeful.

Consider, for instance, Friday night – one of mankind's greatest inventions: up there with the Pyramids, and the Moon Shot – but, by way of contrast, for everyone on Earth.

Emotions

Consider that last dizzy hour of celerity at work, where you're running for the finishing line like a horse at the Grand National. Feeling the whooshing, unstoppable up-draught of walking out of this building, into the evening, and metaphorically throwing your name-tag and tabard in the bin.

You can hear the hiss of the fizzy wine calling – the ridiculous-est friends starting stories that never stop, and the Daft Punk album on a loop as you dance on a table, and this evening won't end when you go to bed, because then, of course, you're going to *sleep* – which is *amazing* – and then you'll wake up on Saturday morning and have *breakfast in bed,* with coffee in your favourite cup, and jumble-sale copies of Adrian Mole to read *in the bath.* A hot bath. A hot bath that smells of roses, or lime blossom.

Consider, for instance, Friday night – one of mankind's greatest inventions.

Consider the nearest animals get to this kind of day-to-day euphoric experience: wallowing in a puddle that's had a double-glazing flyer dropped in it. Yes, there are the Japanese snow monkeys, which you may have seen on that Attenborough documentary, sitting in thermal pools, in the snow. And, yes, I have to give those monkeys my respect. They have done their very best to create joy, aping – literally – the bathing modes of humans. But when those monkeys get out of that thermal spring, they have *no fluffy towels* – and the consequent unhappy, cold dripping will essentially negate all previous achievements.

Indeed, humans are so far ahead with the ability to create, manage and increase joy that we *don't even need to get in a bath* to prompt a quick hit of it. All we need do is wake in the morning and think, 'Wow – I didn't die in the night! I'm already ahead – and I haven't even cleaned my teeth yet!'

And there we are again – hot with joy, aching with it like effervescent brandy in our bones: not dead, in bed, with a whole day in which anything could happen, and even if 'nothing' happens, you still have lunch, and pictures of cats that look like Hitler on Twitter, and putting on your favourite shoes, and looking up at the sky, and reading *Wolf Hall* on the bus, and putting your key in the door, and smelling stew.

You know how some people have religion – God, and such – to guide their lives, and provide comfort and support? Brought up by atheist hippies, I have The Beatles instead – four working-class lads from Liverpool who shook the world: the *real* Greatest Story Ever Told.

And from the Bible of their life, my favourite gospel is The Gospel of the Day They Finished *Sgt. Pepper.* In the wee small hours of late April, they finalised the mix, and took the tapes over to Mamma Cass's house, in Chelsea. And they hugged, and poured drinks, and lit fags, and had long hair, and dragged the speakers of the stereo over to the window, where they flung the sashes open, and balanced the speakers on the sill. And as the sun came up, they pressed 'play'.

And when the opening track started out across the rooftops – *'It's Sgt. Pepper's Lonely Hearts Club Band/We hope you will enjoy the show!'* – the neighbours opened their windows and started to complain. Until they realised it wasn't Sgt. Pepper's Lonely Hearts Club Band at all, but The Beatles, and that they had turned into something else – something astonishingly other from anything that had gone before – during the night.

And, as Paul McCartney tells the story, all the people just sat on their windowsills too, and lit cigarettes, and poured drinks, and listened to the decade changing from forty feet away. They joined in.

And when the album finally ended – 'A Day in the Life'! 'A Day in the Life', released for the first time, among the chimney pots, by the river, for this tiny village gathered above the rest of London. *The rest of the world–* they all applauded. And The Beatles bowed, from their window. And it was still only 6 a.m.

So whilst I appreciate ants' nests, and baleen filters, and the head-rotating abilities of the owl, what makes us human is joy, and the joy we take in our joy. And that we can plan it and build it and shape it as perfectly as a silver jet-plane, and then fly it over drizzle, and Monday, and Mount Ararat, and up towards the sun.

ROBERT WEBB

Comedian

As one might expect from the acclaimed comedian Robert Webb, his answer is both touching and hilarious: arguing that humour is the proof of both consciousness and imagination.

If I said that 'a sense of humour' was an important part of what makes us human, you might think this is a case of special pleading.

Given that, for twenty years, I've earned a living by trying to make people laugh, you might think I've got a fair bit of 'comedy skin' in this game. 'Ah yes,' I seem to be saying, 'the websites have already replaced the travel agents, the androids will soon replace the estate agents (let's assume we'll notice the difference), but I, a comedian, have no robot challenger. No funny Terminator doing a pratfall in the rear-view mirror; no HAL 9000 writing an especially whimsical episode of *Father Ted*; no C-3PO falling through the open bar like Del Boy, despite how much I'd love to see it.'

But I choose humour because it has a special place in my heart as well as a special place in my mortgage. For most of us, life without it would be scarcely worth living. That's why to accuse someone of lacking a sense of humour is one of the cruellest insults. Nobody wants to be the person in the room on whom a joke is lost. We've all been there, but some people are more regular visitors than others. Know them by the controlled panic in their eyes as they search the faces of companions who keep laughing at seemingly random intervals. My heart goes out to them; especially in Britain, where we – for no good reason that I can see – pride ourselves on our sophisticated use of irony and self-deprecating understatement.

I must say, there's been a marked absence of both in public life lately; since, shall we say, the EU referendum. I was a Remainer, but on both sides there's been a collective failure of humour, which is bad news, because that also entails a failure of tolerance and a failure of imagination. Some jokes thrive on bigotry, but the comic spirit in total is much bigger than that; wider, more generous.

If I said that 'a sense of humour' was an important part of what makes us human, you might think this is a case of special pleading.

To go back to the robots, I can imagine a time when Artificial Intelligence reaches a stage where my saying that machines don't have a sense of humour could itself be viewed as a form of prejudice. I'd be accused of being . . . a what? A 'carbonist'? A 'chip-phobe'? It'll be 'PC gone mad' all over again. You'll have noticed, by the way, that political correctness is never sane – it's always one step ahead of current mainstream opinion: that's what it's for. If the term had been around a few centuries ago, you'd have had people saying, 'Okay, drowning suspected witches was a bit much, but those women who live alone and show an interest in herbal medicine – what are we supposed to do with them: welcome them? Allow them to drive or vote? It's PC gone mad!'

If we ever start caring about the feelings of machines, I think humour will provide an important test. A few years ago, there was an enjoyable reboot of the sci-fi drama *Battlestar Galactica*. The robots, called Cylons, had updated themselves to look human, but their human enemies still referred to them dismissively as 'toasters'. The Cylons had other human attributes: they felt hatred and envy as well as love, wonder and religious faith. However, even in their proud individuality, the Cylons in the show had one thing in common: none of them were funny. It's almost as if the writers had to draw the line somewhere and they knew that, when it came to deliberately funny robots, the audience just wouldn't buy it.

Similarly, I can imagine an android of the future so amazingly dextrous that it could sit down to play a piano concerto every bit as well as a renowned concert pianist. What it won't be able to do is to get some of the notes deliberately wrong, like Les Dawson, in a way that's hilarious. You could ask it to get the piece slightly wrong and it could do it, and maybe sometimes, at random, it would be funny, but the thing lacking would be intention. It wouldn't know what it was doing. Watching such a sad spectacle would be no different from laughing at a chimpanzee dressed in a bowler hat to sell tea bags.

So, I choose humour because it shows proof of consciousness and imagination. As profound as the heaviest, funniest line in Chekov or Shakespeare, as daft as the urge to giggle when somebody breaks wind at a funeral. To err is human. And so is to laugh.

MARIAN KEYES

Writer

In an essay full of both deep pain and hilarious warmth side-by-side, bestselling novelist Marian Keyes argues that, through all our struggles, the capacity for laughter is the key that makes it possible for us to be, and keep on being, human.

My father was lying in a hospital bed, with a chest infection that just wouldn't go away. He'd been in hospital for a month, he'd stopped eating and drinking, and the prognosis was bad. He wouldn't even take his medication, and without that, he would certainly never be coming home.

A nurse tried to coax the antibiotic into his mouth, but he kept twisting his head away, like a petulant child. From the sidelines, my mother and I cajoled him to cooperate and, finally, the nurse got the tablet into Dad's mouth. My mother and I loaded on the positive reinforcements. 'Well done, Dad', 'Good man', and suchlike. We were so relieved. He'd taken his tablet, he was going to get better!

The nurse tilted a glass of water to his lips, to help him swallow the pill. Dad lifted his head up just an inch or two, paused for a moment – and spat the tablet into the glass of water. In dismay, I jumped to my feet and said, 'No, Dad!' The disappointment was crushing and the fear was terrible. He turned a mildly astonished gaze on me and, beseechingly, I looked at my mother.

Then, suddenly, out of nowhere, she and I were in absolute convulsions. Helpless with laughter, we howled. We laughed and laughed until tears ran down our faces, and every time it seemed like the bout had run its course, all we had to do was make eye contact and we were off again. Afterwards, despite the fact that Dad still hadn't taken his medication, we felt better than we had for ages. Our mood was elevated. In fact, we were positively giddy, and even our muscles felt relaxed.

This made me think about people laughing at terrible times, sometimes at the most unlikely and inappropriate occasions. Because clearly it's not inappropriate at all. One of the things that makes us human is that we use laughter as a survival mechanism.

It seems there are actual physiological reasons. Laughter triggers the release of endorphins, the body's natural feel-good chemicals. They give an overall sense of well-being and apparently can even relieve pain temporarily. Laughter also boosts our immune systems, decreasing stress hormones and increasing infection-fighting antibodies. A good, hearty laugh relieves muscle tension. Interestingly, we are thirty times more likely to laugh with others than alone. Laughing is very much a group activity, and when we share a laugh with people, it's very bonding. And connection with others has its own positive benefits.

Then, suddenly, out of nowhere, she and I were in absolute convulsions. Helpless with laughter, we howled. We laughed and laughed until tears ran down our faces.

I've used laughter to navigate countless grim episodes in my life, but nothing can illustrate its power better than Edith Eger's account of her time in Auschwitz. In her memoir, *The Choice*, she writes, 'I peel potatoes for our supper and hide the skins in my underwear. When the guards are in another room, I toast the peels in the oven. When we lift them to our mouths, the skins are still too hot to eat. "We've escaped the gas chamber but we'll die eating potato peels," someone says, and we laugh from a deep place in us that we didn't know still existed. There's power in our laughter.'

CARDINAL VINCENT NICHOLS

Archbishop of Westminster

Cardinal Vincent Nichols's answer to the question is a unique exploration of how shedding tears contains multitudes of human experience.

Recently I visited one of the centres in Erbil in Iraq where thousands of Christian refugees are living. One woman told me of their frightening and rapid flight from their home in the city of Mosul as ISIS terrorists advanced. She told me that her Muslim neighbours of many, many years wept to see them leave. Here, in the midst of the most awful suffering, is a true sign of what makes us human. We weep.

The tears of true weeping are powerful in all that they can express. They flow because we are heartbroken at what is or has been lost or destroyed. As human beings we know, at the deepest level, what is truly good for us, and it is not the latest car or mobile phone. Perhaps we shed a tear over them occasionally, but we do not weep. We weep at the death or departure of a loved one. We weep at wanton destruction of friendship, even at the destruction of our much-loved environment.

We weep because, in fact, we are not indifferent to goodness. We care passionately about all that is good – and not just about 'my personal goodness', but all that is truly good, objectively good, good for others, for our common good.

Sometimes we weep with rage. These tears are born of our innate sense of justice, when we see a situation which is 'crying out to heaven for justice'. Often those tears will be fuelled by our sense of helplessness, for the evil being done is beyond our influence. But that does not dull our sense of outrage at innocent suffering, at horrendous abuse of a person's integrity or dignity. Pope Francis says that we will never truly tackle the problem of human trafficking, modern day slavery, until we learn again how to weep.

Such tears come from the heart, from our inner selves, from our souls. They point to that dimension of being human which goes beyond the immediate, which sees beyond the facts, to an awareness of the deeper values. They mark us out from the animal world with its refined instincts but absence of moral sense and decision-making.

> **Here, in the midst of the most awful suffering,**
> **is a true sign of what makes us human.**
> **We weep.**

There is another source of tears which we must not hide away. Each of us is capable of shedding tears of regret and of repentance. Here, perhaps, we come to the most inner part of ourselves. We reflect on our behaviour. We judge our behaviour. We face the uncomfortable truth of our waywardness and we repent. This is the realm of conscience, that inner capacity within every human being, by which we recognise in what we do the difference between good and evil.

These tears of repentance are the most valuable. Through them, we set out on the road of forgiveness, the road of new possibilities, the road of a new freedom to start again. Tears of a confession, when shed in the embrace of love, evoke mercy and forgiveness. That is certainly true of the love of God. And when we seek and find forgiveness we, as human beings, appear in all our nobility as most powerfully reflecting the image and likeness of God in which we have been created.

Emotions

Then, of course, come the tears of joy. They being in sheer relief that a burden has been laid down, a locked door sprung open. But then they become tears of wondrous gratitude that I am loved and that life again is filled with light.

Long may we weep. Then we will discover again our humanity.

DOMINIC LAWSON

Journalist

In a poignant and heart-warming answer, Dominic Lawson leads us through a consideration of laughter and humour. Filtering his own personal experiences through philosophical musings, this is a delightful portrait of human happiness.

Are we the only species that laughs? And, if we are, does that mean a sense of humour is one of our distinguishing characteristics? Well, I know that hyenas are said to laugh, and there is a type of bird called the laughing gull. But these designations owe more to our desire to see creatures as reflections of ourselves than anything about their minds.

Why we laugh, outwardly or inwardly, is a little mysterious. One person's joke can be another person's insult. That's hardly surprising. Making fun of other people appears to be at the basis of humour – the fat well-dressed man slipping on a banana skin – but, in fact, we are laughing at the human condition. Or, as the philosopher Francis Bacon put it: 'Imagination is given to man to compensate him for what he is not, a sense of humour consoles him for what he is.' It's hard to imagine enduring all the misfortunes which existence can bestow without that consolation. As the saying goes, you've got to laugh, because otherwise you'd cry.

I can think of one example from my own family. When my mother was given a completely unexpected diagnosis of terminal cancer, she invited a funeral director to our home and asked him to give a quote for his service. 'May I ask,' said this impeccably smooth figure to her, 'who is the deceased?' She replied: 'The deceased will be me.' His startled and confused reaction perhaps owed something to the fact that my mother was in her forties and had no outward signs of sickness. But when she told us what had happened, mimicking the palpable consternation of the previously inscrutable funeral director, we, her soon-to-be-bereaved children, were reduced to uncontrollable laughter.

What other people are thinking is generally hidden from us. This lies behind so much misunderstanding between humans. But when we laugh together at the same time, there is a glorious feeling of mutual recognition: we are alike.

This is shared laughter, the bond that binds us together. What other people are thinking is generally hidden from us. This lies behind so much misunderstanding between humans. But when we laugh together at the same time, there is a glorious feeling of mutual recognition: we are alike. We are very far from alone.

Perhaps this is one reason the most commonly seen initials in what used to be called lonely hearts columns are GSOH. While I would be suspicious that someone claiming to have a good sense of humour might not actually be in possession of one (like the short man claiming in his ad to be 'average height'), this code is an acknowledgement of the fact that a close relationship without a shared sense of humour would not have much of a future.

But the modern belief that happiness is our due, and that we can consciously plan such a blissful state, is illusory. Happiness is not an end-point, but an accidental and ephemeral result of circumstances, most of which are outside our control.

Indeed, it is the unexpected which most makes us laugh: the sudden shock of recognising the truth in absurdity. This helpless exhalation called laughter renders us, for a few moments, like the carefree infants we all once were.

SHARRON DAVIES

Swimmer

Sharron Davies' highly personal answer speaks to the power of having a dream to guide you through the worst experiences a human being can go through. She recounts how, in times of grief, learning to be kind to yourself is one of the greatest and most powerful acts of compassion many of us can experience.

My life has always been about training, preparation, focus and setting targets . . . from as far back as I can remember. Some would agree that the ability to have a dream, and aim for it, maybe spending years or even a lifetime, is part of what makes us human.

If you can't dream and feel hopeful that one day that dream will come true, it can leave a void that means that life has no purpose. A dream can be a multitude of things, from becoming a doctor, helping others, being an astronaut, exploring space, being a teacher, passing on knowledge, or becoming an Olympic champion; even being a mum or a wife and loving your family and nurturing your children. No one has the right to say what that dream is, and what your journey will be on your quest for it, but it gives humanity a purpose, and can change from time to time, with life's twists and turns.

Recently I had my toughest challenge ever. I lost my mum, who had always been my safe harbour, and my daughter lost a good friend to suicide, a young man of only nineteen with the world to discover in front of him. All just before I was due to do a rather crazy TV show that put me on a deserted island with a bunch of strangers, the clothes I stood up in and a knife to survive. For me, the timing was terrible. It put me in a very dark place which I've had to recover from. It was as if my misery bucket was full and every little thing seemed to tip me over the edge, where my coping mechanism was to get angry and take it out on those closest to me rather than ask them for help.

As humans, we deal with grief in a multitude of different ways, but the ache grief brings can be unbearable, and I'm not sure any other species feels it in quite the 'all-consuming' way we humans do when we're sad.

So, I've discovered I need to be kinder to myself. Surround myself with those that have compassion. That I need to offer more compassion to my friends, and be more patient with those that I love. To have fewer targets and more understanding of the deep pain loss can bring. Grief can be about so many things: it can even be about the loss of your dream.

My life has always been about training, preparation, focus and setting targets . . . from as far back as I can remember.

After my recent experience, I've modified it slightly, what it is that makes us human. For me, it's still to dream, but with the compassion to support others whilst they strive for their dreams, being there when life throws curve balls at those you love, and the understanding that we can't all achieve our dreams, but that potentially, without them, we don't have a purpose. Striving, failing, learning, and trying again is being human.

People and Family

While many essays in this book consider
the common traits of individual humans, these
answers focus on how our humanity lies in our
interconnectedness – our connections with others,
our friendships, our families, and our care
even for strangers.

ROSE HUDSON-WILKIN

Bishop of Dover

Drawing on the African philosophy of _Ubuntu_, meaning 'I am because we are', Rose Hudson-Wilkin argues that we become the people we are through our relationships with others. It's an inspiring vision of the power of community.

To respond to this question, I have to go back to my roots – as a woman of African-Caribbean heritage – and draw on the African philosophy of '_Ubuntu_'.

This word comes from the Zulu and Xhosa language and it means 'I am because we are.' It is part of the Zulu phrase '_Umuntu ngumuntu ngabantu_', and this literally means that a person is a person through other people. Credit must be given to Archbishop Desmond Tutu for popularising the word. He spent a significant part of his life for so many years stressing the need for others' humanity to be taken seriously: not just black people in South Africa, but people all across the globe.

As a child growing up in Montego Bay, Jamaica, although I did not know the word '_Ubuntu_', I knew I was human because I had a sense of belonging. I did not have a perfect nuclear family, as my mother was in the UK and my father was 'around'; I grew up with my father's sister, Aunt Pet, and I was aware of other aunts and uncles. And, interestingly, there were a whole host of people that we referred to as aunty this or uncle that (who were not blood related). But that is what we did. During slavery, when the Massa referred to our menfolk as 'boy', we gave them back their dignity and we called them uncle. We enabled each other to feel a part of humanity, to have a sense of belonging; a family to be part of.

Personally, what makes me human, therefore, is, firstly, my sense that I belong to a family. This family is beyond my blood relations. For example, so many people who I do not know in Jamaica have sent messages of congratulations to me on becoming a bishop. One message that has been repeated daily since my appointment was announced is 'you make me proud'. They are proud because they see me as part of them. I belong. When I was installed in Canterbury Cathedral – wow, the welcome that I received from those present was also telling me clearly that I am and that I was a part of them.

> **What makes me human is being able to recognise that I share a common humanity with people from across the globe. It means that I can rejoice with others as they rejoice, but, equally, I can weep with them too.**

Secondly, what makes me human is that I am connected to my creator. At the start of each day, there is a conscious connecting to God. Throughout the day there is a constant rhythm of prayer and song; silence and words and, if I am lucky enough to go by a florist or go through a park, I feel blessed to be able to pause and admire God's handiwork in nature. An act of kindness by someone enables me to see another expression of God with us – in humanity.

Finally, what makes me human is being able to recognise that I share a common humanity with people from across the globe. It means that I can rejoice with others as they rejoice, but, equally, I can weep with them too: those who are homeless on our streets in the cold; the refugee or asylum seeker who is trying to make a life for their family; the child that is abandoned; the parents who have lost their child; those who are abused; the person who is lonely. I am human because I am interconnected with the rest of humanity.

KRISS AKABUSI

Olympic athlete

When we consider what makes us human, it's easy to think in individual terms. But Kriss Akabusi instead focuses on the 'us', and makes the compelling argument that the primary way in which we understand the world, and ourselves, is through each other.

There are few questions as powerful as 'What makes us human?'. But, ultimately, what makes us human is the ability to even cogitate on that question. We might be reminded of Descartes' 'I think, therefore I am' here, but, to me, being human is more than that. We think both on our own, and in relationship to others – because being part of a society is what makes us human.

Just imagine, if there were no other people in this world, would I speak a language? Would I even know I could speak? With nobody to reflect back our discourse, we don't have that realisation.

I'm born alone, I die alone, but, in the space in between, I meet others and I interact with them. And that interaction is what makes me human: those relationships with all the others who have ever been and ever will be.

I'm born alone, I die alone, but, in the space in between, I meet others and I interact with them.

When animals act on instinct – perhaps to protect their young – they respond fiercely without consideration. However, as a human, I can stop and think before acting. I think about the situation in relation to all that I've seen, all that I've heard, all that I know, all that's been passed down to me, and I can respond accordingly. And that knowledge, which has been passed on from everyone else, is vitally important.

So, to me, it's our relationship with others, and the impressions they leave, that are key to making us human. We are the sum of all the people we have ever met, and those half-a-dozen we reinvent ourselves with the most.

And with those others around us, we ascribe meaning to our lives. Without that meaning, our lives are essentially meaningless; we come into the world simply to die. As existentialists have mused for centuries – the likes of Kierkegaard, Sartre, Camus – we are all dealing with the reality of the meaninglessness of this life, and yet we make it meaningful.

And by doing so, we are human.

I look back at my life, I see a series of events, and I create a meaningful narrative that informs how I will act today. However, another aspect of our humanity is that we can reframe those narratives. We might meet new people, have new experiences, causing us to reflect and change the way we do things, enabling us to choose to do something different.

This leads us to contemplation, so we can live our lives to the full. We can contemplate the life we've already had, and what we'll do with the life we have left. It's so important to live a life you can sum up as 'a life well-lived', and so, by contemplating, adapting and acting, we can put ourselves in the right position to live, to die.

I can think about everything that's been before, and think about how I will tie it up in the years to come, to know I've lived life well. I can think about how I want people to remember me, the legacy I want to leave my children, and, because I am human, I can do something about it now. When we watch movies, we're given the impression that death is a neatly done thing. But, in reality, it's not always like that. What will go unsaid? What will go undone?

So, the things you want to do now? Do now. The things you want to say now? Say now. Thereby reframing *Cogito ergo sum* to 'I die, therefore I am!'

GEORGE OSBORNE

Former Chancellor of the Exchequer

A positive and personal consideration of the things that bring us together as human beings: from religion to politics to music. For George Osborne, politics itself is a very human thing, driven by people figuring out how to create communities.

What makes us human? Other humans. It's the stories we tell each other, the words we use to speak to each other, the music we play to each other that make us a human race.

The poet told us that no person is an island. We spend time by ourselves, but we are not solitary creatures – in fact, I hate being alone for too long. We are born to parents; we're raised by families; we form bonds of love and friendship with others; we have children together; we look after those children, and hope they will look after us some day; and when we die, our greatest fear is that we will die all alone.

Of course, we share this planet with other sentient and social animals – and I understand better than I once did that we would do well to share it better. But none of these other animals is able to reflect on its own existence as we humans do. My pet, Lola, lovely as she is, isn't thinking about a dog's life; she just wants her next meal.

But, when we're freed from the tyranny of hunger and subsistence, we start to wonder about human life, and what its purpose is. And we do it together. We form religions, we get carried away by causes, we volunteer time and money to help people we have never met. We listen to songs, laugh at jokes, watch sport. And we find it more rewarding when others watch and listen alongside us. I sing to myself in the car when the best tracks come on the radio; but it's even more fun with someone sitting beside you.

I'm not a philosopher, but I used to be a politician. I'm happy to ask that they ask the big question 'why?', but while I wait for an answer, I want the hustle and bustle of this world. People say they hate politics. But politics is just the word we use to describe how we work out how to get along with each other. For all the arguments, and sometimes terrible conflicts, it always amazes me that, for most of the time, in most places, we do. Here on this island, there are 65 million of us rubbing along.

People say they hate politics. But politics is just the word we use to describe how we work out how to get along with each other.

That's because we tell a history of how we came to be here, and the deeds and mistakes of those who came before us. We share a culture, which we draw from across the world – and we add to it. We're interested in each other, we watch and read about what we do.

And we construct a set of rules. Sometimes we say God gave them to us, and we call it a religion. Other times, we say it's a constitution or a set of laws. Either way, they are codes of common behaviour that help us live together. I relish the complexity and understanding that involves. It's not abstract; it's real. It's human. And I love it.

SIR PAUL SMITH

Fashion designer

Sir Paul Smith takes us back to the beginning of his career, in a small shop in Nottingham. The key to making the shop work was communication – and it is that ability, he says, that makes us human.

My first shop measured twelve feet by twelve feet. It was in an alley in the centre of Nottingham, down a nondescript corridor behind some other shops – an old-fashioned tailor and a jeweller. The room had a solid door and no windows. As a retail space, it couldn't really have been worse.

I had an Afghan hound called Homer, who I promoted to shop manager. The room was so small that it was crowded with just the two of us there. To start with, we opened on Fridays and Saturdays, and I spent the rest of the week doing other work to earn money to get the shop going. I opened it on 9 October 1970 – and I knew that, if I wanted to stay in business, I had to find ways of attracting the attention of the sort of customers I wanted, and then of keeping them interested.

Of course, I was selling what I thought were very nice shirts, jackets, jumpers and so on. The idea was to offer clothes that were more stylish and better made than those of the competition. But the key to making the shop work was communication. And behind that were the lessons I'd learned from my father.

He was something called a credit draper – a job that doesn't exist any more. He'd go from door to door selling clothes that people paid for in instalments. He was good at it because he was good with people – good at making them feel comfortable. They were pleased to see him. He could talk to anyone, whatever their age or class, and he was quite charismatic. He had a great sense of humour and he was good at breaking the ice.

When a customer came into my shop, it was so small there was nowhere to go. To keep them, I needed to engage with them in some way. So as well as the clothes I was selling, I made sure there was always an unusual object to use as a conversation starter. It might be an old poster I'd found at a flea market in Paris, or a penknife from a fishermen's shop in Greece. They were like props, and they helped me to make a customer feel relaxed about staying and looking through the clothes while we chatted.

When a customer came into my shop, it was so small there was nowhere to go. To keep them, I needed to engage with them in some way.

I can only speak English, but somehow or other I've managed to build a business with shops in seventy-three countries, based on communicating with people. All the shops have art on the walls or unusual objects on display, as ice-breakers and conversation starters. It helps to sell things, of course, but it's also a reminder that, as far as I'm concerned, communication is what makes us human.

MELVYN BRAGG

Writer and broadcaster

In this moving account, the legendary Melvyn Bragg reflects on his childhood and long-lasting friendships. For him, a full life comes from sharing it with others, and being able to reflect on the shared experiences of decades past.

I am picking out long-lasting friendships. People I have known since I was about five years old, known for more than my three score years and ten, are, in a sense, my chroniclers, my witnesses, as I am theirs.

For instance, there are three men from Wigton whom I see regularly but not enough, with whom I feel at ease in a way not possible with anyone else. It is always the smallest, even the most trivial things. When we raided another gang's bonfire – High Moor was the prime target, David Pearson's gang always built the biggest in the town; when we took sledges to the snowfields in those bitter winters; when we pinched apples and tried to eat as many as we could to hide the evidence and ended up with stomach cramps; when we used the hassocks in the church for trench warfare before choir practice. Catching tiddlers in jam jars. Climbing tall trees to find the best chestnut.

We recall characters from the town in the 1940s. Do you remember Kettler and Lol and Patchy and his disgracefully talented dog? Then there were the games around the banana slide in the park, where the thing was never to go up by the steps but to find other ways to scale it. And the empty town in the evenings was an adventure playground and our own jungle.

And playing football in the street with a bald tennis ball until it got so dark that we were moving by instinct, the gutters marking out the width of the pitch, a couple of jackets marking the goals, diving to save a shot, scraping knees. Always finding things to do.

Setting up a gang of us – well, six – who met every week or so in each other's kitchens to play Ludo and Monopoly and Tiddlywinks. And later, in the Scouts, pegging down sodden tents in the perpetual rain and coaxing flames out of reluctant twigs and yet managing to laugh a lot. And all the things that went wrong. That's the best bit. When we set off on an expedition or a mission which collapsed.

And later we would bike to dances in church and village halls, biking there in the half light, biking back in the dark. On it goes. A shared life. Your own life multiplied, mirrored, enriched, memories released that you never thought you had retained. The past, that other country, taking over the present and giving it a fine new flavour. When we first got drunk (on a couple of pints), when we, when we . . .

In the archives of the brains of close friends, there is a privileged museum to which only we have access and it brings out a full sense of a lived life.

> **People I have known since I was about five years old . . . are, in a sense, my chroniclers, my witnesses, as I am theirs.**

When a long-standing friends dies, I know that part of me has gone and can never be recovered. It is a particular kind of sadness and regret, but it's always seasoned with gratitude that it happened at all. That we knew each other so well and took time to look out for each other and put up with each other and understood what we were sharing in: friendship.

So here's to William, Eric and Brian. See you back in Wigton.

FLOELLA BENJAMIN

Broadcaster

Through her experiences of presenting children's television, Floella Benjamin talks about the lasting impact that those early moments of connection can have on the course of a child's life.

If you were to walk down the street with me anywhere in the UK, you would be amazed by the amount of people who come up to me and say 'Thank you for my childhood.' People from all walks of life who become little children all over again. You see, childhood lasts a lifetime, and everything children experience, good or bad, stays with them for ever.

Luckily the memories they have of me are loving, affectionate ones, all because of my appearances on television programmes like *Play School* and *Play Away*.

It was forty-two years ago I first appeared on children's programmes, and I finished *Play School* thirty years ago, but the memories still linger deep in people's minds.

I must admit, at the time I wasn't fully aware of the impact I was having on those young lives. I just enjoyed doing the programmes and put my heart and soul into them because I believe, whatever you do, you should give it your best shot, otherwise it's not worth doing. That philosophy must have filtered through the screen into those young minds because, even now, every day people say to me: 'You had such an influence on my life . . . because of you and *Play School*, I'm now a teacher, a musician, an artist, or a doctor.'

You see, what *Play School* did was to lay a foundation that made children confident about learning and discovering; it opened their minds to the world. It was like a mini culture show exposing them to art, music, storytelling, drama, dance, even humour. Many say that I was the first black person they had ever seen and that it changed their perception about people from different cultures.

As a child, I dreamed about being a teacher and I suppose I did end up being a sort of teacher, working in children's television, taking millions through the round, square and arched windows, introducing them to their world. But I too have benefited from those experiences, because they made me realise that everything we do affects children. I also realised children are not considered in a way that will benefit society in the future. Time and time again, children are treated as second-class citizens, and not enough attention is given to their early development or the long-term consequences.

That's why, back in 1983, I started campaigning for a Minister for Children. It took twenty years to finally get one put in place by the Labour government. My vision was for government to have joined-up policies, because every decision they made would directly or indirectly affect children. I also campaigned for there to be diversity in children's books, especially picture books, so that all children could see themselves reflected in the stories, giving them a feeling of belonging.

I am still campaigning on behalf of children, and whenever I stand up in Parliament, I always speak up for children's well-being, to change their world for the better, through legislation. Children don't have a vote, their voices are silent, but the way the world exploits them is shocking and shameful. I also do numerous school visits and take assemblies in which I encourage children to feel worthy, and talk about how to deal with temptation. I try to pump unconditional love into their worlds and give them the confidence to face the challenges they are likely to come across as they grow up.

We are now living in the internet age, and children are under huge pressure from social media. The challenges are even greater to nurture and protect them from an increasingly dangerous, unforgiving world. For some children, life is like a marathon; it's relentless, so they need guidance on how to cope. People say children are resilient – NO – they're good at covering up pain, but more and more are suffering with mental illnesses, including depression.

Time and time again, children are treated as second-class citizens, and not enough attention is given to their early development or the long term consequences.

We have all been children, but somehow we forget the importance of childhood – that is, until we have our own children. But, sadly, after a certain age, when our children are grown up, we forget to put children first. So my mission in life is to focus everyone's minds on giving all children, not just your own, the best beginning in life, and seeing every child as a gift to the world. Because, remember: 'childhood lasts a lifetime'.

SHAPPI KHORSANDI

Comedian

Told in Shappi Khorsandi's inimitably funny and relatable fashion, her essay teases apart how the unconditional love a parent has for their child illuminates the very best (and some of the very worst!) things about being human.

When I was about six, I was sat on the Underground with my mum and she found treasure in her handbag. It was an unfinished Dairy Milk chocolate bar. She unwrapped the foil to discover that there was only one piece left. Without a moment of consideration, deliberation or calling a lawyer, she gave it to me. That was the moment I realised my mother loved me more than I could ever imagine. I sat munching the chocolate, in awe of such a love existing. There wasn't a soul in the world I would give my only piece of chocolate to. I was so moved by it, I managed to brush off the shock of discovering that my mother was the sort of person who didn't finish off chocolate bars.

Trying to imagine how much you will love your children before you have them is trying to imagine a colour that doesn't already exist. The writer Elizabeth Stone put it perfectly when she said that having a child is to 'decide for ever to have your heart go walking around outside of your body'. I would add 'central nervous system' to that. You can't lose yourself to hedonism any more, because it's now of critical importance that you stay alive and alert, because there is a gorgeous bundle of your DNA relying on you to clear a safe path in the world for them to walk on – and to empty the dishwasher.

We create a universe to lose when we have children, yet somehow, on most days, we manage to go about being parents, swinging them on swings, shouting at them to hurry up, without sinking to our knees and shrieking 'BUT WHAT IF SOMETHING TERRIBLE HAPPENS?' But this fear is somewhere within us all of the time. It flares up and subsides, depending on where we are in life and how much broccoli you can get them to eat, but it is always there and will never leave.

**Trying to imagine how much you will love
your children before you have them is trying to
imagine a colour that doesn't already exist.**

If you're not a parent, the chances are you will, at some point, have had parents, and witnessed the madness that can descend on them when they feel you're in peril. The simple decision not to wear a coat on a cool evening can send your mother into a vortex of fuss and worry. Making every moment, every decision, about the well-being of children, no matter how badly you get it wrong sometimes, is the most universal trait of human beings.

Of course, some parents are duds; they are cruel and selfish. But, as humans, the instinct of even a stranger when they suspect neglect of a child or cruelty by a parent, is to help the child, to take it somewhere where it is safe and can be loved. Sometimes I hear people say 'I hate kids' with bizarre lack of self-awareness. It's like saying, 'You know the Childcatcher in *Chitty Chitty Bang Bang*? I was on his side.' The most uptight, grumpy person on the bus will awkwardly return the uninhibited grin of a rosy baby. Grumpy people are, after all, human too.

ANDRIA ZAFIRAKOU

2018 Global Teacher Prize winner

For all the frustrations and eccentricities of family life, Andria Zafirakou writes, her family remind her who she is and inspire her to be better. And she encourages us to think more broadly, about our communities and societies, to show them the same level of love and commitment.

I'm sitting here, staring at my computer screen, trying to contemplate how I am supposed to answer the question: what makes us human? What is it indeed that summarises what the common thread to humans is? My mind is bombarded with ideas and themes to enquire. I can say this about this, and talk about them and about that, but none of these ideas seem to be meaningful and, thus, they start to dissolve quickly. I am desperate for inspiration and consider reflecting on Descartes' quote: 'I think, therefore I am.'

Ten minutes later, my computer screen continues to remain blank and, worse still, it appears that I have finished my tea in record time and I need to put the kettle on again.

I go downstairs into the living room where my daughters are sprawled all over the couch, watching their favourite children's sitcom. They are totally transfixed by the screen, with huge smiles permanently fixed on their faces. Think the Joker from *Batman* and you are not far off. Then, suddenly, both burst into fits of hysterics and stomach-grabbing laughter, and one of them loses all control and rolls on to the floor.

I couldn't resist: I joined them in their chorus of giggles, to the point where my tears were pouring out of my eyes and my legs automatically crossed each other to ensure that nothing else poured out. It was one of those lovely fuzzy moments that you sometimes have where you experience and gain so much warmth, energy and happiness being with your children. It was perfect.

Two minutes later, the doorbell rings and I rush to open the door. My mother is there, carrying a shopping bag filled with plastic containers and saucepans full of food. I say, 'Hi Mum', and then she hands over the shopping bags and proceeds to tell me in one continuous breath . . . 'Hi Andria, I'm not sure if you have guys have eaten, I went to the supermarket yesterday and there were some good offers on, and I decided to cook some *avgolemono souppa*, *dolmades, pasticcio*, and I've also made some apple pie using the apples from the garden, as I know that your girls love it. Here you go, give my love to the girls, I can't stop as I'm going to your brother and sisters to drop their food off as well, see you.'

And off she went. I went straight into the kitchen and started to put the food in my fridge with my own Joker-type smile radiating from my face, knowing that a) she made all of my favourites, b) this must have taken her hours to do, bless her, and c) I won't have to worry about what to cook for the girls for the next few days or even week!

The following day, I go to work at my school and, whilst I teach my Year Seven Art class, I think about the amazing characters that I have in my classroom and how incredibly lucky I am to be sharing the room with and looking at the future of our world.

This is typical and absolutely normal behaviour from my parents. They continue to live their lives providing and helping their children and their grandchildren by doing whatever they can to make things just that bit easier for us. Warm fuzzy feelings hit me again through the onomatopoeic channels of 'Kazap' and 'Zonk'. Just love *Batman*, don't you?

The following day, I go to work at my school and, whilst I teach my Year Seven Art class, I think about the amazing characters that I have in my classroom and how incredibly lucky I am to be sharing the room with and looking at the future of our world. I sense hope and endless possibilities, as I know in front of me are our future presidents, CEOs, changemakers, scientists, artists and sportspeople. I get that warm fuzzy feeling again and notice that it is because I am feeling a sense of pride. They are my students, they are my children, I am their teacher and I am their mother. My role and purpose is to help them become and achieve who they want to be.

I am inspired and start to type on my computer. What makes us human is acknowledging the family.

ALAN JOHNSON

Politician

In a moving and deeply personal answer, Alan Johnson writes of the kind and selfless actions of his mother, who raised him and his sister in difficult circumstances – and their efforts to hold on to her values since she passed away.

I was fortunate enough to spend the first thirteen years of my life with two incredible women, who happened to be my mother and my sister. My sister Linda has been part of my life ever since – but we grew up, raised families and now live on opposite sides of the world. If you asked us to define humanity, we'd both say that it was personified in the tiny frame of our mother, Lily, who had deep compassion, enormous courage and a capacity for selfless love that is the essential element of what makes us human.

After a harsh childhood in Liverpool, she faced an even harsher adulthood in the slums of Notting Hill – with a feckless husband, two children and a heart condition that she knew would lead to an early death. Our father Steve ran off with the barmaid from the village pub when I was eight, and Linda eleven years of age. There is no denying that Steve's cruelty, and his failure to provide for us, reflected aspects of humanity including fallibility. However, he had another defining human characteristic. He was a musician. Steve played the piano entirely by ear, only having to hear a song once before he could play it in the pubs and clubs of our corner of West London.

The ability to translate emotions into music, art, poetry and dance brings joy to our existence, however mundane and difficult that existence may be. We had a big old Radio Rentals contraption wired into one of our rooms in Southam Street, West 10, with a Bakelite switch setting out our three options – BBC Home Service, Light and Third Programme. One day, unusually and perhaps unintentionally, the switch was on three. Out of the huge speaker, in one corner of the squalid room we called a kitchen, came a piece of music that enchanted me. It wasn't the pop music that I was already fascinated by – but it was uplifting and inspiring in equal measure. I found out years later that it was *Pictures at an Exhibition* by Mussorgsky. Its beauty and majesty nourished my soul.

Lily believed in God, although she never went to church. Our moments of worship came when she found a shilling piece to feed the empty gas meter, or a piece of coal as we joined her on the trail of the coalman, picking up the chunks of black gold that dropped from his sacks as he delivered to the big houses in Holland Park. Faith and belief are a very human traits, as are laughter and joy. What I remember most about my mother was her radiant smile, the way she tried to imitate her favourite Hollywood film stars, her little homilies and her terrible jokes. Every New Year's Eve, without fail, she'd tell us that she'd just seen a man with as many noses on his face as days left in the year, and every year we'd try to manage an indulgent chuckle.

> **What I remember most about my mother was her radiant smile, the way she tried to imitate her favourite Hollywood film stars, her little homilies and her terrible jokes.**

After Steve had started another life with his new family, my mother did an extraordinary thing. Having tracked down where he lived, she implored me to visit him, on the spurious grounds that every boy needs a dad. I refused, and in desperation she offered to go with me, to enter the home of a man who'd abused and deserted her and sit exchanging pleasantries with his new wife.

She would have suffered that humiliation because she felt it was in my interest.

After Lily died, Linda displayed all her mother's characteristics in her battle with 'the authorities', as she called them, to keep us together and out of care. Unlike me, she eventually made contact with our father, principally because she wanted to have a relationship with our half-sister, Sandra. The things that make us human aren't common to every human being. I couldn't understand how Linda, who'd suffered much more than me from his cruelty, could bring herself to make contact. But she, like Lily, was far stronger than me.

I don't think that she ever forgave Steve, but her desire to be a sister for Sandra drove her to do what was undoubtedly the right thing. If I had an ounce of that magnanimity, I would be a better human being. Lily died almost fifty years ago. Linda and I have enjoyed an infinitely better life than hers. Sometimes the best things that make us human emerge from the worst things that humans have to endure.

PROFESSOR GREEN

Rapper

Stephen Manderson, better known by his stage name Professor Green, tells the moving story of his difficult upbringing. Many will relate to his experiences with anxiety and depression, and even more will be reassured by the conclusion he draws from his life: though our past makes us, it does not define who we're going to be.

Our past and experiences are what make us human – but they don't have to define us.

Writing my autobiography was the first time I've tried to document the goings-on over the years: the trouble with school, the dealing, the depression, the music and the marriage. Have I been lucky? If I have, I've had to make all the luck myself. I didn't have parents to guide me when I was growing up and, although my nan took that role, it was still hard not to have a mum and dad who were there all the time. By the time I was ready to reach out to my dad, to try and make some of that better, it was too late: I lost him before I got the chance to know him, and to find out why he was hardly ever around.

Accidents used to keep me off school, but I quickly bounced back. But anxiety and depression would stop me in my tracks. They were the hardest to shift and that hasn't changed. Nan did everything she could for me, and with her love I still had a lot of amazing times. Growing up without much money and with my principal carer being my nan was not always easy, but, at the same time, it was very far from a miserable life. She gave me the things you can't put a price on – a home, her love and her patience.

Although the financial situation in our house was so often perilous, I was always dressed smartly and had nice clothes. Nan put herself under tremendous stress for me. She bent over backwards to give me things. There was a constant worry brought on by living outside our means, and through it I learned that I would have to work my arse off for everything I wanted.

Have I been lucky? If I have, I've had to make all the luck myself.

As I grew older, I would find that where I was born didn't have to determine where I ended up, but at the same time, I was aware that none of us are born deserving anything.

We're born where we're born, we try for what we try for. People don't seem to understand that they aren't owed anything, but so many people go through life acting as if they are. It would have been easy for me to sit on my arse and be a victim of my circumstances. From the start, I had had to live my life without support from my parents. Their absence shaped my decisions all the way through my life, but I had come through it. I did what I needed to do in order to survive and succeed.

It was meeting inspiring people through music that was one of the best parts of finding success as far as I was concerned. New experiences were better than making more cash. Money makes it easier to have those experiences, but it was the moments I shared with people that put a smile on my face. Success felt good in itself. Musical recognition was something I'd risked everything for and worked my arse off to get, and it felt good to be succeeding at something that was positive, that was decent, that was legal, that my Nan could be proud of me for doing.

By now I'm feeling more comfortable in my own skin – as well as recognising, however reluctantly, that I'm a proper adult now. I've been trying to be more active in fighting depression. I could have done with an example to show me that successful, happy people didn't always come from perfect families and privileged backgrounds. Society pressures us all into believing that, if we're not happy all the time, then there's something wrong with us. I've come to learn that happiness isn't a permanent state, and neither is sadness.

Speaking out is important. If I can help others who come from disadvantaged backgrounds to believe they can do more than society thinks is right for them, then I'm all for it.

I'll always be that guy those things happened to and I will always draw on those experiences, but they don't define me.

COLIN PARRY

Founder of the Tim Parry Johnathan Ball Foundation for Peace

Colin Parry talks of how a loving family fortifies him against the challenges in life, and how – even when faced with unimaginable loss – humanity can prevail.

I can only answer this question by rephrasing it to 'What makes *me* human?' Self-evidently, I am a product of my family genetics and of where I was born – Liverpool.

If I have one overriding recollection of my childhood, as an only child, it is of laughter. Mostly laughter with my mother, who was both funny and very loving, despite her often being alone due to my father's naval career, followed by his service as a prison officer. My father was not always an easy man to be around, being a product of a 'command and control' environment and, all too often, given to shouting and dark moods. Mercifully, he was never physically violent and, on the upside, he was a fantastic joke teller and would have my mother and me in peals of laughter at his gags, which, more often than not, were not censored for the delicate ears of a young boy.

At school, I always tried to be the joker, either as a self-protection device when confronted by older kids, or to deflect attention away from not having done my homework. Consequently, I spent many a long hour in detention for pushing my luck too far with my teachers. So, looking back, I have to credit my father for pushing me hard at home to get the education I was in danger of throwing away at school.

I got a place at university, but promptly messed up my first year, again larking around. My behaviour was compounded by being from Liverpool at a time when Liverpool was *the* place in the whole world you would have chosen to be from. So, I was never short of mates or girlfriends, just year-end grades, and I faced the risk of losing the place I had worked hard for!

Thankfully, I secured a repeat year, but this time studying Politics and not English, my original degree subject. After graduating, I went back home to Liverpool and became a graduate trainee in personnel management, and, some years later, I met my lovely wife Wendy and we produced three beautiful children in three years! Life was again full of laughter and me telling the same inappropriate jokes my dad had told me.

Tim, our middle child, inherited my mum's love of life and laughter, but his laughter and fun died when he was killed in 1993 at the age of twelve, by an IRA bomb.

Never can a family face a worse nightmare than the death of a child, and so it was with us. Thankfully, however, our humanity did not die, and through this, we survived the loss of our joker. His name is now for ever enshrined in both the charity Wendy and I set up in 1995 – The Tim Parry Johnathan Ball Peace Foundation, and again, five years later, in the Peace Centre we opened in 2000.

Never can a family face a worse nightmare than the death of a child, and so it was with us.

So, what makes me human is my family's humanity, passed down through the generations, filled with laughter and fun – which lifts me when I fall, makes me laugh when I cry, and restores my faith when all seems lost. Tim is, was and always will be the beacon of light and humanity in the lives of Dominic, Abbi, Wendy and me.

HELLA PICK

Journalist

A fascinating answer about our fundamental need for friendship and connection, Hella Pick spares no criticism for the social media that is supposed to bring us together, offering a strong warning against the isolation it can frequently lead to.

Imagine being stranded on an island – all alone, just having to rely on your own wits, without a friend to help, to talk with, even to quarrel with. I wouldn't just feel lonely, I would feel diminished – less than human. I firmly believe what makes us human is friendship. It is our capacity to make friends that helps us to live through good times and bad times and enables us to confront the immense stresses and challenges of the world we live in. The human being has a fundamental need for friendship.

> **Imagine being stranded on an island – all alone, just having to rely on your own wits, without a friend to help, to talk with, even to quarrel with.**

In my own life, I have found time and again that friendship is the most precious commodity we possess. As a small, bewildered child refugee, who had been transplanted from Austria to a school in the English Lake District, I was befriended by a local artist and his wife. They became my anchor, gave me a sense of stability and helped me to adjust to my new world.

When I first became a journalist, women were still a rarity in that profession. For me, it was even more of a challenge, because my job involved spending time in Africa, where women reporters were even more of a curiosity. I would have had a very tough time indeed if some of my male colleagues had not befriended me and made me feel that I was 'one of them'. Probably even more importantly, the African friends I made taught me early on in life to understand that racial discrimination had no place in our society, let alone in my own life.

I have always travelled a lot – often for my work, but also for pleasure. Friends across the globe have been a great bonus. They open horizons, they help me to understand other cultures, they can cut across political divides.

During the Cold War, I spent a great deal of time reporting on the Communist world and soon learned that friendships could be formed even if our politics were far apart. I was also lucky enough to meet some of the brave individuals in the Soviet Union who fought for human rights at great risk to themselves. Winning their trust and making friends with them, they taught me so much about the importance of freedom, integrity and courage.

Of course, friendships are not just about the big challenges but also about our intimate lives. Most of us have hobbies and special interests. What would football be without friends to share the high emotions of a match? Who likes to go to a gig or a show without a friend? Who believes that love can last without friendship between the partners?

I was about to ask who thinks that being alone with a smartphone or tablet is better than being in the company of a friend, a human being? And that has caught me short. We all know what a large role social media has come to play in most people's lives. Still, the fact is that social media has encouraged isolation. Direct human contact takes second place. This diminishes our humanity.

Friendships can have their ups and downs. Thankfully, some last, but some break up; some just fade away; some return. But, to my mind, friends of any shape or mind or colour have one thing in common: they define us as human beings.

ROBERT PESTON

Journalist

This deeply moving tribute to his late wife, Siân Busby, reveals a more private and, of course, deeply human side to Robert Peston. Written about a year after her death in 2012, he speaks about how the physical absence of a loved one does not mean losing the connection you shared, or the wisdom and guidance they gave you in life.

What is it to be human? Since the death of my wife, Siân Busby, about a year ago, I have been thinking a good deal about this. How could I not, having been wrenched savagely from proximity to the person with whom I have been in love for the best part of my life? It is a version of 'what's it all about?'

It is immediately clear to me that a small part of the answer is taking pride in the achievements of those to whom we feel closest, since I feel obliged at this juncture to tell you that Siân was a brilliant writer, wonderful mum, devoted sister and all-weather friend. And she was my soul mate.

Her last year demonstrated another quality of many humans: bravery. She was much braver than me, and her courage during five years of body-wracking lung cancer was exceptional. Siân hoped for the best and was never pessimistic; she only ever revealed to me her fears and anxieties, protecting our children and friends, so that life could be as normal as possible; she rarely complained when wracked with acute pain.

If she occasionally remarked that, as a non-smoker, rare drinker and healthy-living person, it seemed a bit unfair that she was afflicted with a disease more normally associated with a life of indulgence, would that be so shameful?

Siân was not a saint. She could be intolerant and damning of those she considered vain and stupid. But she was the best human I will ever know.

What I really want to explore is the link between the social, our connections with people, and the essence of being human. Siân built her life around mutually supportive, intimate friendships, which were often artistic collaborations. These connections for her were largely in the private sphere. In this sense, we were a 'Jack Spratt' couple, because she did not enjoy public life, whereas I revel in trying to reach out to a wider audience – both through my work as a journalist, and through founding an education charity, Speakers for Schools.

One motive for setting up Speakers for Schools was a conviction that everything works better – the economy, communities, society in the broadest sense – when we are connected to as many varied people as possible. And the connection has to go both ways. It is a two-way pipe. Life is dull and poor for those with limited knowledge and a narrow outlook. There are fewer opportunities to create wealth – material and spiritual – in the absence of challenging conversations. It is other people who help us both to see more of the world as it is, and to understand more about ourselves.

That is why I often think the eminences who go into state schools under our scheme derive as much benefit as the students whose ambitions they are trying to spark, because they are asked challenging questions that their entourages would never put to them, and they are taken out of their cosseting monied ghettos.

But the kernel of my reflections on human-ness are about what it means to lose the physical presence of the person to whom you feel closest. What happens to the connection to the one you love when he or she dies? As you will have gathered, in an important way I feel lucky because, for all my recent trauma and heartache, with Siân I had the kind of bond that for years I had thought impossible.

And just because Siân isn't sitting next to me, that does not mean the bond or connection has gone.

Of course, there are really important things that I miss, beyond what words can convey. She was beautiful in every way, and just entering a room to be with her made me feel happy. The loss of physical intimacy is brutal, horrible. But we also had an unusually deep intellectual and spiritual connection. That intangible connection cannot be destroyed; it is manifest in a continuing integral dialogue with Siân in my heart and head, or through the warmth that memories generate.

For all my recent trauma and heartache, with Siân I had the kind of bond that for years I had thought impossible.

We were always confident of the connection between us, not possessive of each other, or jealous of each other. This does not mean we were similar people or agreed about everything. She was (is) a Celtic artist; I am a Jewish hack. She kept my ugly vanity in check, and I helped her become more ambitious in her art and writing. We were more as a couple than we could be apart. And more than anything, I do not want to be made smaller by her departure; I will not allow myself to lose her wisdom and guidance.

Even when Siân was ill, all I could see was the two of us growing old together. We knew, intellectually, that there was a high statistical probability that the lung cancer would kill her, but that was not a prognosis we accepted in an emotional sense. Neither of us was ready for or reconciled to her death. We would talk frequently of being together for ever. And I am only a bit embarrassed to say that I still believe that.

So here is another thing about being human. Many of us put a quest for the eternal at the centre of our lives. As a Jew by birth and an agnostic through choice, I do not look for immutable truth in conventional religion. But I found something that transcends physical existence in my connection with Siân, my love for her. That is what defines me, as a human.

DR SARAH JARVIS

GP

It is our ability to care that makes us human, according to Dr Sarah Jarvis. In her decades of work as a GP, she has seen the best and worst in humanity – but she believes that the need to care for others is a core trait of humankind.

On a chilly winter's morning in Shepherds Bush, I sat on the floor in a tiny flat with three other women. We were all crying – for some of us, there was the occasional chest-wracking sob. For others, a silent trickle down the cheek. The floor was a default position because it was the place we could hold hands as we shared stories about the person – or now the body – lying three feet away from us on a bed.

To one of us, she was a sister: to two, a mother. To me, she was a patient – but to all of us, she was special. I had cared for her for almost twenty years, through her decline from robust health through weakening courtesy of the chronic lung disease COPD, and finally the ravages of cancer.

The body that lay there was a pale shadow of the vibrant woman I had first known – but we were not sad. She had had a good death: she had had the death she wanted. She had slipped away quietly and peacefully at home, surrounded by the family she was so very proud of.

This sort of death does not come easily – a 'good death' takes planning, and despite our best efforts, it isn't always achieved. That peaceful end had involved a small army – district nurses, home care assistants, occupational therapists, physiotherapists, cancer nurse specialists and, of course, her family – who had all played a part in caring for her.

And to me, it is our ability to care that makes us human. Of course, we are hard-wired to care for our offspring – it's an evolutionary imperative. And, of course, even that doesn't always happen: as a GP, I have seen the worst of humanity as well as the best, and abuse of children, partners and older dependents never loses its power to horrify.

But I have also witnessed more examples of human caring and compassion than I can possibly count. Often from professionals – not just doctors and nurses, but care home assistants, cooks and porters, who go above and beyond to provide comfort. And, very importantly, from the army of unsung heroes, 'informal' carers, without whom the very fabric of our society would disintegrate. But all too often from volunteers, neighbours, strangers who just want to make a difference because they care – not for one person, but for any person in need.

I have witnessed more examples of human caring and compassion than I can possibly count.

When I informed my parents at the age of eight that I wanted to become a GP, I had been inspired by the GP who came to our home to see my father. We had complete faith that he would make my father better – and that's what I wanted to do for other people. Of course, my idealised view of the profession was very different from the reality – being a GP involves infinitely longer hours than much of the public realises: acting on results, making referrals, attending case conferences. We are not expected to be experts in the minutiae of every condition, but we do have a duty to know enough about every condition to recognise and act on the signs the vast majority of my specialist colleagues will never see. We live with the knowledge and the constant pressure of knowing that every decision we make is important.

People and Family

A close friend of mine – a prominent journalist – for many years covered many of the most important issues of the day and, in effect, set the national news agenda. I was musing one day on how he coped with the responsibility: he raised one eyebrow and remarked 'When I make a mistake, nobody dies'. But while spotting an early case of cancer and saving a life is gratifying, it's being able to care that means I have never regretted the decision my eight-year-old self came to.

Society

These essays consider the structures that
bind us together as a society: a world of work,
economics and politics. What place does humanity
have in the cut-throat world of politics?
Does money define or distract from our true
nature? Can a vocation give us purpose –
or is there more to life?

FRANCIS FUKUYAMA

Political scientist

It is not our intelligence that makes us human, but *'thymos'* – the recognition of one's dignity – says Francis Fukuyama. This thought-provoking answer peels back the layers of humanity until we are left questioning the true motives of our daily decisions.

Living as I do in Silicon Valley, the most typical answer to this question given by the people around me would have something to do with intelligence or rationality. There are a number of technology enthusiasts and rich entrepreneurs who one day hope to be able to upload themselves into a machine, as if their entire being consisted of cognitive abilities and memories. There is a long tradition of putting intelligence at the front of the queue in describing the essence of the human, as in the very term *Homo sapiens*.

I've always thought this was a very limited view of the specifically human. Plato understood better, and divided the human soul into three parts: reason, desire, and *thymos*. The latter is a Greek word that can be translated into English as 'spiritedness', and is closer to what I think makes us uniquely human than our intelligence.

Thymos is the part of the human personality that demands recognition of one's dignity. It doesn't want food, shelter, sex or money, like the desiring part; rather, it wants other humans to recognise one's dignity or worth. One feels angry when one's dignity is not adequately recognised, and pride when it is; one feels shame when one is properly condemned, and guilt when one has failed to live up to one's own standards and recognises one's own unworthiness.

I believe that *thymos* is very specific to human beings. Many animals exercise both reason and desire; human beings just have a lot more of both. (Some dogs, it would seem, have human-level quantities of both.) *Thymos*, on the other hand, is much harder to find in the non-human animal world; some higher primates seem to fight over prestige, but it is not clear that they can feel either pride or guilt.

Economists think that human history is largely a story of fights over resources. They have no room in their model for *thymos*, which is actually the driver of the behaviour they think of as economic. People want things not necessarily because they're needy or greedy, but because they want recognition. Why do I really covet that Mercedes? Is it because I need such a good car, or is it rather that I want a marker of my social status? The well-to-do female executive can still get terribly angry when she learns that she is not being paid as much as her male counterpart, not because she necessarily needs the money, but because her relative pay signifies a lack of respect.

**Human beings . . . can invest many other things
beyond their own persons with dignity:
a flag, an altar, a piece of parchment
bearing a constitution.**

Human beings, moreover, can invest many other things beyond their own persons with dignity: a flag, an altar, a piece of parchment bearing a constitution. They get angry when other people or causes they value are treated with disrespect or injustice. Much of our contemporary conflicts arise out of 'identity politics', in which some group suffering past discrimination – whether race, gender or sexuality – seeks recognition of its dignity.

Today, we seem to be returning rapidly to a world of geopolitics, as Russia and China make territorial claims and ISIS seeks to take over the Middle East. The former two are driven by nationalism;

the latter by religion. But both nationalism and religion are species of identity politics in which the demand for recognition lies front and centre. Russia feels it was despised by the West after the breakup of the Soviet Union; China talks about the '100 years of humiliation' it suffered at the hands of the West. The young militants fighting in Syria and Iraq similarly feel that Islam, or their particular sectarian version of it, has been inadequately recognised.

Thymos is not just the source of violence and conflict, however. All human beings are driven to do great things by pride and approbation, and are enjoined from doing bad things by shame and guilt. Much more than reason and desire, *thymos* drives human beings into society, since what they seek is the recognition of other people. The struggle for recognition, as the philosopher Hegel noted, is therefore in many ways the basis for politics and for the evolution of human history. Were it not for *thymos*, human beings would probably still be living in tiny bands on the African savanna – happy, perhaps, but not dominators of the whole planet.

JASON COWLEY

Editor of the *New Statesman*

We might sometimes be tempted to think of politics as the least human sphere of life, but this essay, interwoven with personal insight, serves as a powerful reminder of what politics can and should be.

I've long been haunted by a scene in George's Orwell's great novel *1984*. Winston Smith, the hero, is being forced to watch propaganda films depicting acts of war and destruction. Winston is moved by something he sees, a woman protecting a child by wrapping her arm around him. It's a futile gesture. She can't protect the boy or stop the bullets. But she still embraces him, all the same – before, as Orwell writes, 'the helicopter blew them both to pieces'.

For Winston, what Orwell calls the 'enveloping, protective' gesture of the woman's arm comes to symbolise something profoundly human – an expression of selflessness and of unconditional love in an unforgiving world.

I read *1984* for the first time in my late teens. I'd dropped out of sixth-form college without completing my A-levels and was commuting on a coach from my parents' house in Hertfordshire to London, where I worked as a junior clerk in the Electricity Council, a vast labyrinthine public sector bureaucracy. During this long daily journey – sometimes two hours each way – I started to read seriously for the first time.

I was just getting interested in politics – this was the high point of the Thatcher years – and Orwell's portrayal of a dystopian future in which Britain (renamed Airstrip One) had become a Soviet-style totalitarian state was bleakly fascinating. Fundamentally, the book seemed to me to be about the deep human yearning for political change – about the never-ending dream of preserving or creating a good society.

1984 was published in 1949, during a time of rationing and austerity in Britain – but also of renewal. Led by Clement Attlee, who'd been Churchill's deputy during the wartime coalition, the Labour government was laying the foundations of what became the post-war settlement.

The NHS and the welfare state were created. Britain's independent nuclear deterrent was commissioned. New towns were established – such as Harlow in Essex, where I was born and brought up. To grow up in Harlow – I now understand – was to be part of a grand social democratic experiment. Our lives were socially engineered. Everything we needed was provided for by the state – housing, education, healthcare, libraries, recreational facilities. This hadn't happened by accident. As my father used to say, we owed the quality of our lives to the struggles of those who came before us.

The conservative philosopher Edmund Burke described society as a partnership between 'those who are living, those who are dead, and those who are yet to be born' – and I find this idea of an inter-generational social contract persuasive.

But progress isn't inevitable. There's no guarantee that things will keep getting better, as Winston Smith knew. History isn't linear, but cyclical and discontinuous. And these are disturbing new times in which we are living. A terrible civil war has been raging in Syria for many years. Europe has been destabilised by a refugee crisis and by the emergence of insurgent parties, from both the radical left and right. We have entered a new era of great power rivalry as China rises and the liberal world order is fragile. And many millions of people in the West feel locked out or left behind by market-driven globalisation.

But we shouldn't despair. To those people who tell me they're not interested in politics, I often say: 'But politics is interested in you!' And part of what it means to be human is to believe in politics and the change politics can bring.

What, after all, led so many Americans to vote for an anti-establishment maverick like Donald Trump? Trump promised to 'Make America Great Again' – and enough people believed him, or at least wanted to believe him, to carry him all the way to the White House. They want to believe in something different, because the status quo had become intolerable.

So politics matters.

To those people who tell me they're not interested in politics, I often say: 'But politics is interested in you!'

The decisions we take collectively as humans have consequences. We are social beings and rational agents, yet we can be dangerously irrational. This is why long-established institutions, as well as the accumulated wisdom of past generations, are so valuable, as Burke understood.

Politics makes us human. It changes our world and ultimately affects who we are and how we live – not just in the here and now, but long into the future.

PETER TATCHELL

Human rights campaigner

Peter Tatchell's essay is a rousing answer about the power and importance of protest, citing historical movements that have led to monumental change in all our lives. What makes us human is our drive to fight for good.

Protest makes us human. Without it, where would we be? We'd still be living in the dark ages of serfdom, tyrant kings, slavery and child labour.

Every social reform in history has been the result of dedicated and brave women and men who've protested against injustice – from securing the Magna Carta to the freedom of colonial peoples in countries like Kenya, Malaya and Cyprus.

None of our precious rights and freedoms were freely given to us by people in power. They were hard-won and came about as a result of protests.

It is thanks to the Chartists and Suffragettes that we've all got the right to vote.

Likewise, it was protests that secured social welfare provisions like pensions and child benefit, plus the National Health Service and free schooling.

It is our capacity to comprehend injustice, and our willingness to challenge it, that makes us human. Using reason, ethics, logic and science, we work out what's wrong and protest to stop it.

Our sense of conscience, and ability to empathise with others, motivates us to resist wrong and advocate for what is right.

We would not be human without our instinct and drive to protest against things we disagree with. It is a key defining element of our humanity.

Vastly more than any other species, our brains are hard-wired to question, criticise, dissent and rebel. It is our unwillingness to accept bad things and our willingness to fight for good things that makes us truly human.

Of course, what is good and what is bad is a subjective judgement, so you can have protests from the right as well as from the left.

Vastly more than any other species, our brains are hard-wired to question, criticise, dissent and rebel.

Either way, protest is the lifeblood of democracy. It is the means by which we, the people, hold the rich and powerful to account – a vital mechanism for the defence of democracy and liberty against the abuse of state and corporate power.

Indeed, you could say that protest is the most direct from of democracy. Protesters don't leave it to MPs. They do it for themselves and, through their own efforts, bring about social change.

Securing a fair society is far too important to be left to politicians. They are often the last people to wake up to the need for change. Much of the time, pressure for social reform is first initiated outside of parliament by campaign groups, such as Amnesty International, Greenpeace and Animal Aid. Their extra-parliamentary protests are nearly always the initial sparks and catalysts of social reform.

Three of my inspirations are Mahatma Gandhi, Sylvia Pankhurst and Martin Luther King. They all used protest as a way of winning human rights and social justice. Faced with unresponsive governments, they staged street demonstrations, refused to pay taxes and organised hunger strikes and sit-ins. By these means, India won its independence, women got the vote and racial segregation was ended in the United States.

Here in Britain, Margaret Thatcher's much-hated Poll Tax was defeated when hundreds of thousands refused to pay and protested in the streets. Opposition MPs had proven powerless to stop the Poll Tax. But when people protested en masse, Thatcher's flagship policy collapsed in one the biggest political climbdowns in modern British history.

Far from threatening the democratic process, protest from outside the parliamentary system protects and enhances democracy – acting as a much-needed counter-balance to the frequent arrogance, self-interest and elitism of political parties and politicians. Protest is power to the people! Protest is what makes us human.

ALEXEI SAYLE

Comedian, actor and author

Few essays manage to take in their childhood experiences, a chance meeting with hypnotherapist Paul McKenna and the history of capitalism, but if anyone can do this and make it thoroughly entertaining, Alexei Sayle can.

Several years ago, I attended a summer party where one of the other guests was the stage hypnotist and motivational speaker Paul McKenna. For some reason, we got talking about environmental issues, in which I know he has an interest. I was talking about how so much of my own and other people's supposed environmental activity, such as recycling wine bottles or buying organic bread, is just a mask for continuing rampant consumerism and he replied, 'Yes, if you were truly serious about trying to save the planet then what you would do is, you would kill yourself.'

I had never heard this opinion expressed before. As the child of Communists and a vestigial Marxist myself, my belief had always been that mankind's depredation of the planet was as a result of our exploitative economic system. I had unthinkingly subscribed to the view that capitalism was the problem and, if we had a different, fairer economic system – such as socialism – then we could heal the scars we have inflicted on the earth in our pursuit of the wilder excesses of capitalist consumerism. Socialist man would walk arm and arm with nature into a kinder, greener future.

But what McKenna seemed to be saying was that what makes us human also makes us destroyers of the earth, and that – given human nature – there is no way that we could live in harmony with the environment. Therefore, the only hope for the planet was if mankind disappeared completely. Once we had disappeared from the face of the planet, a great peace would descend – wars would stop, the destruction of the rainforest would be halted and gradually green growth would cover the landscape scarred with our buildings. The beauty of this wonderful blue-green planet would be restored and its only inhabitants – the animals – would live in harmony with Gaia.

A few days later, I was having my breakfast and chewing on a piece of toast when the unbidden thought popped into my head, 'this toast is a bit dry, I might as well hang myself'. Of course, this was Paul McKenna, who at the party had clearly planted a suicidal post-hypnotic suggestion in my brain. I managed to avoid committing suicide, but continued to wonder whether to be human means that I will inevitably be part of destroying the natural world, or if there is some way in which we can live in harmony with the earth.

So, given that every other creature except us has always had a benign relationship with the planet, and that, before the invention of agriculture, we did too, and that there remain tribal societies in a few remote corners of the earth who still do no harm to the biosphere while the vast majority of us live profoundly unnatural lives, how did this come about, and can we reverse at least some of the worst effects of what it is to be part of the disease that makes us human in the twenty-first century?

Pascal said: 'All of humanity's problems stem from man's inability to sit quietly in a room alone.' And that has got to be at the root of what has gone wrong with our relationship to our environment. We basically can't leave well alone; we are never satisfied. This perpetual search for novelty may have made us reach for the stars, but it has also led us to constantly seek the better, bigger exercise bike. Capitalism has seized on this flaw in our make-up and refined it so that we think that happiness will come from the next thing – the very next thing – that we buy. Our last phone did not make us happy, but this new one with a 13 billion pixel camera will do it. Or if only I had the £300 pair of trainers instead of these crappy ones that I bought last week for £129. Why did I ever imagine they would make me happy?

What obsesses all industrial societies is ceaseless growth, making more and more things, building more and more buildings, eating more and more food. Without continuous expansion, all manufacturing economies will collapse. In order to continue this expansion, people must be convinced that their happiness lies in buying new stuff. So what makes us human right now in the industrial economies is to be permanently dissatisfied, because, for our economies to grow, we must believe that it is not any of the things we already own, but the very next thing we buy, the very next holiday we take, that will finally push us over the top into serenity. Of course, as soon as we buy the thing or finish the holiday, that sense of dissatisfaction returns. The happiness doesn't last, but what is continuous and increasing is the brutal excavation of the earth's finite resources.

Millennia ago, in pre-agrarian societies, one day was much like another and people lived together in harmony with each other and with nature.

> **The thousand-year experiment to see if happiness can be bought, if possession of more and more stuff can give life meaning, has failed. We need to realise that the best things in life are not things.**

There existed a primitive form of communism: since there were no surpluses, nobody could accumulate more possessions than anybody else, and without more possessions, there was no incentive to grab more power – decisions were reached more or less by consensus. We are never going to get back to this Garden of Eden, but surely it should be possible to live more in harmony with both our planet and our better, truer selves? The thousand-year experiment to see if happiness can be bought, if possession of more and more stuff can give life meaning, has failed. We need to realise that the best things in life are not things.

Perhaps we need to look at and learn from the animal world: few animals living in freedom fail to reach their full potential.

To quote D. H. Lawrence: 'If men were as much men as lizards are lizards, they'd be worth looking at.'

BRENDAN O'NEILL

Journalist and writer

Brendan O'Neill's answer is a deft exploration of the question of personal and societal change. A forceful argument against determinism, his essay characteristically pulls no punches.

If I was playing a word-association game and someone said the word 'humanity', I would respond with the word 'change'. For me, that is what human beings are all about – change. Change at both an individual level, where we aspire to be the masters of our own fates, where we refuse to accept the hand dealt to us at birth and instead seek to change our fortunes. And change at a social level too, where humanity comes together and consciously transforms the world around us. Where we refuse to live at the mercy of disease or capricious, amoral Mother Nature, and instead change our physical surroundings to make them more amenable to human life.

If we look back at the past 6,000 years of human history, we can see this really powerful disposition to change and transformation. It was best summed up in the Renaissance of the 1400s and 1500s, when Giannozzo Manetti published a book called *On the Dignity and Excellence of Man*. Manetti said men could shape their own fates by 'the many operations of intelligence and will'.

Looking at my own family history, I can see how the individual urge to change and our exercise of social change can crash together and improve human life. My grandmother lived in the bleak west of Ireland from the early to the late twentieth century. She was illiterate, she never travelled more than forty miles from where she was born, and she suffered many physical ailments.

In contrast, her grandchildren, my generation, have travelled to every corner of the globe; we are literate, well-educated, in fact; and, statistically speaking, we're less likely to suffer from disease. That upward shift is a product of both the individual and social thirst for change. It was through my parents' generation's individual decision to leave the west of Ireland, to trek to other parts of the world in search of work, that we now find ourselves in a better position than my grandmother's generation was ever in.

If we look back at the past 6,000 years of human history, we can see this really powerful disposition to change and transformation.

And it was through mankind's social transformations – his war on disease and development of technology – that life in general is far better today than it was in the early twentieth century. Back then, in 1900, global life expectancy was thirty-one years. Today, it is seventy. We are all of us beneficiaries of earlier generations' stubborn refusal to accept their lot or to bow down before nature.

But sadly, today the human urge for change is under attack. It's being hemmed in by a dangerous new idea – that humanity is fundamentally destructive and therefore our instincts must be tamed.

At the individual level, our desire to determine our destinies is trampled on by a fatalistic belief that we are determined by our genes or our biology. New neuro-scientific claptrap tells us that everything from our political leanings to our propensity for violence is determined by neurons in our heads. Or we're told that how we are parented in the first five years of life determines our future personality and fortunes. These deterministic theories tell us that our character and life's path are fixed by forces beyond our control. In the depressing words of Lady Gaga, we are all 'born this way'.

And at the social level, our urge to transform our surroundings is now treated as something dirty and dangerous. Our impact on the planet is now referred to as a 'footprint', a horrible, eyesore eco-footprint. Our conquering of this planet is now treated as something wicked and toxic – humans are a plague, say extreme greens.

What is striking about today's reaction against both individual and social ambitions is that it comes from secularists, scientists, from activists who claim to be rational. In the past, it was priests and other moralists who told us to accept our lot. Today, such instinct-muzzling lectures come wrapped in scientific terminology; they are made by neuro-experts or greens waving scientific journals.

The backward desire to restrict human beings' aspirations, to tell us our fate has been written for us by powerful external forces, is today expressed by those who conceive of themselves as radical.

Well, we need to change this, too. We need to challenge and overthrow these emerging misanthropic ideas. We need to reassert the virtue of humanity's impact on the planet, and remind people of 'the dignity and excellence of man'.

LIONEL SHRIVER

Novelist

This answer hit home with something present in our everyday lives: money. According to Lionel Shriver, money is the glue holding our society together – and those who are reckless with our economic stability threaten our capacity to be human.

Money. Sorry to sound crass, but money makes us human.

It's thanks to money that our complex social arrangements are possible. Money can store energy – of labour and materials – to use in the future, which enables us to make plans. Money is divisible, and converts like and unlike into the same quantity. Without it, how would a writer manage at the supermarket? Could I trade a paragraph for a kilo of carrots? All our contraptions – the trains, planes and automobiles, the smart TVs: we'd never organise the production of all this junk without money.

In much of my fiction, money articulates relationships. What does it mean when a well-off grown son still expects his poor father to pay for dinner? Money can express beholdenness, gratitude, greed, justice, charity, celebration, spite . . . We use money to be nice, and to screw each other over. Disposition towards money betrays character. Savers convey caution and self-reliance – but sometimes also an inability to accept their own mortality. Easy spenders convey a you-only-live-once abandon – but sometimes also a willingness to burden others with their problems later on.

Ironically, money itself is worthless. It's only valuable when converted to something else. Offer two people £1,000, and one sees a holiday in Jamaica; the other sees central heating. Our projection on to money of positively anything we might desire is what makes it so alluring.

Yet what most of us want, above all, isn't available for purchase: love, loyalty, respect, wisdom, talent, admiration; notoriously, happiness. Why, you can't even buy a passable sense of humour. When you consider how little money is capable of securing, it's a wonder that we're so obsessed with the stuff.

Older people like me often want money to buy safety. Yet while writing *The Mandibles*, about the collapse of the dollar in a future United States, I grew sobered by how dependent we are for safety, especially in cities, on a functional currency. Civilisation has made urbanites biologically incompetent. So how will this Londoner eat, if Tesco no longer accepts the paper or plastic in her wallet in exchange for a chicken?

When money doesn't work any more, the world gets Darwinian, fast. It gets animalistic.

We rely on a viable currency for maintaining social order. When people can't buy the means to survival, they take what they need by force. Incinerating a population's lifetime savings invites incendiary rage, and breaks down the mutual trust that makes complex societies possible. When money doesn't work any more, the world gets Darwinian, fast. It gets animalistic.

Money is the glue that binds, the grease that lubricates, the cartilage that keeps the body politic running. Which is why I am alarmed by 'quantitative easing' – the frenetic conjuring of money out of thin air by central banks. I'm alarmed that private banks are allowed to loan scads of money they don't actually have to people who won't necessarily pay it back. I'm alarmed by financial institutions that trade in high-stakes yet impenetrably convoluted investment instruments, as if participating in an amusing video game called *The End of the World As We Know It*. I'm alarmed that global non-financial debt now stands at more than three times as much as worldwide GDP – hundreds of trillions of dollars. When does that money get paid back – that is the principle – and if it never will be, well, you've heard of fake news? I call that fake money.

I'm no economist, but I've concluded that these people, in government and the private sector alike, don't know what they're doing. Historically, the money folks have never negotiated a financial world this interrelated, this complex, or this dependent on computer algorithms, which can send the international fiscal superstructure into freefall in seconds. They are not simply playing with abstract digits, or corporate profits, or whether or not you and I can afford to buy a boat. They are playing with our ability to walk down the street without getting hit over the head with a cricket bat for our bag of potatoes. They are playing with our capacity to be human.

ROBERT SKIDELSKY

Economic historian

Robert Skidelsky argues against the cold view of humankind proposed by economists, and says that humanity instead happens when we live without weighing up the cost-benefit analysis.

Let's start with an addled view of what it is to be human. According to economists, it is the ability to calculate. Their picture of the human is that of *Homo economicus*, 'economic man', a calculating machine who is always weighing up the costs and benefits of every course of action.

Economics is about 'economising' – eliminating waste, including waste of time, so that all behaviour becomes efficiently purposive. The task of economics, according to the economist Dennis Robertson, is to 'economise on love, that scarce resource'. We need to economise on love because we live in a world of scarcity and cannot afford to spend too much time on wasteful activities, such as love. Economics offers us a way of getting what we want without love. Excluded is the idea that we might 'want' to love and be loved, that we might want beauty, leisure and many other things that make life worth living.

In order to make the construction *Homo economicus* plausible, economists assume that human behaviour is self-interested and that wants ('preferences') can be measured in money. It is money that makes possible the calculation of costs and benefits from different courses of action. Every activity has a cost and a benefit measurable in money. Love has a cost. If I spend time on love, I forgo the opportunity to make extra money to buy the iPad I crave, because 'time is money'. The best form of love for *Homo economicus* is quick sex, because that wastes very little time.

Robert Skidelsky

Most people believe that marriage is about love, but the economist Gary Becker has shown that individuals, in making their choice of partner, calculate the costs and benefits of different types of relationships.

Economics offers us a way of getting what we want without love. Excluded is the idea that we might 'want' to love and be loved, and many other things that make life worth living.

Similarly, there are costs and benefits in telling the truth, not cheating at cards, buying one's partner flowers, listening to music, reading a poem. Indeed, there is almost no form of activity one can think of that does not have attached to it at least the pretence of costs and benefits calculable in terms of money. And if one habitually makes this calculation before deciding to act, one will slowly but inexorably cease to be human.

The alarming thought is that, exposed to training in economics, human beings *do* start acting in the way economists say they should. In a marvellous book, *I Spend, Therefore I Am*, Philip Roscoe reports on research that shows that students studying economics are markedly more calculating than students of other subjects. Economics contaminates all our motives, forcing, in Amartya Sen's words, 'smallness on us'.

The dilemma in defining what is human is this: calculation is an integral part of the human outfit; animals don't calculate. Without calculation, there could be no economising behaviour. And without economising behaviour, there would be no growth of wealth. But if calculation is all we do, then we cease to be human. For the alternative forms of existence are not human and animal, but human, animal and robotic. Robots can be programmed to act exactly as economists think human beings should: efficiently, purposefully. There is no waste in a robotic civilisation.

So, as I would see it, the essence of distinctively human activity is action without thought of the consequences, without counting the cost of the activity and weighing it against the prospective benefits to be obtained.

And I would also claim that for many, if not most activities, this is the only rational form of action. For, contrary to Dennis Robertson, the truly scarce resource is not love, but knowledge. The great advantage of acting from motives of love is that it economises on the need for knowledge.

Usually we have only the foggiest idea of what the consequences of our actions will be, especially further in the future. And the net of delusion is being cast ever wider, as we are bombarded with more and more information masquerading as knowledge, more and more material for the calculus, which far outruns our ability to sift it into truth and falsehood.

Therefore, to follow our hearts rather than our heads, our intuitions rather than our calculations, is the distinctively human way of being. And if economics tells us the contrary, down with economics.

FRANK GARDNER

BBC security correspondent

You can still feel the excitement in Frank Gardner's words as he remembers walking into a global newsroom for the first time, and finding the vocation that is truly his passion. His answer serves as a reminder that what is comfortable is not always best for us.

Is this a scientific question? I just ask because, if it is, then I have absolutely no idea. You see? Line one, and I'm already out of my depth. Probably should have stuck to writing about security or counter-terrorism. But if we're talking about emotions, feelings, what makes us tick, what gets us out of bed in the morning, then I can offer this: it's about doing what we are really passionate about.

I'm not talking about mundane necessities here. Every creature knows instinctively it has to sustain itself, whether it's the lioness stalking the wildebeest, the ivy creeping its way up the tree trunk and sucking the life out of it, or the office worker pushing their tray around the canteen at lunchtime. This is all a given: it's just the essential, everyday run-of-the-mill business of surviving. But being human involves something very different over and above this. It's the luxury of choice.

After I graduated in Arabic and Islamic Studies – that, in itself, was a very conscious and unusual choice for the 1980s – I drifted inadvertently into investment banking. With no background in finance or economics, I never expected to pass the initial interview, most of which I didn't understand. To my amazement, I was offered a job and got sent to New York for training. My time in investment banking was relatively well-paid, comfortable, and occasionally quite interesting. But, at the end of the day, all we were doing was shuffling other people's money around the world. I found it hard to get excited about a product I never saw or touched.

When I reached my zenith in banking and departed the industry in a blaze of mediocrity, I opted to retrain in broadcast journalism. I was thirty-three. My parents were horrified. How would I survive? Why on earth would I want to trade in such a comfortable existence for long hours and low pay? This was a choice no sensible animal would have entertained. But it was what I wanted to do, and I have never regretted it for one moment.

The buzz I felt on walking into a global newsroom for the first time was irreplaceable. Suddenly, I was in a space where real live stories were coming in from all parts of the world, being turned around in double-quick time by people who were passionate about news and current affairs, and broadcast to a waiting audience of millions. It was infectious and I was hooked.

**If we're talking about what makes us tick,
what gets us out of bed in the morning, then
I can offer this: it's about doing what we are
really passionate about.**

Today, twenty-three years on, I still view every broadcast I make as an immense privilege, something never to be taken for granted. The experiences I get to have are ones I could never have had in banking: speeding up an Amazon tributary in a Colombian assault hovercraft, flying fast and low over the Horn of Africa in a Blackhawk helicopter, interviewing an undercover FBI agent, accompanying a police raid in the backstreets of Tunis. This stuff is fascinating to me, entertaining to my friends, and explaining it to our loyal audiences is a perpetually worthwhile challenge. It's what makes me human.

MARY PORTAS

Businesswoman and retail consultant

Mary's story is one of having achieved huge professional success against the odds, but still feeling there was something missing. A wholly original exploration of the money-can't-buy-happiness moral, it is a captivating tale with an important message.

When I was sixteen years old, my mother died suddenly of meningitis. A couple of years later, my father died too. Aged nineteen and only just out of school, I was left with no support and with a younger brother to look after. The final kick came when our family home went to my father's new wife after his death, leaving my younger brother and I homeless. No, it wasn't a great time. But out of the darkness came light, and for the first time ever, I experienced how powerful kindness can be.

My brother Lawrence and I were taken in by friends of my parents, Sheila and Harry. Not relatives, I must add. They were good people with a small three-bedroom house and four children of their own. They were people who could have done without adding to their busy household. But they knew that this act of kindness saved two teenagers from loss and grief. And ultimately helped us go out into the world.

This is still one of the greatest acts of kindness I have ever experienced, and it has had a profound effect on me. It influences all that I do today. In fact, it eventually became my guiding principle in life and business. But it wasn't always thus.

When I first went into the world of work, I didn't see much kindness. In fact, I saw much that was opposite, especially in leadership. Behaviour that was competitive, tough, aggressive and sometimes offensive. I even remember a colleague (a father of three), up on being fired, being told, 'Don't take it personally, it's business.'

The business game they played was an alpha one, and regrettably I joined them. And I was good at it. So good that, by the time I was thirty-one, I was on the main board of Harvey Nichols. I had money. I had status. I had power. But at what cost? At the cost of who I truly was.

I suppressed my natural energy, my instinct and sensitivity, and put thoughts of kindness to one side. I became a completely different person at work to the person I was at home. I set up my own agency. I started in TV, I advised global retailers, lectured worldwide, wrote books – all driven by the alpha behaviour I'd learned in retail. The money rolled in. I worked like this for years, until I couldn't any more.

I had money. I had status. I had power. But at what cost? At the cost of who I truly was.

In 2012, my youngest son came into the world in the same week my eldest one went out into it, off to university. I took some time out to think and be with them. And at that time, I realised that work wasn't making my soul sing. I needed to work out why. I spent many months reflecting, reading and working out the qualities that I, as a woman, felt reflected my best self. At the heart of all of these values was kindness. The value that connects me with my formative years and, most importantly, to myself. The value that I learned through the kindness of the couple who took me in. The kindness I learned through caring for my younger brother and, later on, for my own children. The kindness that was built on strength.

Once I'd crafted my list of values, I sat with my managing director and together we worked out how we could place kindness at the core of our business. Kindness is not the same as being soft or a pushover (I'm certainly not that); it comes from a place of respect and compassion. We treat the people we love with kindness, but it's rarely spoken about as the key to a successful business – but, I assure you, it is. It's even possible to fire people with kindness. I have. Many times.

I truly believe kindness is the future currency that businesses will structure around and trade in. And for those sceptics, it's also commercial and profitable. I'm proud I have created a kind working environment at my agency Portas. One built on support, strength and honesty. One that reminds me where I've come from. And one that guides me where I'm going. Who wouldn't want that?

If you believe in caring and being kind to people, you bring out the best in them. It gives them confidence and strength. It allows them to be who they are. To be honest and open. There really is great power in kindness. There is strength in it. In fact, I believe it's the most important part of life's success.

Equality

Can we answer the question of
'what makes us human?' when all humans
are not treated equally? These essays explore how
we find acceptance in a world of discrimination –
racism, sexism, ableism, transphobia – as well as
hearing from those who are fighting for human
rights and equal opportunities in the fields of
immigration, education and poverty.

NAZIR AFZAL

Lawyer

During a twenty-four-year career, Nazir Afzal has been the prosecutor on some of the most high-profile cases in the country, but despite the injustice and suffering he has seen, he has hope for mankind.

If we think about it for one moment, whether we are born in this society or have joined it as an immigrant, there seem to be fundamental things that we would expect: things that we crave as a human being.

I'll run through the list as I see it:

— decent length of life
— bodily quality of life
— freedom and political expression
— ability to forge ahead
— relationships
— respect from others and self-respect
— the goods of culture

There have been some hard-won freedoms, but we are witnessing immense pushback from a variety of sources that are putting all these gains at risk. 'We've gone too far' is the new mantra. If you take action against racist abuse, they say you're a snowflake. If a woman reports sexual abuse, they say 'we don't believe you'. If a disabled person wants benefits they're entitled to, they say 'prove it'.

I am hungry for justice. I have been fed on a diet of injustice, of victims' pain and unnecessary suffering. I have lived in a system that I have not felt part of. One that prides itself on process largely at the expense of empathy and understanding. I have seen the worst that humans can do to each other and the best. It is a privilege to serve: some people have forgotten that.

The trust deficit between those in power and those they supposedly lead is greater than at any time in living history. The lies we are told have been amplified, and have been adopted as a strategy by people who should know better. When we see others break the rules we all abide by, and with no apparent consequence, then our faith in justice is diminished. Humans have rights *and* responsibilities.

**I have seen the worst that humans can do
to each other, and the best.**

People routinely asked me how, having seen the most horrible things that humans do to each other, I can remain calm and contented in myself. It's simple: each one of us has it in them to save lives, to make the lives of others more bearable, and to deliver justice where it is needed.

ALAIN DE BOTTON

Philosopher

Alain de Botton argues for an education system that truly equips us for life by teaching us not only how to do maths, but also how to put our time on the planet to good use.

I want to suggest that what really makes us fully human is education.

Now, education gets taken really seriously in our society. Politicians speak about it constantly, as do public figures. At the moment, the consensus is that education needs to get better, by which people mean that exam results have to get more impressive and that we have to become more skilled at competing with other countries, especially China – and particularly in maths. In this account, the point of education is really to make you a good worker, able to pull in a good salary, and help the GDP of the nation.

This is a really great ambition – but is it the *only* ambition we should have for education? I want to argue that the real purpose of education is to make us fully human. By that I mean, education should help us with the many ways in which we end up less than we can be.

Of course, entering adult life without any technical or professional skills is a disaster, for oneself and society. But there are other equally problematic ways to be. And the one that interests me is emotional health. I think our education system leaves us woefully unprepared for some of the really big challenges of adult life, which include:

— how to choose a life partner
— how to manage a relationship
— how to bring up children

— how to know ourselves well enough to find a job we can do well and enjoy
— how to deal with pressures for status
— how to deal with illness and aging

If you took any of these problems to any school or university in the land, they would look a bit scared and tell you to go and talk to a GP or a therapist.

There are plenty of insights out there – they're on websites and in books, films and songs – but rarely are they systematically presented to us. You can be in your late fifties by the time you've finally come across stuff you would have needed to hear in your late teens.

We have constructed an intellectual world where educational institutions rarely let us ask, let alone answer, the most serious questions of our deeper human nature.

That's a real pity. We have constructed an intellectual world where educational institutions rarely let us ask, let alone answer, the most serious questions of our deeper human nature. We shouldn't be surprised at the levels of divorce, mental breakdown and general sheer unhappiness in the nation. We aren't taking these issues seriously. It's very important to know the capital of New Zealand and the constituents of the periodic table, but such facts won't enable one to sail through life unscathed.

What we need, above all, is to grow more familiar with the idea of transmitting wisdom down the generations. That's one of the key roles of education, in my eyes. The purpose of all education is to spare people time and error. It's a tool whereby society attempts to teach reliably, within a few years, what it took the very brightest and most determined of our ancestors centuries of painful effort to work out.

We accept this principle when it comes to science. We accept that a university student enrolled today on a physics degree can in a few months learn as much as Faraday ever knew – and within a couple of years, will be pushing at the outer limits of Einstein's unified field theory. But this same principle tends to be met with real opposition when it comes to wisdom. Here, educationalists often say that wisdom is not something that one person can ever teach another.

But it is: there is more than enough information about overcoming folly, greed, lust, envy, pride, sentimentality or snobbishness in the canon of culture. You can find answers in philosophy, literature, history, art and film. But the problem is that this treasury is not sufficiently well filleted and skilfully dissected to get the good material out in time.

No existing secular institution sets out to teach us the art of living. Religions, of course, have a shot at this – they constantly want to teach us how to run a marriage or find the meaning of life. They're not wrong to do so. It's just that more and more of us aren't convinced by their specific explanations. But what they're trying to do is hugely important, and something that non-believers should learn from.

In my ideal school of the future, you might learn about geography and maths, but you would also be systematically taught about the really big challenges of life: how to be a good partner, how to stay sane and how to put the small amount of time we all have on this planet to the best possible use.

These are subjects that we need to monitor with all the manic attention we currently give our maths scores. At the end of the day, they are as important, if not more so, in deciding whether this country will be a flourishing and happy place.

MAHAMED HASHI

Community leader

Mahamed Hashi tells us about the community he grew up in and the people he meets now through his charity work. Despite being affected by violence, neglect, poverty, and mental health issues, he argues that as long as we're empathetic with each other, even the most vulnerable in our communities can stay hopeful.

What makes us human is our resilience and our empathy, our ability to recover quickly from our adverse experiences, but also, despite this, our ability to think of others.

I've worked with young people for over twenty years as a youth worker – young people who have been affected by violence, neglect, loss and even death. Over the last seven years, I've also worked through the Brixton Soup Kitchen with people who have been dealt the worst cards imaginable. But I've also found that those who have gone through these experiences are some of the most humble and empathetic people ever.

Now, looking at the kind of community that I grew up with in Lambeth, we had the highest rates of youth violence, highest incidents of mental health problems, highest rates of HIV, second highest rates of teen pregnancy – one in three children were born into poverty. As a black man, you were six times more likely to be stopped and searched, three times more likely to be arrested, and more likely to receive a custodial sentence for the same crime as your white counterpart.

It is so easy to look at this through the kind of lens of trauma, and just look at it and say, 'Ah, that's so sad. We need to do more.' But, we should also look at the resilience that we had to build in order to survive, and I think that's a place to celebrate.

If you look closely at our community, you'll find so much value in it. We have people like Karl Lokko, who despite being a gang member, having been featured numerous times on the fronts of newspapers with different kinds of weapons and involved in various kinds of violence, was able to turn his life all the way around, to the point where he was invited to Harry and Meghan's royal wedding. People like Terroll Lewis, who built the Block Workout up because he couldn't afford the gym. They share the same origins and same places of birth as people like David Bowie. You know, we have a former mayor of London from Brixton, a former prime minister from Brixton.

The real tragedy behind poverty is not the actual poverty itself, but what it does to your hopes and dreams.

Sometimes it's important that we empower local communities in addressing the issues that they are most affected by. We must learn to bridge the gap between the most vulnerable people in our communities so we can learn from their experiences, and they can learn from ours. But, sometimes, we expect them to be thriving when they are barely surviving.

The real tragedy behind poverty is not the actual poverty itself, but what it does to your hopes and dreams. It's so important that we continue to inspire people by sharing our experiences, being empathetic to the different experiences various people go through, and really celebrating the resilience that you have to build through these experiences. Every experience is a good experience as long as you can learn to grow from it.

JULIA GILLARD

Former Australian Prime Minister

Julia Gillard writes an essay that challenges and inspires, arguing that a sense of fairness must be at the heart of humanity. She demonstrates how her fight for gender equality is far from complete, and calls on us to use our humanity to create a more equal world.

Every good blockbuster needs a theme song. And so it is with *Wonder Woman*, with its theme song always circling back to the refrain that 'to be human is to love'.

Have Hollywood and Gal Gadot, who brings Wonder Woman to life, and the Aussie singer Sia, got it right? Is being human about love? And, if so, does that necessarily mean being human is also about knowing how to hate? My answer is yes. This time, perhaps unusually, popular culture has brought us part of an essential truth.

Being human is about emotions, but it is also about something more. The essence of being human is the combination of our ability to feel and our capacity to think. Ultimately, what makes us human is a sense of fairness, which can overcome prejudices.

To take one timeless example: as human beings, we can grow up in cultures that teach us to fear the 'other'. To give a wide berth to people of different skin colour. To fear those who worship some other god. To make decisions about who is inferior based on factors that people are born with, like their gender or sexuality or race or disability. Much of history has been about the struggle of human beings to face and defeat their tendency to fear or shun the other. To convince themselves, through the powers of the mind and indeed the soul, to embrace a shared humanity. And this struggle continues on so many fronts today.

Julia Gillard

My chosen front to fight on is the continuing discrimination in our world based on gender. As the first woman to lead my nation, I desperately want other women to have fair access to positions of leadership, and for women to be fairly judged once they reach such positions. This drive has led me to King's College London, where, with an amazing team, I am building the Global Institute for Women's Leadership. Our mission is a simple one. It is to deepen our understanding, through research, of what works to eradicate gender discrimination – and to promote this evidence – until it is equally likely that any leadership position is held by a woman or a man.

With global level data showing women make up just 23% of national parliamentarians, 26% of news media leaders, 27% of judges and 15% of corporate board members, there is much to do to achieve equality. Certainly the current rate of change won't enable us to see it in our lifetimes. Improvements in the number of women political leaders has stalled and there was only a one percentage point movement in the last decade in the number of senior female managers globally.

> **Our sense of fairness is at the core of our humanity. It is what powers our progress as a species and it is what will drive us to create a better, more equal world.**

But for all these depressing statistics, I feel we are at a pivotal moment. Although it originated in Hollywood, the familiarity of the experiences described by the #MeToo movement has meant the wave has reverberated through journalism, politics and beyond. The stories collected are visceral illustrations of the career consequences suffered by women who are forced to manoeuvre around problematic men. The energy and enthusiasm generated by this movement has led to an awakening for many and spurred action to guarantee the rights of women.

Equality

So in this time of change, at the Global Institute for Women's Leadership, we are taking a broad perspective as we analyse women's journeys to leadership and the barriers that keep them back. At every point in a women's life journey, we want to address the points where she is treated differently and less fairly than a man. This can include everything from the old boys' network dictating who gets jobs, to the challenges of balancing work and family life, to the unconscious biases that tell us women are too hysterical or too hard to be promoted.

Our sense of fairness is at the core of our humanity. It is what powers our progress as a species and it is what will drive us to create a better, more equal world.

CAROLINE CRIADO-PEREZ

Writer and campaigner

Men, not women, are the universal template for humanity, writes the feminist campaigner Caroline Criado-Perez. In this powerful essay, she invites the reader to question why, when we think of the standard human being, many of us revert to this as the default template.

Imagine a human. What did you picture? Statistically, most of you pictured a man. It's okay, I did too. And there's a very good reason why so many of us picture a man when we think of a human. It's because, for millennia, men have been represented as the universal, default, gender-neutral template for humanity. Women, while technically human beings, are really seen as a niche, atypical variant of men, with some bits added on and some bits taken away.

Back in the fourth century BC, the philosopher Aristotle could be found articulating this viewpoint in his biological treatise, *On the Generation of Animals*. 'The first departure from type,' he wrote, 'is indeed that the offspring should become female instead of male.' Men were the type from which women deviated. Indeed, Aristotle saw the female body as a mutilated male body.

**Imagine a human. What did you picture?
Statistically, most of you pictured a man.
It's okay, I did too.**

Through the Renaissance, anatomical drawings continued to firmly label the female body as a variation on the male body, with female testicles (the ovaries), and a female scrotum (the uterus).

Equality

The female body was the male body turned outside in – the reason given for this bizarre location of the reproductive organs inside the body rather than outside the body, as in normal humans, was because of a female deficiency in vital heat – which is itself telling. Why a female deficiency? Why not argue that men have too much vital heat?

This thinking continued into the twentieth century, with the development of the human scale by the influential Swiss architect, Le Corbusier, which was meant to centre the needs of humans in architecture. Of course, by human, Le Corbusier meant a six-foot man – specifically, a six-foot British police detective, because it's important to be precise about these things. Supposedly, it was pointed out to Le Corbusier that women are humans too, and they also used buildings, and, to be fair to him, a modular woman was belatedly considered. Ultimately, however, the female body was rejected as a source of proportional harmony.

Now, I know what you're thinking: okay, this is all very funny, but no one thinks the female body is too proportionally inharmonious to be used in complex calculations any more. Do they?

Well, I'm afraid that we very much do – and it isn't funny at all, because the results for women can be deadly. Because we have designed cars to protect a dummy with the measurements of an average man, women are 47% more likely to be seriously injured and 17% more likely to die than a man in the same crash. Because the majority of medical research has been carried out on men, women are 50% more likely to be misdiagnosed if they have a heart attack and, consequently, more likely to die from it.

And this all continues today because we still think of men as a universal template for humanity, with women as a dispensable complicating factor. I think it's probably time we stopped – don't you?

STEPHANIE HIRST

Radio presenter

Stephanie's journey as a transgender woman is incredibly moving and inspirational. Despite the uniqueness of her story, her quest for self-acceptance is one that all humans will relate to.

We all feel the need to be accepted, loved and cherished. The feeling of being in complete agreement with something, giving it 100% support and approval, is a powerful emotion. Being part of something that is looked upon by others with satisfaction makes us feel good.

Every single day we compare how others behave, judging them good or bad, right or wrong. Those who fit our personal ideology are accepted; those who seem not to fit in are shunned, bullied, and – in certain areas of the world – maimed or even killed for not conforming to society's 'normal' box.

But what is 'normal'?

When we are born, the majority of us are cherished, loved and adored by our parents and families, spending those first few formative years being unconditionally accepted. It is often at school where we will find our first experience of non-acceptance. Here is where we forge friendships and form our social skills, learning to find our level in life, which will go on to either help or hinder us during our time on earth.

I most certainly wasn't accepted by everyone during my schooling. Seen as effeminate and attention-seeking, I was pretty much doomed during my time in the tough Barnsley schools I attended.

At home, though, is where I felt warmth and love, away from the preconceptions and judgement that were outside the front door of 5 Wilford Road.

Equality

I'd known from a very early age that I was female, and just praying that the boy's body I was born with would one day develop into a woman's gave me naive hope as a child – but once reality hit, the years of inner torment and denial followed.

However, I was blessed with a distraction. From the moment my father sat me down in front of our seventies Fidelity radio, which at that very point was playing Queen's 'Bohemian Rhapsody', I was instantly captivated by this thing called 'radio' and, of course, the ground breaking song it was playing. Radio was different. It was like a club where everyone was welcome, no matter where you were from or who you were. I needed to be in that club, inside that radio, the voice that people heard.

My parents could see that I was happy creating their own radio shows in their bedroom: who were they to argue? It was the escapism I needed away from the gender dysphoria, along with the continuing bullying and beatings I got at school. But clearly, I needed to be heard. Maybe that's why I love the medium of radio so much – it's a one-to-one connection.

The world is still full of those who cannot accept someone's desire to find true happiness.

The acceptance I got from my childhood radio heroes was unbelievable to me. On the one hand, I had the circle of friends at school, who were clearly judging the book by its cover, and on the other hand, I had a group of professional broadcasters who saw a glimmer of talent in me, and wanted to nurture and grow it. I'd been accepted somewhere at last.

Once I'd accepted myself, the pathway to a happy existence was right there in front of me.

But I was terrified. The world is still full of those who cannot accept someone's desire to find true happiness, or indeed cannot accept the way they were born. Would becoming female mean I'd lose the one thing that I'd loved so dearly since childhood?

It was a risk for my career to transition from male to female. But by then I'd passed the point of suicide, because I deserved to live. Just because I was born in the wrong body, I shouldn't take my own life. No one should die because of their fear of being ostracised.

The unconditional love, warmth and support I received from my family, friends, listeners and the general public as a whole, confirms to me that I've been accepted for who I am. We've all been blessed with the wonderful emotion of acceptance, and for us to use this powerful tool in a positive way will make the world a better place.

Always have the courage to be yourself. I love the person I've become, because I fought to be her.

ALISON LAPPER

Artist

Alison talks about how the feelings that make us human are often denied to people with disabilities, and that what we all need is love, acceptance and respect.

The problem with this question is that you have to find universal characteristics that link people like Hitler with Mother Teresa.

I could have a stab at it and say freedom of choice, and the desire to humanise everything, but an anthropologist may hiss 'What about X?' A human rights campaigner may snap 'Saudi Arabia, huh?' And you'll always get that plonker who'll yell 'You don't even look human, love, so how can you talk?'

However you cut it, humans are incredibly different, so this is a nightmarish question. Unless you are an expert, of course. But I'm only an expert on *my* life, and the challenges disabled people face. Based on that, I think there are four vital things that make us human: the need to love, the need to *be* loved, and the need to be accepted and respected as a human being in the first place.

In *The Elephant Man*, there was a scene where John Merrick was chased into a railway toilet and trapped between two rows of urinals. With his back against the wall, he screamed at the mob: 'I am not an animal! I am NOT an ANIMAL! I am a human being!', and of course he was. But to be treated like a human being, you have to be accepted as one.

When I was trapped at Chailey Heritage school, I was too afraid to scream – but, then, I was only tiny and didn't even know that I was different. I understood that I was one of the 250 'strange little creatures' that lived there. But we were in the majority, so acceptance wasn't an issue. It only became an issue when we were faced with the outside world. That was a whole different ball game. As toddlers, we were taken to Brighton Beach, and we emptied it in ten minutes! We were never asked if we minded being repeatedly sprawled naked in front of ten to fifteen medical professionals, and endlessly poked, pulled, rotated and photographed. Every Wednesday afternoon, wealthy donors would peer at us through the classroom windows. They didn't seem to see children, just poor, pathetic, unloved creatures.

**Disabled people aren't a different species.
We are human beings with the same needs and
aspirations as everyone else, and everyone
has a basic need to be accepted.**

Although we've come a long way since then, I'm still stared at; some passers-by will do a double-take if I'm heard making an intelligent comment; I'm told I intimidate people; I make people feel uncomfortable, or even turn their stomachs. *Why?* Disabled people aren't a different species. We are human beings with the same needs and aspirations as everyone else, and everyone has a basic need to be accepted.

I think that is why John Merrick said to Treves at the end of the film: 'My life is full because I am loved.' Now he could die in peace, because society had finally accepted what he had always been; a human being who just happened to be disabled.

Merrick also mentioned love, and I believe that loving, and being loved, also make us human.

When I was little, the ward sister would say: 'Put that crying baby down. They don't need a hug.' In her eyes, children like us didn't need human contact, let alone love. We were all treated the same way, so we grew up thinking that that was normal. Mind you, at the age of five, I also thought it was normal to be taken to Lewes

Prison to visit the inmates. Our surroundings were so alike that it seemed that the only contrast between us was that we were locked away as punishment for being different, and they were locked away as punishment for doing wrong.

Yet, I was aware that kindness made me feel loved. Kindness, that I had experienced from my foster parents, my sister, some of the nursing staff, and all the teachers at Chailey. But, of them all, my rock was always Nurse Mary Shepherd. Because of her, I recognised that humans were more than just fed, watered, educated and disciplined.

Despite my upbringing, the need to love and be loved was instinctive. As I grew up, I felt love and respect toward my friends and myself. As I grew older, I fell in love, I made love and experienced the joy of parental love.

I still do, but these feelings, feelings that make us human, are often denied to people like me because of our disabilities.

So, what do I think makes us human? Four needs: to love, to be loved, to be accepted and to be respected.

SINÉAD BURKE

Writer, academic and disability activist

What makes us human is our ability to acknowledge that we do not know everything, writes Sinéad Burke. In her answer, she looks back on her time as a teacher in Dublin, and compels us to embrace the conversations and situations that make us uncomfortable.

What makes us human is our ability to acknowledge that we do not know everything, and, more importantly, that we do not know what we do not know. It sounds obvious, but the reality is anything but.

It was first made clear to me when I was in the classroom. I taught six classes of boys in the inner city in Dublin. I remember other teachers, parents and friends asking questions about how I would control them, how I would assert myself and how, with the design of the classroom, I would be able to teach at all. Without malice, these adults were underlining the notion that teachers should be authoritative, facilitators of praise and punishment, and they probably shouldn't smile until Christmas.

I didn't believe in that kind of teaching, at least not for me. My teaching centred on creating a classroom environment that was a haven: a safe space for children to be introverted or extroverted, vulnerable or confident, to explore who they were and who they could be. It was created through shared experiences and shared learnings.

On the first day, the boys asked, 'Why are you so small?' I told them that I had dwarfism, a genetic condition that I had inherited from my dad. A specific gene called FGFR3 had been mutated and the growth receptors in my arms and legs had been turned off, meaning that my limbs were shorter than most other people's.

295

It sparked a broad conversation about genetics and how it impacted their lives – why some of them had brown hair, or were mixed race, or how the tallest and the smallest boys in the classroom had parents and siblings who were similar in height. Using my lived experience and physicality as a case study, it opened up a conversation that would often be considered too adult for children. Instead, by using language that they would understand and examples within their reality, it brokered respect and a common understanding.

We need to refrain from trying to fit each person within the one mould.

As adults, we need to learn from children and mirror their curiosity and empathy. We need to acknowledge that the spectrum of human experience is diverse and our knowledge of who people are and what they can come to be is unlimited, unlike our knowledge. We need to refrain from trying to fit each person within the one mould.

I often hear my friends say, 'Sinéad, I don't see you as a little person. I just see you as you.' They mean well, and probably think that they are paying me a compliment. But why do they strive to see me as 'normal', and what does that antiquated term even mean? By not acknowledging what makes me different, there's an erasure of the accommodations that people require and the systemic biases that exist that make it difficult for me to just be me and for you to be you.

We need to embrace the conversations and situations that make us uncomfortable, that spotlight the gaps in our knowledge and awareness. We need to research and educate ourselves on the spectrum of human existence. We need to recognise what makes us different and be brave in our attempt to find the answers and solutions to the systems, societies and classrooms that were designed for one type of person.

KATIE PIPER

Author and broadcaster

This answer directly addresses society's issue of beauty standards. As a burn survivor, Katie has a unique perspective on how rediscovering her confidence has made her feel human and helped her to connect with others.

I am unaware of any evidence that any species other than *Homo sapiens* appreciates beauty. The ability to admire, even be moved by, the beauty of both the natural and the human-made seems, in fact, to be part of what makes us human.

In every culture on earth, people decorate their possessions and themselves, and enjoy visual art. They stare in awe at vast landscapes and the starry sky, and they sing and dance, and make instrumental music. Why? The answer seems obvious: it gives them pleasure. Observing beauty around us – in art, nature, our environment.

Here in the West, we live in a culture that worships beauty. I am mainly referring to personal beauty – the type that drives women and some men to have plastic surgery in the endless pursuit of physical perfection. We're pressured to look a certain way. We, many of us, may even measure our worth by how we look, by whether we measure up to some standard of beauty we hold in our heads. I've often questioned where this standard comes from.

The world we live in bombards us with messages about what ideal beauty looks like. We're inundated with images of unreal, airbrushed, anorexic women, and led to believe that this is the ideal we must strive for – and, if we are to be accepted, that we must achieve.

As humans, I feel it's important to get a balanced perspective on what is beautiful. Every human is already beautiful, and every human can be even more beautiful! A person defines their own beauty. The sign of a beautiful person is they always see the beauty in others. If I used the cliché 'it's what's on the inside that counts', I'm sure my critics (in more unkind terms – social media trolls!) would shoot me down, perhaps with suggestions this is consolation for someone who is facially disfigured, a made-up patronising quote to help those who are considered less attractive feel okay about it.

There is no denying it is our faces that project our deepest essence, that interact with other people when we speak with them, when we look in to their eyes, when we laugh. We show our opinions or feelings through our facial expressions. Our faces are where people look when they want to know us or understand us.

Many of you will have confidence problems or lack of belief in your own beauty – perhaps you think you're unattractive, overweight or you just don't like yourself. I want you to know about one of the most powerful tools we all have – the human spirit. If we exercise it, it can be incredible and get us through the lowest times.

My confidence, my strength, has projected beauty. Finding and defining my own kind of beauty is what has made me feel human again.

You can't see it: it's inside each and every one of us, and that's what radiates true beauty. We have all experienced being touched by someone's human spirit, their kindness, the support they have shown us, even their ability to make us laugh – no one has ever been touched or moved by the most perfect skin, the neatest nose or the smallest waist.

Beauty is a state of mind. It's not question of whether you're 'pretty' or 'plain', young or old, thin or not thin . . . it's a matter of your own self-image. This visual aesthetic of beauty is fleeting. No matter what lengths a woman or man goes to in order to preserve their youthful beauty, it cannot last. Confidence makes you beautiful and beauty makes you confident!

As a burn survivor, it wouldn't be wrong of me to suggest there are now some people who wouldn't be physically attracted to me, or perhaps don't consider me to represent beauty in their heads any more. But my confidence, my strength, has projected beauty. Finding and defining my own kind of beauty is what has made me feel human again and made others able to feel that they can relate to me – human to human.

Helen Keller was a woman of many great qualities – beauty being one of them – and this quote from her summarises my thoughts perfectly: 'The best and the most beautiful things in the world cannot be seen or even touched – they must be felt with the heart.'

MARY ROBINSON

Politician and former UN High Commissioner for
Human Rights

**As human beings, we are nothing without our dignity. Consider-
ing the responsibilities we all hold to our fellow humans across
the globe, Mary Robinson's answer is a moving call for action.**

To me, what makes us human is best summed up in the African concept of *Ubuntu*, which Desmond Tutu explains as: 'I am because we
are.' Another way of saying it is the old Irish proverb: '*Is ar scáth a
chéile a mhaireann na daoine.*' This translates as: 'It is in each other's
shadow that we flourish.'

My early interest in human rights stemmed from being the only
girl wedged between four brothers, two older than me and two
younger. I became profoundly influenced by the first sentence of
Article 1 of the Universal Declaration of Human Rights: 'All human
beings are born free and equal in dignity and rights.'

I like to discuss with students why the word 'dignity' comes
before 'rights'. What is this concept of human dignity? To me, it is
the inner sense of self-worth, the spiritual and cultural factors that
are imbued in an individual, which make each one of us distinctive. The true poverty of the homeless person, lying in a doorway,
invisible to the passer-by, is the lack of any sense of that self-worth
and dignity.

Human dignity evokes an empathy with the other, connects us
one to the other. Empathy is extraordinarily important in family,
in community, in country, at so many different levels. Now, in our
interconnected world, that empathy must expand to tackling the
gross inequalities that raise important issues of justice.

Mary Robinson

In recent years my sense of what makes us human has been affected by an awareness of how destructive our activities are becoming to the planet and the ecosystems of which we are part. We have not been good stewards in many ways over the centuries, and our fossil fuel-led economic growth has had a toll on human health, biodiversity and the atmosphere. In 2013, for the first time in millions of years, we reached 400 parts per million of carbon in the atmosphere.

This number is significant for at least three reasons: first, because a significant amount of the carbon was put there as a result of human activities; second, because we are leaving the realms of a safe climate and heading for a 3–4°C warmer world; and third, because the results of a warmer world are already being felt as seasons change, rainfall becomes more unpredictable, the sea level rises and extreme events such as floods and drought increase in frequency and severity.

Climate change arguably poses the twenty-first century's starkest challenge to human rights – including the rights to life, shelter and an adequate standard of living. This is particularly the case for many people in the developing world, who have contributed the least to causing climate change but are disproportionately suffering the impacts each and every day. The poorest people and parts of the world emit negligible amounts of carbon into the atmosphere, while the wealthiest places and people emit the most, yet have the capacity and resources to adapt and build resilience to climate impacts.

We know it is already tougher being a human being in some parts of the world than others because of inequalities related to power and poverty. The impact of climate change further undermines the human rights of the most vulnerable. As human beings, we should be moved to address this injustice; this is climate justice.

If human dignity evokes empathy and connects us to other people on the planet, then we have to care about climate change. Empathy – which is, I believe, what makes us human – must compel us to take responsibility for our actions and make a choice; a choice to change the way our societies operate to realise a safe world for all who inhabit it.

What is this concept of human dignity?
To me, it is the inner sense of self-worth,
the spiritual and cultural factors that are
imbued in an individual, which make
each one of us distinctive.

We must empathise with those who are most affected by climate change – we have to hear the voices of the most vulnerable and then we must demand the action needed to keep the world safe. We also have to consider the needs of future generations and have a sense of intergenerational justice; to think of what our grandchildren and their grandchildren will say if we fail to act when we have the information and capacity to do so. This imaginative ability to hear future voices accusing us of failure to protect them is also part of what makes us human. It keeps me awake at night.

A Force for Good?

As human beings, we are capable of
unspeakable horrors but also limitless generosity.
These essays explore everything from war and
murder to altruism and forgiveness, and together
question whether we should define our humanity
by the worst in us or by the best we're able to be.

PETER BLEKSLEY

Author, broadcaster and former undercover police officer

Many of us are fascinated by murder mysteries and true crime documentaries – but, as human beings, we all abide by Peter Bleksley's 'fundamental rule'. Those who break it, says the former Metropolitan Policeman, have a mindset so alien to us that they occupy an entirely different world.

'The Fundamental Rule' binds us together. It allows us to go about our business, to enjoy our lives, and it makes us human. What is that rule, you may ask? Well, it is basic, it is easy to understand, and we abide by it. It simply says, do not kill one another.

During the coronavirus pandemic, we have seen parliament enact temporary laws that restricted us to our homes, prevented the majority of people from going to work, and stopped us having family and friends round for a barbecue. Those were mere variations of the fundamental rule. In pre-virus normal times, only 0.001% of people breach the fundamental rule every year.

When they do, enormous police resources are dedicated to finding the culprits, to gathering the evidence against them, and to putting the defaulters in front of a court of law. If they are found guilty, then they are removed from society, generally speaking, for a very long time, if not for ever.

A tiny number of those who break the rule may find their own lives extinguished courtesy of a police officer's bullet. So be it. Because the rule is the very bedrock of our civilised society, those who break it, and seek to spread fear that the rule will be broken again and again, can expect their punishment to be unforgivably severe.

However, in all other cases, those who break the rule in our great union of countries are not punished with a noose, a fatal injection, or an electric chair, because not only do we abide by the rule as individuals, we abide by it as a collective. Our standard default position is that we do not kill our fellow citizens, no matter how seriously or how many times they break the fundamental rule. That is what makes us a flagship nation.

A whole industry of TV drama, films, documentaries, books, podcasts and more thrives on telling us the stories of those who broke the rule. Numerous writers create fictional characters that break the rule, and readers devour their works in enormous quantities. Why this fascination? Because the rule-breakers, be they real or make-believe, are not like you and me. They occupy an entirely different world and have a mindset so alien to us that we feel a need to learn about them, their motives, and, sadly, their victims.

'The Fundamental Rule' allows us to go about our business, to enjoy our lives, and it makes us human. What is that rule, you may ask? Well, it is basic, it is easy to understand, and we abide by it. It simply says, do not kill one another.

Unfortunately, an increasing number of offenders are breaking the fundamental rule and getting away with it. Our criminal history books are littered with examples of murderers who have killed once, not been caught, and have then gone on to kill again. If you break the rule, you simply must be caught, because, if not, then we are all in a bit more danger.

This is why my working life is dedicated to researching and writing about those rule-breakers, and trying to find them, wherever they may be . . .

VAL McDERMID

Crime writer

Bestselling novelist Val McDermid has spent her career researching and writing about the worst of humanity. But, paradoxically, it is through this that she has discovered the best in human nature too.

Human, as opposed to what? Animals? Zombies? Vampires? The differential varies from case to case. Evolutionary biology, the level of vital signs, the lack of a need to consume blood . . . All of those mark us out as human, as distinct from the alternatives.

Some people say what makes our species unique is laughter. And laughter is a wonderful thing. When it comes to making us feel good, it's better than chocolate. Probably even better than sex, because anybody can make us laugh, but sex only works well with certain individuals. But we're not the only species that can laugh. Most primates laugh when you tickle them. There's even evidence that they can crack jokes and play tricks on each other. Now scientists believe rats laugh when they're playing with each other. So that quick and dirty differential doesn't work.

Others say we're unique because we ask questions that don't directly affect our survival. Why is the sky blue? What is Jeremy Clarkson for? How many ways are there to skin a cat? Are angels real? Is there honey still for tea? I don't imagine many porcupines occupy themselves with notions like these.

Nevertheless, it seems to me that the key marker, the aspect that most particularly speaks of our humanity, is our capacity to be humane. To show love, compassion, generosity of spirit and kindness – that is, I believe, what makes us human.

A Force for Good?

Some people might say I spend my working life considering the opposite of those things. After all, I write books where people do terrible things to each other. I make my readers catch their breath and shudder at the depravity human beings are capable of. Perhaps some might even argue that this aspect of my work illustrates profoundly what makes us human. That we are the only species who devote their intelligence and their energy into devising unspeakable tortures and gruesome ways to kill, then putting those things into practice.

Certainly there have been times researching my novels when I've found myself wondering what twisted the imagination of these perpetrators so badly that what they came up with seemed like any kind of an answer. I still shiver at the memory of my first visit to a torture museum, in San Gimignano in Tuscany, a town so lovely it's a UNESCO World Heritage Site. There, in the midst of man-made beauty, was the worst of man-made ugliness.

And yet . . . the most disturbing thing about those instruments of torture was that some of them were beautiful. If you didn't think about what they were for, if you just looked at them as mechanical objects, some of them were elegant and graceful. And my job as a writer is to try and figure out why the people who created and used those objects were impelled to do what they did. What they still do.

> **It's compassion that makes it possible for us to move beyond the bad things to the possibility of something better.**

And that's why my books are not ultimately about the evil things we do to each other. They're actually about how, in the thick of that darkness, we can find redemption. How we can get beyond the idea of revenge to a place of forgiveness. How we can help those who seem beyond help to move towards some sort of rehabilitation.

It's compassion that makes it possible for us to move beyond the bad things to the possibility of something better. It's clear that something akin to love exists in the animal kingdom. Swans mate for life; wolves mourn when members of their pack are killed; black vultures attack unfaithful partners. But only humans show compassion and forgiveness. That's what makes us human.

ANTHONY LOYD

Journalist

It's a common observation that irrationality is part of being human, but few people are forced to confront it in such extreme conditions as Anthony Loyd. His essay is about the power of lasting friendship, and how, even in the worst of places, we can find unexpected hope.

After I had had my hands tied, and had been beaten and shot, my captors took the brass phial from my neck. It is a small, narrow cylinder about three centimetres long, and hangs from a piece of green nylon.

Inside are the ashes of my friend and mentor, the Reuters war correspondent Kurt Schork, who was killed in Sierra Leone in May 2000.

Part talisman, part juju, part tribute – that phial is mostly an emblem of spiritual memorial – a way by which I remain related to a dead friend who was one of the most inspiring influences in my life.

When that little cylinder of his ashes is with me in war – and it is always so – then I am empowered: a little stronger, more enduring, braver, luckier; my moral focus clear and my humility and humour intact – mostly, anyway. For those are the positive attributes I learned from Kurt Schork – a uniquely chivalrous and gifted man – in the wars in the Balkans where we had worked together a quarter century ago, and those are the qualities to which I still aspire.

Each of the component feelings I have around that brass phial – the sense of supernatural, of inspiration and spirit – is in some way irrational, but that doesn't matter: irrationality is an integral human attribute, part of our core make-up and belief system. I am not irrational despite being a man: I am irrational because I am a man.

So when my captors took his ashes from me that day in May 2014, when I was abducted in Syria by an armed Islamist gang, I felt especially bereft. The loss of the phial held exponential impact. I had the sensation of teetering on the edge of darkness: reduced and alone, my protection gone. The sense of nakedness gained added physical dimension when all my clothes were cut off, so that soon I was lying there wearing nothing but the plasticuffs binding my wrists, and a thin layer of blood which coated my face and my left foot from where I had been shot twice in the ankle as punishment for trying to escape.

Kurt is not the only dead friend I remain close to. I have many dead friends, and I keep them all near. If you are a friend of mine and you die, I will never forget you. I will think of you often, and I will recite your name to myself in solitude, or in prayer, and whenever I am in a spiritual place.

When that little cylinder of his ashes is with me in war – and it is always so – then I am empowered: a little stronger, more enduring, braver, luckier; my moral focus clear and my humility and humour intact.

But in war, where I spend my working life, Kurt's ashes are the most obvious emblem of the way I keep my dead with me, because war can be full of fear, sometimes dread, and is ruled by the dynamic of chaos, so you need every ally at hand, dead or alive: and in terms of the force being with you, you aren't going to do much better than having Kurt Schork's ashes around your neck.

Luckily, my captors in Syria respected these irrational sentiments too. They would not have known exactly what was inside that worn brass phial they took from me, but they must have had some echoed sense of its significance. For, later, one of them approached me. By that time I had difficulty seeing out of an eye due to the series of beatings I had received, and I could not walk. Dehumanised – for I had been treated like an animal – I was at least no longer naked, having been given tracksuit bottoms and a T-shirt to wear.

'Here,' the man said gruffly, pushing the brass phial back into my hands, 'you need this.' With that gesture, a skein of hope flew through me. In my hour of loneliness and fear, the ashes of my friend were with me again, and I became myself once more: irrational enough to believe, of course, that somewhere out there in the cosmos, my dead friend was going to save my arse.

MAX MOSLEY

Former F1 president

A provocative look at the worst of human behaviour, which pulls no punches in criticising world leaders. In a vividly honest answer, Max Mosley (1940–2021) laments that being able to admit wrongdoing is viewed as a sign of weakness rather than intelligence.

So, what makes us human? Is it good things humans are capable of, or is it our almost limitless capacity for cruel and irrational behaviour? The good is what one would expect, given the intellectual ability of humans, but our defining characteristic seems to be the nasty side. We see it everywhere, even in religion. Practitioners of one religion will inflict unspeakable horrors on their rivals, for no better reason than they believe something different. We did this in Europe at one time, and it continues in the Middle East to this day. The main problem seems to be that those concerned are absolutely certain that they are right. Therefore, anyone who disagrees is a heretic who deserves the worst.

In politics, irrational certainty is everywhere, no matter how certain the facts. To admit that one might just possibly be wrong is seen as a sign of weakness, not intelligence. Politicians are always ready to sacrifice thousands of lives in wars to settle disputes. Each side blames the other with absolute certainty that they are right. They use force because they can, with little thought to the families left devastated. The fact that disputes can be settled without resort to killing and armed conflict doesn't deter them.

They don't just waste human life in wars. For more than twenty years, I have been involved in global campaigns for road safety. Every year, about 1.3 million people die in road traffic accidents worldwide. That's some 3,000 per day. It's the biggest global killer of young people, those we can least afford to lose. The number of deaths on the roads is more than a thousand times greater than the deaths worldwide from terrorism. Yet the reaction to terrorism has been massive, with millions of dollars spent and civilised restraint often abandoned. Meanwhile, until very recently, it has been impossible to persuade governments to take road deaths seriously. If a fraction of the terrorism effort had been devoted to reducing road casualties, tens of thousands of lives could have been saved globally.

Take just one country: India. According to government figures, about 370 people die on Indian roads every day. The steps needed to reduce that figure drastically are well-known and proven. Yet until the recent arrival of the Modi government, almost nothing was done. But imagine what the reaction would be if terrorists massacred 370 people in India in one day. Then imagine if they started doing that every day. The whole world would unite to stop it. Yet the 370 daily deaths on the road were virtually ignored. That is just one example, but everywhere you look there is cruelty and irrationality, with America and the UK often leading the way. Our interventions in Iraq, Afghanistan, Syria and Libya have killed and maimed hundreds of thousands, and have made the lives of ordinary families so intolerable that thousands of them are trying to flee to Europe despite appalling risks.

> **The good is what one would expect, given the intellectual ability of humans, but our defining characteristic seems to be the nasty side.**

So, in my view, what makes us human is our ability to override or suppress our capacity for kind and rational thought in favour of actions and policies which are at best stupid, and at worse barbarously cruel. It's a thought I find depressing.

GEORGE ALAGIAH

Journalist and broadcaster

George Alagiah spent much of his career covering war and disaster zones – but, even in the worst of times, the human spirit shines through. He writes that caring for one another is what makes us human, and reminds us that, even in the darkest moments, we must find the light in life.

It's a while since I used to roam around the world's disaster zones for a living, but, if I had to distil all those years of reporting down to the one image that sticks in my mind, it would be this: a boy, not yet a teen, sheltering under a tree, his spindly arms wrapped around two younger siblings, comforting them. I remember his face and the country that had failed him and millions of others. I never got his name. But, in a sense, the detail doesn't matter, because he was one child and every child; it was one country and every country.

What that image tells me every time I conjure it up is that caring for one another is the most basic of instincts. In fact, it is what makes us human. That boy knew it, it was in his bones. In a cruel world, one in which the adults had reneged on their duty, he knew it was his turn to take up the burden of caring. To be sure, that responsibility had fallen on his narrow shoulders too early, robbing him of the childhood that was his right, and yet he did it without question.

In our rich and comfortable country, perhaps in all wealthy nations, it has become much harder to understand that to care is to be human. We are not called to act on that instinct in the way that young boy was. It's as if we have outsourced that responsibility, transformed it into a duty to be performed by others. How much easier it is to point the finger at the government, or an institution. How convenient to be able to blame an unseen bureaucracy instead of looking at ourselves in the mirror and asking the question: when is it my turn to care?

Well, for all its deathly potency, the coronavirus pandemic has forced us all to answer that question with the words 'now is the time'. From Captain Tom to countless other acts of heroism, this disease has helped us to rediscover what it is to be human. This does not mean we are about to absolve the state from playing its part, but I think we understand its limits. Our taxes cannot buy tenderness; our votes do not ensure kindness. Those are things we have to do for ourselves. We know that now, just as some eighty years ago, in the adversity of battle: a previous generation forged a kinship that defined it.

In the worst of all possible times, in the most desolate of places, I have seen a million little miracles, acts of solidarity and care, that defy description.

People still say to me: after all you've seen, you must have a dim view of our world. My answer to them is this: precisely because of what I've witnessed, I have a *hopeful* view of our world. In the worst of all possible times, in the most desolate of places, I have seen a million little miracles, acts of solidarity and care, that defy description. I have seen this thing we call the human spirit, and I feel all the richer for it.

BRIAN MAY

Queen guitarist and astrophysicist

Most people would admit that the human race isn't perfect, but Brian May's profound essay questions whether we have any good in us at all. With undeniable passion, he questions why, if kindness defines our humanity, it is so lacking in the world.

What makes us human? Well, we'd have to define 'human', wouldn't we? Apart from the trivial meaning of simply 'pertaining to a member of the *Homo sapiens* species', the word is usually used in two ways, which are related:

1) Characteristic of people as opposed to God or animals or machines, especially in being susceptible to weaknesses: they are only human, and therefore mistakes do occur; the risk of human error.
2) Characteristic of people's better qualities, such as kindness or sensitivity: the human side of politics is getting stronger.

These definitions are straight out of Apple's Dictionary and are probably typical.

Here we see the qualities that we hope are to be found in us . . . and it's noticeable that they are not the qualities of accumulating riches or power, or dominating what surrounds us. On the contrary, the qualities that we instinctively feel make us special as a race are the opposite of what so much of the world actually strives for. We apparently admire vulnerability, consciousness of our own weakness, and consideration of the sensibilities of other beings around us.

A Force for Good?

So it doesn't take 700 words to define what makes us human – by common consent, it's kindness. But if this is the general perception of what there is to be proud of in human behaviour, why is it that, when we look around, so often we see the very opposite? We see decisions being made purely on the basis of money, or to benefit the careers of those wielding power. We see people being cruel to children, to the disadvantaged, and to the other creatures with whom we share this glistening blue planet. We see people enjoying the pain they can inflict on other beings, and vigorously defending their right to do so as a 'civil liberty'. It's almost impossible to believe, but there are people at this moment working night and day to keep hold of their right to indulge in despicable cruelty.

Once upon a time it was legal to keep black men in chains, to burn so-called witches at the stake. It was legal to dig out badgers and use them as 'bait' for training dogs to be vicious, to hunt wild animals with packs of dogs that would rip the quarry limb from limb. All of these things are now illegal, but there are still teams of people working to bring back blood sports – these inhuman behaviours. And they are supported by many rich and powerful people in Britain today.

It's worse than this. Just as the laws that protect children from abuse are flouted behind closed doors, and time and time again atrocities are exposed, the laws, such as they are, against wildlife crime are routinely being broken in our countryside. Law and order have broken down. Thousands of badgers are being slaughtered and thrown on the roads. Fox hunts regularly hunt foxes to death, in contempt of the law, which the present regime is refusing to enforce. The sickening practice of badger-baiting is rife and actually increasing.

It appears that the inhuman side of humans is winning. But it will win only if we let it. It has been said that, for evil to flourish, it takes only a few good men to do nothing about it.

Perhaps, after all, the almost laughable, simplistic generalisation is true. Perhaps there are two kinds of human being. On the one hand are those who understand that we are all – human and non-human – just animals, and that the gift which has been given to Man is awareness, to make the world a kind place for all. And, on the other hand, are those who don't 'get it'; who cling to the idea that Man, or more accurately they, are the only thing that really matters on this planet, and that all other beings – men, women, children and animals – are to be used and abused at their pleasure.

**The rich get richer, the poor get poorer,
and the weak become persecuted to extinction.
I seriously wonder if we have the right to
call ourselves, as a race, human.**

It is shocking. But in a world with so much awful cruelty, and so much shining goodness, it seems to me that the good can never persuade the bad to change. The amount of wasted effort is enormous and depressing. All we can hope for is a decent, benign, compassionate government one day which will outlaw cruelty of all kinds, and enforce decent behaviour on those who cannot see that they are doing anything wrong. That has been the pattern in the past.

But are we human? Are we a humane race? Looking around at the concrete world we have created, in which the rich get richer, the poor get poorer, and the weak become persecuted to extinction, I seriously wonder if we have the right to call ourselves, as a race, human. We have a hell of a long way to go.

YASMIN ALIBHAI-BROWN

Journalist

This answer is a direct challenge to our selfish natures. If having a borderless heart is what it means to be human, then how many of us are truly human?

My first day at secondary school in Kampala, Uganda. Our class teacher, Mr Patel, delivers a pep talk on education, hard work and aspiration. Then, a little hysterically, moves on to teenage rebellions and sexual desires. '*Remember*, girls and boys. Stay inside the family and community. It is the rule of life. A TIGER DOES NOT GO WITH A LION.'

No, a tiger does not go with a lion. Animals, in their natural habitats, stick with their own type. The herd instinct is powerful and potent, defensive and offensive. Although humans belong to one biological species, we have the herd instinct too. And also the opposite instinct: to break out of our tribes, nations, cultures and ethnicities. We can and do reach out to those with whom we have no historical or genetic connections.

Strangers help each other in the most terrible circumstances; kindness breaks through group allegiances. Peasant Russian women gave apples and bread to German prisoners of war in World War I; some Germans helped Jewish people during the Holocaust; white Americans walked with Martin Luther King as he fought for equality. In Rwanda, good Hutu men and women tried to stop their own tribe from massacring Tutsis. I once met a Christian Iraqi doctor in Jordan whose family had been killed by Iraqi Muslim militants. A Palestinian Muslim couple gave him refuge and he married their daughter.

This is a good story without end. I knew the wise Rabbi Hugo Gryn, who sadly died of cancer some years back. He'd been in a concentration camp, felt the Nazi burn on his skin. Suffering made him empathetic. He said we all had an obligation to the wretched and wounded from faraway places and unfamiliar cultures. It was a test, of our humanity and civilisation. It's a hard test.

Sometimes self-protection becomes a cold, thick wall. Compassion and warmth cannot penetrate it. That wall is going up across Europe, grappling with austerity and an unprecedented flow of people from elsewhere. Some are desperate escapees from brutal regimes, others want a better life: another natural imperative.

> **Men and women who care about those outside their tribes, whose hearts are borderless, show what it is to be truly human.**

Thankfully, millions of Europeans do feel the pain of strangers and reach out. When that little boy washed up on a beach in Turkey, looking as if he was asleep, he became every child, our child. People with no connections to Syria, where the family came from, rushed to help, offered to house and look after these wretched refugees.

When we Asians were forced out of Uganda by Idi Amin in 1972, thousands of us moved to the UK. The country was as tense as it is now; Enoch Powell was the anti-immigration folk hero. But generous Britons gave the exiles warm clothes, free English lessons, nappies and towels, vouchers for essentials, books. They didn't know us, but saw us as people in distress and need.

Men and women who care about those outside their tribes, whose hearts are borderless, show what it is to be truly human. And so I say again: yes, Tigers do not go with lions, but *Homo sapiens* do. That's what separates men from beasts. If we lose that capacity, we will have given up civilised impulses and turned from men and women to beasts.

STEPHANIE SHIRLEY

Businesswoman and philanthropist

As a child refugee from Nazi Europe, Stephanie Shirley experienced the gift of generosity from strangers, who gave her a loving home. In her thought-provoking answer, she talks about the benefits that true altruism bring to the person giving as well as receiving.

Many animals behave in ways that benefit their kin. But philanthropy is a distinguishing characteristic of the human species.

I was an unaccompanied child refugee from Nazi Europe. Generous strangers gave me a loving home. Their Christian ethic was that it was better to give than to receive. I believe in only the last six of the Ten Commandments – those enclosed in the Golden Rule: 'Do as you would be done by'.

Quakers usually give anonymously, always without any fuss. Muslims do not give to charity but rather 'in charity' to individuals (much more difficult) and – like practising Jews – think of giving as a duty, not an option. Sikhs believe life has three equal dimensions, one of which is giving one's earnings, talents and time to the less fortunate. Buddhists recognise philanthropy as the gift of service and teaching, rather than of wealth or material possession. The various faiths may all seem different but – like picking individual mushrooms – if you dig down and look underneath, they are all one. All equally valid givers. The important thing is that they all give.

What drives the giving spirit? Most of us are taught as children to share and to give. Perhaps as part of family tradition. Many families struggle to make do, but some mega-wealthy people want to limit the amount their heirs inherit so as to release them to make their own way. Devout people give to satisfy divine will. Enlightened self-interest is when we give to others and so, indirectly, help ourselves; perhaps as insurance – such as giving to Age UK for possible future benefit ourselves. Or as entry into some elite group. Or with reputation – to show moral dignity, not just our spending power. Unfakeable authentic advertising.

These drivers contrast with the altruistic: 'it's the right thing to do', 'giving makes me feel good'. The positive-psychology movement swears that doing good has fabulous mental health benefits, and brain scans show the pleasure centres in the brain are stimulated when we act unselfishly. My own giving is some sort of repayment for all that I've been given.

**Giving is high on the list of virtues.
Anyone can do it.**

Perhaps the motives hardly matter. Giving is high on the list of virtues. Anyone can do it. We might not be particularly 'moral'; we might be partial to a drink too many; we might have a roving eye; or we may prefer light reading to philosophy. We may not see ourselves as all that spiritual. But we can all give. That's what makes us human.

ANN WIDDECOMBE

Politician

Like all other creatures, we are, to a great extent, preoccupied with survival. But Ann Widdecombe's essay celebrates all that cannot be reduced to this simple aim. We have laws, and we have norms, but there is so much more that goes beyond this.

In the Genesis story, the knowledge of good and evil is obtained uniquely by man, and a nuanced sense of right and wrong is what continues to distinguish us from the rest of creation. We are more intelligent, but we are not alone in possessing intelligence. We have complicated speech, but we are not alone in communication. We can analyse emotion, but we are not alone in possessing it. The animal kingdom demonstrates both family and pack loyalty. Parents discipline their young, and rogue members of the pack are set upon or driven out. But in each case, the reaction is driven by the instinct for survival. The sense of right and wrong, by contrast, goes right beyond what is necessary for the survival of the human pack.

If we are irritable with someone, but we don't show it, we will still feel we are guilty of wrong because we can have an objective sense of morality: the sense that pronounces: 'I will not do that, even though nobody else will know, because it's wrong.' Christ himself set the standard when he said, *of course* the Lord said murder was wrong, but it was also wrong to feel angry. Quite obviously, adultery was wrong, but so was secret lust. In short, there is a morality beyond law itself, which each individual interprets in thought as well as action.

Law is limited simply to the categorising of thoughts and actions to right or wrong. But it's extended to cover moral imperatives. 'I can do no other,' said Luther, as he pinned up the ninety-five theses and prepared to take on the entire religious establishment. Some may say he was wrong, that he unleashed a religious civil war and cost thousands of lives. But he was driven by his own moral urgency. One man might hide Jews in his attic despite the danger to his entire family. Another might decline, saying his first duty is to look after his wife and children. One man's freedom fighter is another man's terrorist. One man might stand against oppression, another set up an underground movement, while in public professing loyalty to the regime. The scenarios are limitless, but they all involve the same question: what is the right thing to do?

These dilemmas, sometimes dramatic but usually mundane, confront all human beings. It's their recognition and resolution that marks out humankind. That internal activity which we call conscience. A dog or a cat caught thieving in the kitchen will look guilty, because it knows that it has taken food that was intended for the humans, and ownership of prey or food is an established law of the jungle. A law based on survival. But what Fido cannot do is feel guilty because the humans were looking forward to that beef, or to reason that he should have been content with the extra treat he got for lunch. He can fear punishment, but he cannot internally punish himself. He can understand forbidden, but not wrong. The ability to distinguish between forbidden and wrong goes to the core of our humanity.

The scenarios are limitless, but they all involve the same question: what is the right thing to do?

In the rest of creation, the boundary is between forbidden and allowed. But, for us, it is between morally acceptable and morally unacceptable. Human beings are forever debating what falls into which of those categories, sometimes with others, sometimes alone. We debate whether the state should have a role in determining good from bad conduct over a full range of behaviour. And when we do acknowledge the role of government, we debate which penalty is moral. Is the death penalty justifiable if it can be shown to save lives? Should we smack our children?

We have a sense of right and wrong which is not pragmatic. So that we can say, even if that will work, it's still wrong. We have a sense of right and wrong which does not depend on others. As in, I would have to live with the knowledge I had done it. The already well-fed cat sprawled in the sunshine, lazily eyeing up a bird, is said to be just acting in accordance with its nature. But the nature of the human is to form a view on want and killing.

GEORGE MONBIOT

Journalist and activist

George Monbiot's inspiring answer spurs hope into a world where stories of murder and devastation take precedence. Through his essay he encourages us to find the good that accompanies the bad, and urges you to re-evaluate who we really are.

Most of us have a strong belief about our own species: that human beings are fundamentally selfish and greedy. I mean, it's obvious, isn't it? Just watch the news, or look at how our politicians and business leaders behave. Selfishness and greed, unfortunately, are what humans are all about.

But, weirdly, the science tells us nothing of the kind. Study after study, experiment after experiment, shows that while we all have some selfishness and greed in us, these are by no means dominant. In the great majority of people, empathy, generosity and community spirit are all stronger values.

It turns out that we have a distorted view of human behaviour. We have a powerful instinct to look out for danger, so the bad things people do are more salient in our minds than the good things. The news reinforces this tendency: if it bleeds, it leads.

We remember, for example, the two terrorists who murdered twelve people in Paris in January 2015, and our recollection of that horror persuades us that evil is a central feature of the human condition. But we forget the 3 million people in France and the millions elsewhere who gathered, lit candles and marched in public places in solidarity with the victims. These people, not the two terrorists, represent the human norm. We stand together against threats to our well-being.

A Force for Good?

As for our leaders, well, they turn out to be highly atypical. They are more likely to be selfish and greedy than the majority of people, which is perhaps how they got to where they are. But they dominate the TV screens and fill our minds, so we think, 'That's what we're like.' We are, broadly speaking, a society of altruists dominated by selfish people.

Only because it is so familiar do we fail to notice that kindness is central to the human condition.

The reality this obscures would make us gasp if we saw it in another species. Only because it is so familiar do we fail to notice that kindness is central to the human condition. Every day, I see people helping others with luggage, giving up their seats for someone else, giving money to the homeless, setting aside time for others, listening to friends in distress, volunteering for causes which offer no material reward. This is not reciprocity. When you give money to a homeless person, you do not expect them to give you money back.

Occasionally, we risk everything for the sake of other people. I think of my Dutch mother-in-law, whose family, during the German occupation, took in a six-year-old Jewish boy – a stranger – and kept him in their house for two years. Fed him and everything as well. The house next door was occupied by the local German commander; the street was often thick with soldiers and officials. Had the boy been discovered, the whole family would have been sent to a concentration camp, where they would have been likely to be murdered. They were not alone – thousands of Dutch families did the same.

This is what we are. This is what makes us human. And we forget it at our peril.

PARIS LEES

Journalist

Forgiveness can be one of the greatest challenges we face as human beings. Paris Lees tells her own story of how her journey to forgive her father became the most empowering experience of her life.

I used to fantasise about killing my father. I'd wait down an alleyway for him to come home from the pub. Maybe I'd stand on a wall, hidden by a tree, and hit him around the head with a baseball bat. I'd wear a balaclava so no one could see who I was. I'd beat him up. I'd tell him I hated him.

He was a hard man. When I was growing up, he was cruel. Always getting on at me, criticising me, calling me names, shaming me – simply for being myself. People used to say, 'Paris, he's your dad. He loves you, he's just got a different way of showing it,' but it made me furious because I just thought that, surely, if anything, that made it worse? Your parents are meant to love and protect you – right?

I was adamant: I hated him and nothing would ever change that. It was a vigorous, venomous hatred that came, in many ways, to define me. But then you grow up. You live a little. And you make terrible mistakes that hurt the people you love most, too. One of the big breakthroughs I've had in therapy is that I have to forgive myself if I'm going to break the cycle of shame and move forwards and be a better person.

An unexpected side effect of this process is that one night I lay alone in bed and empathised with my father for the first time in my life. I don't believe he meant to hurt me any more than I've meant to hurt people I've loved. And I know he had a really tough child-hood too. I understand now how my upbringing has impacted me, so I can't forgive myself without forgiving him. I'd be a hypocrite.

It's not easy to forgive people – and people have every right to be angry when they've suffered abuse.

Forgiveness is not the same as excusing, ignoring or condoning bad behaviour. It's acknowledging that something was wrong, and then choosing to let go. We all love a revenge story – it speaks to something deep within us. But forgiveness is an incredibly power-ful drive too, and, I believe, much more complex. It doesn't mean that you tolerate abuse – and you shouldn't – but you don't let it continue to poison you.

**Forgiveness is not the same as excusing,
ignoring or condoning bad behaviour.
It's acknowledging that something was wrong,
and then choosing to let go.**

For years, I'd wanted my father to acknowledge the impact he'd had on me. Maybe then, I thought, I could start to forgive him. But I realised that this was simply giving him power over me. In that mindset, my power to forgive him rested with him – and whether or not he asked for my forgiveness. And that was disempowering. I realised that it didn't matter if he ever 'got it' – I could choose to forgive him anyway. The power to forgive was mine.

Weirdly, a few months later, I was blown away by Eva Mozes Kor, a woman in her eighties who had suffered horrific abuse in a concentration camp as a child. In a film called *The Power to Live and Forgive*, produced by Buzzfeed, she describes her journey from being a naked ten-year-old being experimented on by Josef Mengele, the Nazi 'Angel of Death', to forgiving him. Her story is horrendous – at one point Eva was left crawling around on the floor for weeks, believing she was dying.

It's worth watching the film and hearing her story in full – and seeing how, decades later, she came to a point where, incredibly, she felt able to forgive Mengele. But what struck me most was how personally empowering Eva found the process. As she says, 'What I discovered for myself was life-changing . . . I had the power to forgive. No one could give me that power and no one could take it away. It was all mine to use in any way I wished.'

I'm not religious, but I pray to the universe every day now that I might be forgiven for hurting others, and for the strength to forgive those who have hurt me – isn't that human?

JEAN NEALE

Radio 2 listener

A heart-warming account of life from one of *The Jeremy Vine Show*'s most dedicated listeners. Jean concludes that kindness is what makes us human, quoting acts of kindness she continues to receive in her life now.

I was born in November 1930 . . . a very long time ago. That means I was eight years old when World War II began. I don't feel as if I was affected too much by it. That is, until I was older and the Germans started with the doodlebugs, the flying bombs which were an early form of cruise missile. My uncle was an air-raid warden and used to tell us whether the planes overhead were ours or the German's. I don't think he actually knew, he just guessed most of the time, but it put us all at ease when he used to say it was one of ours.

My mum and dad were ordinary working-class people. My mother was a housewife and very house-proud. My father was a lorry driver. He had exemption from the war effort due to the loads that he carried, often working nights. Although my mother didn't show it much, you could tell every night of the raids she worried about my dad coming home safe the next morning.

I left school at fourteen and started work in a department store, which was all right until I found another job at Hadfields steelworks as a telephonist, which is where I met my husband Joe. We married in 1977 and lived a very happy life together. Joe passed away some years ago, so now there is just me left on my own, listening to the radio and occasionally passing on my views and opinions on Jeremy's show.

When I think back on my eighty-eight years, and ponder what makes us human, the answer I come to is kindness. To my mind, these days, values have changed, and caring all too often seems to have gone by the wayside. This doesn't apply to everyone, I'm glad to say, and I have had many examples of kindness being shown to me in my life. I like to think that, if you are kind and considerate to people, it is very often returned.

When I think back on my eighty-eight years, and ponder what makes us human, the answer I come to is kindness.

Doing something nice is often easier than being nasty. It's difficult for me to understand why there is so much killing in the world today, and people don't seem to understand that what they are doing is wrong. Helpfulness is good. Giving someone a helping hand will always be appreciated, by the helper and the helped. If everyone in the world tried to do these things, I suppose you would call this place heaven.

Recently I have had a few mishaps, as one does – it's all down to age, I think. But the kindness I have received from family and friends and all the National Health Service is immeasurable. Everyone has been kindness itself. And I can't thank them enough – it really is very much appreciated. It's that sacrificial kindness that makes life worthwhile, and that's what makes us human.

OWEN JONES

Journalist and activist

**Owen Jones recalls his experiences interviewing refugees –
people who were fleeing the atrocities of war and humanitarian
crises, yet who also found room for kindness, love and compassion. It is that capacity for both, he writes, that makes us human.**

What makes us human is our capacity for almost limitless compassion, and almost boundless horror.

Four-and-a-half years ago, I arrived at a refugee camp in
Djibouti. It was filled with people who had fled Yemen, just over
the water: with the help of British weapons and support, a Saudi-led
coalition has bombed that country into the worst humanitarian
crisis on earth. There, I met little children who drew pictures, like
little children do, but they were not pictures of animals or smiling
families, but dead bodies, surrounded by blood, lying in rubble as
airplanes overhead dropped bombs.

Many of these kids played football or hide-and-seek amongst
the tents of the refugee camp – the capacity of children to adapt
in the most adverse circumstances is truly astonishing – but, with
some, the light had gone out in their eyes, traumatised by what they
had seen and felt.

At the end of last month, I went to Folkestone and met refugees
– from Iraq, Iran and Sudan – who've fled horrors that, thankfully,
remain unimaginable for most of us. Yet when they arrive on our
shores, they find themselves scapegoated and blamed for problems
they clearly had nothing to do with – on newspaper front pages and
in the speeches of mainstream politicians. One had converted from
Islam to Christianity in Iran and, fearing death, fled here. He's now

semi-imprisoned in an old military barracks, crammed together in tiny buildings with complete strangers, with no privacy. He can only sleep with sleeping pills.

But I found compassion too. In Djibouti, I saw the love and care of the UN Children's Fund workers as they tended to some of the world's most vulnerable people. They were talented and capable, and they could have chosen jobs with less stress and more financial renumeration. Their compassion took them to a different place.

> The capacity of children to adapt in the most
> adverse circumstances is truly astonishing – but,
> with some, the light had gone out in their eyes,
> traumatised by what they had seen and felt.

In Folkestone, too, I met local people who, rather than blaming refugees for the failure of politicians to provide enough affordable housing, defend well-paid jobs or deliver well-funded public services, instead spend time fighting and campaigning for the rights of refugees. They don't get paid for it, it takes up lots of time in already busy lives, they get screamed at by far-right extremists: they do what they do purely for love and compassion.

There are those who talk incessantly of human nature, often to argue that building a society free of injustice is a naive and impossible dream. Humans are selfish, greedy creatures who fear and hate outsiders in this narrative. But humans are infinitely malleable: we're all to play for.

It's comforting to look back at, say, the Nazis and say they were sociopaths, but they're the ultimate lesson in what we are capable of if we stop seeing others as human beings: people who would gladly have helped an elderly person across the road in their home town committed the most unspeakable atrocities against Jews and Slavs on the Eastern Front. But that period, too, was full of people who risked their lives to protect others, often strangers, from death.

A Force for Good?

No one could say they did it to 'virtue signal', a phrase now used to discredit any show of love for others; they did it because their love and empathy dictated it.

To be human, then, is to have the power to do immense good or evil. It's not innate, it's not hard-wired into us: it depends on what the societies we grow up in nurture. It's a conclusion full of optimism, because it tell us that horror and injustice aren't inevitable: they can be overcome.

BILLY BRAGG

Singer-songwriter

Now more than ever, we need empathy, says Billy Bragg, writing that this quality not only helps us feel less alone, but also forces us to think outside of our own bubbles.

We live in increasingly divided times. Cynicism has become the default response to anyone suggesting an issue might be more nuanced that it appears. Everything has become black or white. If you're not 100% with us, then you must be against us. And woe betide anyone showing compassion for those outside their own group.

Accusations of political correctness or virtue signalling are levelled at those who stand up for the rights of outsiders – meaningless taunts that seek to shame the impulse to show some understanding for the plight of others. It's as if there is a war on empathy.

As a musician, this troubles me deeply, because empathy is what music is all about – it's the currency of songwriting. When a song moves you, it's because you feel that the singer somehow understands what you're going through. The power that music has is not that it can change the world – trust me, I've tried – but that it can make you feel as if you're not alone.

It may be that you've had a deeply emotional experience that you identify with a certain song, the lyrics of which articulate feelings that you struggle to deal with. If you attend a concert by the artist who recorded that song, when they perform it and you and 1,000 others sing along, it's a moment of solidarity; that your struggle is recognised, your experience validated by all these strangers singing your song. You can't get that online.

A Force for Good?

And the crucial thing here is that you are among strangers. We all expect and deserve sympathy from our nearest and dearest, but empathy draws its power because it requires us to feel compassion for those outside of our family grouping. The impulse to protect one's own flesh and blood runs deep throughout nature. However, it's the ability to have feelings for the plight of those with whom we have no connection that separates us from the animal kingdom.

**When people talk of 'our better nature',
they are referring to the altruistic impulse
that encourages us to overcome the selfish
dog-eat-dog urges that ultimately
impoverish us all.**

When people talk of 'our better nature', they are referring to the altruistic impulse that encourages us to overcome the selfish dog-eat-dog urges that ultimately impoverish us all. You only have to look to New Zealand to see how the response of Prime Minister Jacinda Arden to the terrorist attack on a Christchurch mosque in 2019 was met with overwhelming approval. In her willingness to comfort the families of the victims, we saw our better selves. Social and ethnic differences were suspended. Empathy overcame division.

Compare her reaction with that of Donald Trump, turning a mass shooting in Texas into a grinning photo op, using the victims to promote his own agenda. The then-President of the United States was a driving force of the war on empathy, demonising outsiders, whipping up intolerance, portraying any act of compassion as a form of a weakness.

Hostility towards strangers undermines our humanity and is ultimately bad for our health. When a song moves you, it's not just because the writer has touched a nerve in your own personal experience. It's also the recognition that a stranger, someone who may not even be from your culture, is offering you some solace in what feels like an increasingly uncaring world.

That's empathy, the thing that makes us human.

Philosophy and Spirituality

The essays in this chapter tackle the magnitude
of the question 'what makes us human?' at a
philosophical, religious or spiritual level.
Grappling with questions of mortality,
consciousness and morality, these responses
capture the essence of human spirit and
how we find a place in the universe.

WILLIAM BOYD

Writer

Novelist William Boyd tackles the question with an illuminatingly philosophical meditation on time, consciousness and mortality.

I want to start with a luminously beautiful – and luminously profound – quotation from Vladimir Nabokov's autobiography, *Speak Memory*. He writes: 'The cradle rocks above an abyss, and common sense tells us that our existence is but a brief crack of light between two eternities of darkness.'

'Common sense'. I believe that the knowledge of this state of affairs is the fundamental truth about our human nature: the fact that our lives simply amount to our individual occupation of this 'brief crack of light between two eternities of darkness' shapes everything that makes us human and is responsible for everything good – and everything bad – about us.

You might argue that if you believe in a religious faith – where life and an afterlife is ordained and somehow controlled by a supernatural being – a god or gods – then this awareness of our temporal, bounded existence in time doesn't apply. In response, you might counter-argue that religious faith is created *expressly* to confound and disprove this primordial conviction: a faith created, as Philip Larkin put it, to 'pretend that we never die'.

But whatever the nature of a faith in a supernatural being, or beings, and whatever its unprovable postulates, I'm convinced that what makes our species unique amongst the fauna of this small planet circling its insignificant star is that we know we are trapped in time, caught briefly between these two eternities of darkness, the prenatal darkness and the posthumous one. That consciousness we possess – that this is it, that the time we have on earth is not a dress rehearsal for immortality in some notional heaven, nirvana or paradise – is hard-wired into our very beings at an elemental and immovable level.

None of the other animals on this planet shares this self-awareness, this consciousness, except, perhaps, chimpanzees, our closest cousins, separated from us by the tiniest difference in our DNA. No one can yet scientifically establish that chimpanzees possess a kind of self-consciousness similar to our own, but the fact that chimpanzee society is as Manichean and as spookily similar as our own – light and dark, very altruistic and loving and simultaneously very evil – backs up the supposition that what we share in our genetic make-up may include a form of time-awareness: that we know instinctively our lives are irrevocably finite, and that therefore determines what we are and how we act.

I'm convinced that what makes our species unique amongst the fauna of this small planet circling its insignificant star is that we know we are trapped in time, caught briefly between these two eternities of darkness, the prenatal darkness and the posthumous one.

Is our viciousness, the manifest, unspeakable evil in our behaviour, as much a sign of that self-consciousness as the unselfish, sacrificial good that we are also capable of? Only human beings and chimpanzees gratuitously and knowingly inflict pain on themselves and other species. Only human beings will knowingly sacrifice themselves for the greater good of others. Recognising these opposing tendencies in ourselves, we – *Homo sapiens* – have evolved, over centuries, moral codes to try and check our worst excesses, and, to a significant degree, these self-imposed edicts of behaviour work, broadly, in our various societies – though you just need to switch on your television set or open a newspaper to see where and how they can lapse all too easily.

'The prison of time is spherical and without exits,' Nabokov says. What to do in the face of this universal, inescapable penal servitude? My own feeling – and this again is what makes us human – is that we all – all of us sentient denizens of the earth – yearn for one thing. Just as it's hard-wired into our consciousness that we live between two eternities of darkness, so we search for some factor to alleviate and compensate for that brutal reality.

And the compensation we seek, I believe, is love. We want to love and we want to be loved, every single one of us. As the song says, 'to love and be loved in return' is the greatest thing. That's what makes our sojourn in the time-prison bearable. More than bearable: redemptive, life-enhancing, time-evading. If you're lucky enough to experience that emotion, then you'll have savoured the best, the ultimate, that the human predicament can offer.

ROGER SCRUTON

Philosopher and writer

Roger Scruton (1944–2020) reflects on the self-fulfilling nature of the question: by asking what makes us human, you are identifying exactly what it means to be one. His absorbing essay unites thoughts from influential people in art, poetry, music and philosophy.

If I ask myself what makes us human, then one answer jumps out at me straight away – it is not the only answer, but it is the one suggested by the question. What makes us human is that we ask questions. All the animals have interests, instincts and conceptions. All the animals frame for themselves an idea of the world in which they live. But we alone question our surroundings. We alone refuse to be defined by the world in which we live, but instead try to define our nature for ourselves.

The intellectual history of our species is to a great extent defined by this attempt. Are we animals like the others? Do we have souls as well as bodies? Are we related, in the order of things, to angels, to demons and to gods? All science, all art, all religion and all philosophy worth the name begins in a question. And it is because we have questions that human life is so deeply satisfying and so deeply troubling, too.

Not all questions have an answer. In mathematics and science, we solve our problems as well as create them. But in art and philosophy, things are not so simple. Hamlet's great soliloquy starts with a famous line: 'To be or not to be: that is the question.' The play revolves around that question. Would it be better not to exist? Is there anything in human life that makes life worthwhile? When, confronted by the extent of human treachery and scheming, we fall into complete contempt towards our species, is there some trick of thought, some perception, some argument or some appeal to higher authority that will restore the will to live?

When I look at the great artists of the past, I am often struck by the extent to which their work has evolved in response to a question. Milton asked himself how the flawed world in which he found himself could be the work of a supremely good God, and his answer was *Paradise Lost*. Bach asked himself how variants and permutations flow from the basic moves in music, and his answer was *The Art of Fugue*. Rembrandt asked himself how the soul is revealed in the flesh, and what the lights and textures of our bodies mean, and his answer was his extraordinary series of self-portraits. In art, it is always as though the question is what the work of art is really about. Milton's poem implants the question of man's relation to God in the centre of our consciousness. It does not answer the question, but instead creates wonder and awe in response to it. Wonder and awe are the diet of the artist, and without them the world would be far less meaningful to us than it is.

If I ask myself what makes us human, then one answer jumps out at me straight away – it is not the only answer, but it is the one suggested by the question.

The same is true of philosophy. Although there are philosophers who give answers, it is usually their questions and not their answers that have survived. Plato asked how it is that we can think about the property of redness, and not just about red *things*. How can finite human minds gain access to universal realities? Plato's question is still with us, even though few people today would accept his answer to it. Aristotle asked how it is that there can be time and change in an ordered universe. Is there a prime mover, who sets it all in motion? Few would accept Aristotle's answer to this question: but the question remains. How can there be time, change, process and becoming, in a world that could as easily have been permanently at rest? Kant asked how it is that human beings, who are part of the natural order, can freely decide to do this rather than that, can take responsibility for their decisions, and hold each other to account for the consequences of their actions? Kant was honest in acknowledging that the question lies beyond our capacity to answer it; but until we have asked it, he implied, we have no real understanding of our condition.

In the monasteries, libraries and courts of medieval Europe, the big questions were constantly debated. People would be burned at the stake for their questions, and others would cross land and sea to punish people for their answers. In the Renaissance, and again at the Enlightenment, the big questions were asked and answered. And again, death and destruction were the result, as in the religious wars of the sixteenth and seventeenth centuries, and in the French Revolution. Communism and fascism both began in philosophy, both promised answers to the ultimate questions, and both led to mass murder. Our nature as questioning beings seems to have a huge cost. And maybe we are no longer prepared to pay it. Certainly, if we look around ourselves today, we see a mass of ready-made answers, and very few attempts to define the questions that would justify them.

Should we then give up on the habit of asking questions? I think not. To cease to ask questions would be to cease to be fully human. The challenge which has shaped my own life as a writer, is to ask questions, but gently, and without insisting on an answer.

JONATHAN SACKS

Chief Rabbi, philosopher and author

Even in our modern scientific age, religion still offers unique insight. Drawing on centuries of Judeo-Christian wisdom, Lord Sacks (1948–2020) shared an answer is a rallying cry against the epidemic of loneliness and a tribute to the power of love and forgiveness.

As an answer to the question 'what makes us human?', even in the age of neuroscience, it's hard to improve on the Bible's answer.

First comes the good news of Genesis 1. We are each, regardless of class, colour or culture, in the image and likeness of God. This is the most important statement in Western culture of the non-negotiable dignity of the human person. It is the source of the idea of human rights, most famously formulated in the American Declaration of Independence: 'We hold these truths to be self-evident, that all men are created equal and are endowed by their Creator with certain inalienable rights.'

Like God, we are creative. Like God, we are free. All other life forms adapt to their environment. We alone adapt the environment to ourselves, sometimes with disastrous results, but always extending our powers, making us ever less vulnerable to the random cruelties of fate and the indignities of powerlessness.

Then comes the complication from which all human history flows. 'It is not good for man to be alone.' We are supremely the social animal – part cause, part effect of our ability to use language. What makes us human, according to Judaism, is the strength and quality of our relationships. Jean-Paul Sartre was never more wrong than when he said, 'Hell is other people.' Hell is the absence of other people. Solitary confinement is the worst punishment there is.

So the Book of Genesis is about relationships, focusing on the most important of them: husbands and wives, parents and children, and sibling rivalries. Only in Exodus does the Bible turn to the politics of slavery and freedom. Much of the Bible is about what makes a good society, but it insists on the primacy of the personal over the political. As long as family feeling is alive, said Alexis de Tocqueville, the opponent of oppression is never alone. Without strong families standing between the individual and the state, freedom is eventually lost.

Then comes the complication from which all human history flows. 'It is not good for man to be alone.'

The centrality of the family is what gave Jews their astonishing ability to survive tragedy and centuries of exile and dispersion. I knew this in my bones long before I was of an age to step back and reflect on the human condition. My parents were not well-off. My father had come to Britain as a refugee fleeing persecution in Poland. The family was poor and he had to leave school at the age of fourteen to help his father earn a living.

He had a small shop in London's East End, but he was not made to be a businessman. My mother came from a religious family at a time when it was not considered seemly for a Jewish girl to continue in education after the age of sixteen. So, though we never knew poverty, our parents had little in material terms to give us, their four boys. But they took immense pride in us and wanted us to have the opportunities they had lacked. We all duly went to university and on to good careers. Ours was a story shared by many of our contemporaries.

When it works, the family is the matrix of our humanity. It is where we learn love and self-confidence and the basic values that will serve as our satellite navigation system through the uncharted territory of life. It is where we learn responsibility and the chore-ography of turn-taking and making space for others. It is where we acquire the habits of the heart that help us take responsibility and risks, knowing there is someone to lift us if we fall. A childhood lived in the stable presence of two loving parents is the greatest gift anyone can have, which is why so much of Jewish ritual and cele-bration is centred on the home.

Family life isn't easy or straightforward. The Bible does not hide that fact from us. The stories of Genesis do not contain a single sentence saying, 'And they all lived happily ever after.' Families need constant work, sacrifice and mutual respect. But if you get home right, your children will have a head start in making their own fulfilling relationships, and relationships truly are what makes us human.

Which is why I sometimes worry about the future. A report by the Mental Health Foundation found that one in ten Britons is lonely, and the proportion amongst the young is higher and rising. We invest immense time and energy in electronic communication: smartphones, texts and social networking software. But are virtual relationships the same as face-to-face ones?

This is where, I believe, religion has an immense contribution to make at every level: spiritual, personal and collective. Spiritually, the Judeo-Christian ethic teaches us to see the trace of God in the face of the human other, the most sublime idea I know. Personally, it teaches the importance of love and forgiveness, the two great dimensions of a lasting relationship. Collectively, religions create strong and supportive communities where you have friends on whom you can rely.

Faith is the redemption of solitude, and this is its most human-ising gift. God lives in the space between us when we come together in love and joy.

TERRY WAITE

Humanitarian and author

As humans, we have developed, over millennia, many systems and rules for making sense of our immensely complex existence. But Terry Waite's answer goes beyond rigid moral codes, unravelling the meaning that puts us in touch with life's deepest rhythms.

We have a home in a rural village in the countryside. As there are no street lights, on a clear night the heavens are ablaze with light cast by thousands of stars. I often do what countless generations have done before me – gaze upwards and contemplate the great mystery of the universe of which I am a part. The very particles that constitute my body will one day be reintegrated into this enormously complicated mix, and life will continue – ashes to ashes, dust to dust.

In an attempt to answer the question 'what makes us human?', my starting point is mystery. Life is a mystery. Across millions of years, the planet on which we live our allotted span has developed, and life in all its different forms has emerged. We as human beings are part of that evolving process, and as humans we have certain characteristics that distinguish us from the rest of the animal kingdom.

First of all, we have developed the ability to be aware of, and actively investigate, the universe and life itself. We are able to stand back in wonder at creation, and we are able to advance that process, through scientific enquiry, when each new discovery that we make takes us one step further towards the heart of mystery. Human beings have the ability to reason, analyse and draw conclusions from that process.

As opposed to other living species, we are able to make use of collective cognition. That means we are able to share insights with others and collectively benefit from what we learn. Of course, human beings do act out of instinct, but we are able to go beyond pure instinct and make moral choices. Generally speaking, an animal will act out of instinct, whereas a human being has the choice of taking a course of action that is not determined by instinct alone. Men and women have the capacity to rise above instinct.

This raises the question of how we choose a particular way of behaving. For example, to kill or not to kill another human being. To make such a choice implies a frame of reference. In order to use our ability to choose, human beings have developed a variety of moral codes – some of which have their origin in religion, others of which don't. One well-known code would be the Ten Commandments found in the Old Testament of the Bible. There were other codes, not necessarily formed as a result of the development of conscience – yet another characteristic that contributes towards making us human. Conscience, shaped as it is by a variety of social, cultural and religious factors, enables us to have an understanding of what we believe to be right, and what we believe to be wrong.

In the Bible it says that we are called to be co-workers with God. That implies that we are not simply passive responders, but are called to have a role in the development of creation.

Concepts of right and wrong, good and evil, will inevitably vary between different cultures because conscience is partly shaped by cultural factors. A simple example is the dietary restrictions observed by certain religious groups. For example, some prohibitions originated when it was dangerous to eat certain foods, for health reasons. Now those risks have been considerably reduced, but the sanctions continue through the religious code observed by the group.

Frequently, primitive instinct would dictate that enemies should be killed, but with human beings there is a capacity for forgiveness and compassion. Admittedly not always practised, but there nevertheless.

Speaking from a Christian perspective, religion has the possibility of expressing mystery in human terms. In other words, putting a human face on to what is a profound mystery. Within the beliefs and practices of Christianity, we see the rhythms of the universe demonstrated in ways we can comprehend. Death and resurrection, central to the Christian faith, reflect patterns observed in the universe through scientific enquiry. In the Bible it says that we are called to be co-workers with God. That implies that we are not simply passive responders, but are called to have a role in the development of creation. The personification of good and evil by God and the Devil points to a reality in the world. Negative and positive are both active in creation and within ourselves. As humans, we have the ability to make choices and to determine our moral conduct. Religion, at its best, is far more than a moral code. It is not necessarily to be taken absolutely literally. Rather, it is intended to enable us to be in harmony with the deep rhythms of life, and to begin to touch the hem of mystery which some call God.

JOHN SENTAMU

Archbishop of York

Our search for what makes us human makes us look beyond ourselves, says John Sentamu, in an answer that encapsulates the beauty of religious worship and the curiosity of the human spirit.

A website I visited earlier this year had an interesting tick-box to fill in. It said 'Confirm your humanity'. A rather more profound challenge than ticking the 'I am not a robot' box! How we confirm our humanity is a question which has fascinated people throughout the ages, as they pondered the mystery.

I was ten years old when I encountered Jesus Christ and knew myself to be truly human – God's child, creatively made and wonderfully redeemed in Jesus Christ – called to live out God's characteristics of love, mercy and friendliness. God is Creator, and, for me, this is where my creative and imaginative gifts come from. As the Book of Genesis puts it: 'The Lord God formed man (Hebrew: 'adam) from the dust of the earth (Hebrew: 'adamah). He breathed into his nostrils the breath of life, and man became a living being' (Genesis 2:7).

Yes! Formed from the dust and yet with a close, intimate and self-giving relationship with the Creator-God. Adam, Sentamu, Jeremy Vine is a psychophysical unity. A being, who is alive because I, you, have the 'Breath of God' in us. And, therefore, not a mixture of perishable body and immortal soul.

I think and feel with my whole being. Depending on God for life itself. Adam's, Sentamu's, Jeremy's crowning glory above all other created living creatures is in relation to God. Forever recognising that there is Someone beyond us, infinitely greater than us.

People who have claimed that some human beings are less than human, or not truly human, have committed terrible acts of violence and oppression, thereby violating, blaspheming and spitting on the face of God in every human being they have hurt.

Human beings have an insatiable appetite for worship: to give worth to someone or something – resulting in experiencing a sense of wonder and delighting in beauty. Human beings also have an insatiable appetite for witness: to show and tell. For me, it is bearing witness to God's love affair with humanity. Believing in everyone whether they believe in God or not.

Human beings have an insatiable appetite for worship: to give worth to someone or something – resulting in experiencing a sense of wonder and delighting in beauty.

As I said, being human makes us look beyond ourselves. Let me end by looking at two very different human beings, whose lives demonstrated this gift wonderfully. In the space of three days, back in March 2018, beloved comedian Ken Dodd and world-renowned physicist Stephen Hawking died. Could there be a greater contrast? One was an eccentric Liverpudlian who delighted his audiences by helping them see beyond the everyday to the fantastical, absurd and surreal aspects of life. The other was a brilliant Cambridge professor whose mind reached out beyond the known world to expand our knowledge of the cosmos.

The human desire to explore and to wonder, recognised in these two people, drove them to accomplish so much, in very different spheres of work and different ways of looking at the world. May we, in our humanity, celebrate those who help us take an extra step into the unknown.

JOHNNIE WALKER

Radio disc jockey

An evocative and soul-searching answer to the question from Johnnie Walker that shows what we all have to gain by addressing our spiritual sides.

In 1965 The Who sang about 'My Generation' – no longer would people try and put us down. That repressive older generation and their establishment can just f-f-fade away. Riding a wave of powerful creative energy, young people at last had their own voice, clothes, art, music, and – thanks to the pirate ships in the North Sea – their own radio stations. The Beatles blasted out 'Revolution'. The Theatres Act of 1968 put paid to theatre censorship. I went to see the musical *Hair* and, in 1970, *Oh! Calcutta!* at the Roundhouse, both featuring nudity for the first time on a British stage. The old rule book had been torn up, thrown aside, and there was now a new freedom.

And so began my quest for the meaning of life, of why we are here, what is our purpose and what would be the new rules and morals to guide our lives. Like so many others, I experimented with mind-altering drugs, explored Eastern and Native American philosophies, and devoured books like *Be Here Now*, *The Prophet*, and books on Western and Chinese astrology.

All I learned, together with a number of experiences over the years, has lead me not just to believe in but to have a deep and profound conviction of the existence of a soul and life after death. I found it impossible to accept that we only live once. What would be the point of gaining all that experience and knowledge for it all just to come to nothing at the end?

One of our toughest experiences is dealing with the death of a loved one. Perhaps that dreadful sense of loss and loneliness could be made a little easier to bear with the knowledge that our loved ones do still exist, and that we will reunite with them one day. Many of us are familiar with peoples' accounts of near-death experiences, of being totally aware of their consciousness existing separately from their body, and of meaningful events of their lives passing before their eyes.

As the French Jesuit priest and philosopher Pierre Teilhard de Chardin said, 'We are not human beings having a spiritual experience; we are spiritual beings having a human experience.'

So began my quest for the meaning of life, of why we are here, what is our purpose and what would be the new rules and morals to guide our lives.

So, if our natural state is spirit, what if, before entering this human life, we had some sort of preview or knowingness of the lessons and experiences that this new life could offer us? Maybe that's too much of a leap for our belief system to adopt, but supposing it were to be true, gone would be our lamenting about how unfair our lives are, how dreadful our parents are and how we always seem to be the one who gets all the problems. If we could accept that we actually chose this life, then we can get on with discovering its purpose.

Knowledge may present the signpost, but it doesn't make the road any easier to travel. Frequently, we fail; frequently, I've failed and still do. If we were perfect we wouldn't be here, we'd be vibrating at a super-high frequency, beaming out light and energy in an invisible dimension that is possibly much closer to this dimension that we realise.

Forgiveness sets us free from anger and hate, and learning to give love is what I believe advances us the most. Give some thought to the seven million people in the UK caring for a loved one: it's a very hard role to play. We all show concern for the patient, but who thinks of the carer? Often lonely, struggling with work, children, financial hardship and, in many cases, their own health issues, caused by this extra burden in their lives.

As we think of their selfless acts of kindness, love and support, perhaps we might reflect that loving and caring for others is one of the finest aspects of what makes us human.

JAMES JONES

Former Bishop of Liverpool, writer and broadcaster

James Jones's thoughtful answer links life's biggest questions with the smallest details of day-to-day existence, speaking of the human instincts in all of us as well as the answers he finds in Christianity.

What makes us human? Well, we're different from other animals in the way we handle fire, write, draw, laugh, make faces and wear jewellery. But there's another experience that marks us out – guilt. That might jar with some. But if a convicted rapist showed no remorse, we'd think him less than human.

Guilt proves we are responsible for our actions. Some people feel guilt unnecessarily, and for that they need therapy. But when we've done wrong, it's good that we feel bad about it. Like the rest of the animal world, we are driven by instincts. But being human involves other impulses that override those animal passions. There is a moral instinct in human beings.

Some of the first words a child says are: 'That's not fair!' Sharing sweets or playing a game, kids have an innate sense of fairness. Is that taught, caught, or part of our human make-up? When we say something is unjust, we are behaving as if there is some law over us all that ought to be obeyed. The longing for justice is marbled into the human heart.

The survival instinct, so evident in the animal kingdom, is there in humanity too, but with a twist. Human beings struggle not only to survive but to be free. The story of the human family told in the Bible is a saga that begins with enslavement and ends in liberation.

There is also a spiritual instinct. There are very few people who haven't at some stage in their life prayed. Usually it's when the bottom falls out of our world that we cry out to God. That said, I once met a man who was seeking God because, as he told me, 'I'm getting married soon to a beautiful woman and think life's wonderful, and I just want to know if there's anyone I've got to thank for all this!'

This spiritual side to being human has us wondering about our place in the universe. Sometimes you can hear a piece of music and you become aware of another dimension to life. These mystical moments take you by surprise. Maybe, on a walk or looking up into the night sky, you want to reach out and be at one with the rest of creation.

This spiritual intuition connects with that other basic instinct to find love. What we value most about our humanity is our ability to love and be loved. The Beatles rocked the world with 'All You Need Is Love'. The fact there's such a deficit of love doesn't dull our impulse to go on looking for it.

And the search for love is coupled with the search for truth. John Lennon wrote a song about it – 'Just Gimme Some Truth'. He was pretty cynical. 'From uptight, short-sighted, narrow-minded hypocritics / All I want is the truth'. Lennon, like other songwriters, poets and philosophers down the ages, called out for some answers to the ancient quest for the truth about being human.

> He gave His own unique answer to the question
> about what makes us human. Instead of giving
> us a set of statements, He gave us a true
> human being, a perfect person: Jesus.

If God was listening (and I think He was), He gave His own unique answer to the question about what makes us human. Instead of giving us a set of statements, He gave us a true human being, a perfect person: Jesus. He was passionate about justice, stood by the sick and up for the poor. He was so fuelled with love that, when His enemies drove nails through His hands, He found the power to forgive. He knew it was the only way to break the vicious cycle of hatred that has torn the world apart since Cain murdered Abel.

When our children were small, I would sometimes idle away the time by taking a coin and placing it under a piece of paper, then shading over it with a pencil until the image of the invisible coin came through on to the page. So the image of true humanity comes through to us in the flesh and blood of Jesus of Nazareth. He was so perfectly human that His followers deemed Him divine. Jesus urged the human family to see ourselves on a journey where God is both our origin and our destiny. Finding a purpose to our life brings fulfilment to our humanity.

There's a story of a little boy splashing about in the mud. His mum was about to shout when he looked up innocently and asked, 'Mum, what's mud for?' 'Making bricks,' she retorted. 'What are bricks for?' 'Houses.' 'What are houses for?' 'People.' 'And what are people for?'

Finally, to be human is to worship. There's something deep down that forces us to shout out when we see something truly amazing. Imagine a football cup final or a Wimbledon final, if at the winning shot all the people in the stands stood motionless and silent. It would be weird and unnatural.

When we see something extraordinary, we have to acknowledge its worth. That's worship. It's natural. It's human. When we see something good or noble or beautiful, we have to worship it. And that's the human response whenever we come face to face with the Divine. We're bound to worship. And we do it with music. It's only human.

RICHARD MADELEY

TV presenter and broadcaster

Richard Madeley writes that our self-awareness and our need for answers is what really sets us apart from other species – leading some to religious conclusions and others to scientific ones.

I believe that it's self-awareness that truly defines us. We're the only species that goes through life knowing that one day we'll die. That's very different from the fundamental survival instinct which most if not all animals have, or a fear of imminent death, in the clutches, say, of a predator. It's much more sophisticated than that.

We humans know our personal, ultimate destiny, almost from the time that we learn to walk and talk. Perhaps because we know our time here is short, that provides the spur to discover our place in the universe, literally and figuratively. We've always done this. Greek philosophers and astronomers believed that the stars were chinks of light leaking through holes in the floor of heaven, and that eclipses were caused by gods. They may have been wrong, but they were trying to make sense of what they could see above them. In that regard, we are exactly the same as the ancient Greeks, with our Hubble telescope and robot spaceships probing deep into space. We want to know.

It's our self-awareness that gives us a thirst for knowledge, not just of the observable universe and the laws of physics, but the unobservable one, and the much hazier, looser laws of metaphysics. Why are we here? Do we live on in some other dimension when we leave this one? And, of course, the big one – is there a God?

The search for God, or a god, or a family of gods is fundamental to every human culture that has ever existed. That's because our self-awareness carries with it a basic question, even a haunting doubt. Put at its simplest, it is this: what if there's no point to us? What if we're just a cosmic accident, with no more ultimate import-ance than anything else in the universe: a virus, a desolate asteroid tumbling through space; a speck of sand?

Being self-aware means we cannot tolerate such a question, or at least one of its binary answers, which is of course: there *is* no point to us; we *are* a random happenstance. We're deeply uncom-fortable with this, so we seek to prove the alternative; that there *is* a higher purpose to our existence; there *has* to be, otherwise what would be the point in being self-aware?

I didn't intend this to be an essay about God, but all roads lead to the fundamental question of whether God exists or is simply a necessary fiction to get us through the night. The world-famous cosmologist Stephen Hawking died convinced that there is no God. In his final book, *Brief Answers to the Big Questions*, published posthumously by his children, he argues that the universe spontan-eously created itself. No one made it; no one directs our fate. As for an afterlife? Wishful thinking, Hawking said. But he was pas-sionately thankful for having this one life to try and appreciate the grand design of the universe: and for that, he said, he was 'extremely grateful'. He didn't say who to.

I didn't intend this to be an essay about God, but all roads lead to the fundamental question of whether God exists or is simply a necessary fiction to get us through the night.

I find it fascinating that self-awareness can lead some, like Stephen Hawking, to the conviction that heaven and hell, if they exist anywhere, are right here with us on earth, and others, as fearsomely intelligent and thoughtful as Hawking, to the diametric opposite certainty, that God is real and is, well, as aware of us as we are – or some of us are – of him.

In fact, it's more than fascinating: it's glorious. The sheer scope and breadth of thought that self-awareness brings with it is quite extraordinary. It's truly a gift. It's what makes us human.

BRUCE DICKINSON

Lead singer of Iron Maiden

Bruce Dickinson challenges the reader to not simply accept that we exist, but, instead, to question what it means to 'be'. He urges us not to sleepwalk through life, and instead to look both inside ourselves and outward to a higher purpose.

'What makes us human?' is not so interesting as 'what makes us a human *being*?' It is the 'being' part that forms the enigma of our existence.

I am a mixture of genes; I am a cocktail of chemicals; I am a series of synaptic connections; I am bone and muscle, equipped with opposable thumbs, and an ingenious brain. These things I share with my fellow humans, and many of them are also features I share with reptiles, fish, and my distant evolutionary relatives. Biology is not enough to determine humanity.

Mere intelligence, however measured, is also inadequate. Without interviewing our closest most intelligent species – probably dolphins and other primates – we will never know if they have the concept of spirit, or faith. If they do, then of course we are not unique, which would prove a blow to those religions claiming that God has given us mastery over the earth by right. In any case, we are de facto the top of the food chain, whether God has anything to do with it or not, and, quite frankly, we are not doing a great job with our self-appointed stewardship of the planet.

The awareness of being, and the question of why we are here at all, is the closest I can come to defining what makes us human. Questioning, not the mechanics of existence but its essential meaning is fundamental to our humanity. Is the universe scientific or poetic? Does emotion have energy and power which sustains beyond our mortal existence? Why does a William Blake painting or verse speak across generations?

As we robotically erase many of the physical functions that have preoccupied humanity for centuries, we shall be left with a dark abyss in the soul of man. The sciences condemn us as an adjunctive and inconvenient obstacle. It would be easier if humans did not exist.

As we robotically erase many of the physical functions that have preoccupied humanity for centuries, we shall be left with a dark abyss in the soul of man.

And yet we do, and we must explore the world of art, spirit, music to sustain us. All of us live most of our lives sleepwalking through our brief existence. Those humans who do not, are called geniuses, and they have paused briefly from the menial trudge through survival, to look up at the stars, or inward to our archetypal souls.

This is the difference between human existence, which is simply unfettered reproduction, and human being. The fact that we appreciate the enigma is what makes us human.

What Makes Us Human?

These essays celebrate the ways that humans
contain multitudes: that there is no one answer
to what makes us human, but instead myriad
perspectives within each of us – and that
this itself can sometimes offer the answer.

ANDREW MARR

Journalist and broadcaster

Full of winking humour and subtly, tacitly revealing his conclusion: reading Andrew Marr's answer gives you the impression of following a great mind as it reasons and feels its way through the question.

What makes us human? In the first place, it's being capable of understanding the biological and evolutionary answers to that question (such as the huge growth in the frontal lobes around the same time as the language instinct develops, and, hence, self-consciousness; or the evolution of the erect posture and the opposable thumb); and yet, at the same time, uneasily feeling that all that's not enough. Thus, loftily declaring our kinship with angels while behaving like murderous beasts; and yet being intelligent enough to understand that the word 'murderous' is a libel on fellow mammals trying to stay alive by eating one another.

In the second place, it's making. We are the making animal. Unless we make – that is, in some small way, change the world around us – we are not fully human. The making can be a book, a picture, a garden, cooked food, but the best making is the making of other human beings, kind and competent, through parenting, biological or otherwise. But what we do, is we change the world around us. We are because we make.

However, in the third place, to be human is to be driven by urgent, dangerous and apparently irresistible drives, from hysterical acquisition of 'stuff' through to lust ('perjured, murderous, bloody, full of blame, savage, extreme, rude, cruel, not to trust').

And being a bit sorry about that.

On the other hand, it's also: waking up on a crisp winter morning, with ringing, apricot-coloured sunlight spreading across brick walls and leafless trees, and experiencing delight, an electric crackle which moves from the back of the calf muscles, up the spine and into the scalp; and at that moment trying to sing for joy and then, hearing the result, being a bit sorry about that.

In the fourth place, it's knowing perfectly well, from the moment that we are born, we are dying and yet, when Death amiably lollops towards us, being greatly surprised and personally offended by this, the most humdrum and unremarkable intrusion of all; and it's promising one's children 'not to be a burden'; and then being a burden; and being a bit – but only a bit – sorry about that.

In the fifth place, taking a very long time to understand the difference between happiness and pleasure, but getting there eventually. And being happy about that.

In the sixth place, it's hypocrisy.

In the seventh place, it's having a slightly disturbing relationship with the evolved creatures who we share the planet with, sentimentalising them, eating them and making friends with them; though rarely at the same time. To be human is to weep, oyster-eyed, about biodiversity while eating oysters; to want to save the Galapagos Islands by flying to them and living in a well-appointed hotel on them.

But what we do is we change the world around us. We are because we make.

In the eighth place, it's abdication and loll, refusal and sprawl: brimming with urgency about the day ahead and then rolling over, shuddering slightly, and staying in that nice, warm bed anyway.

In the ninth place, it's learning, just in time, to manage one's addictions; to prefer coffee over cocaine and the scent of hot bread to the smell of marijuana; to drink Scotch and abjure Jack Daniels;

to move from a lot of cheap wine to a little more expensive wine; and thus, to grow up.

In the tenth place, it's learning to substitute the pleasures of being older for the lost pleasures of youth; viz, sitting outside a cafe with a coffee or whisky, and a copy of a decent newspaper, staring vacantly into the middle distance; rather than skiing down a black run; and, of course, wondering where all the decent newspapers have gone.

In the eleventh place, it's having too few regrets to mention; but boring on incessantly about them anyway.

In the twelfth and final place, it's insisting that one has lived one's life 'my way' while having, in fact, behaved exactly like everybody else – bipedal, vainglorious, self-deluded and yet, luckily, just lovable enough . . .

. . . But mainly, to be human is to make.

YOTAM OTTOLENGHI

Chef and cookery writer

Watching our children grow and begin to make sense of the world, Yotam Ottolenghi says, we start to have a whole new perspective on life's big questions. A thoughtful answer about the wisdom that comes with time, that will make you see the idea of change in a whole new light.

I was raised in an almighty godless home, so I can't really choose a spiritual route towards answering this question. My parents would be proud, though, if I chose an analytical angle, a rigorous philosophical path. And since I was always a big pleaser, and still am, I'm afraid, I will take this approach, at least for now.

This means that I have to first acknowledge that the only way for me to even begin answering this colossal question is through my own experiences. I've got nothing but them.

Trouble is, my experiences of today are so very different from my experiences of, say, twenty years ago, and those are so utterly different from those of another twenty years earlier. So, what made me human at four? And is that the same thing that makes me human at forty-four?

When I look back, I tend to think that the first few months of my life I just spent surviving. I don't remember a thing, obviously, but judging by my recently born son, it looks like all I did was make sure that I was fed and allowed to sleep. That definitely didn't make me human; it just kept me alive.

Later on, it seems like some thoughts started entering my head. Not proper thoughts, I don't think, but simple thoughts, such that make my eight-month-old frown when he observes a new kind of food as he examines it carefully, before shoving it into his little mouth. I don't think that counts as particularly human. I've seen many monkeys pull that exact same face.

As for me, a few months after the frowning stage, my mum tells me, I started talking. And let me tell you, I know a few people, especially my older sister, who prayed to God to take this gift away from me. Even today, my beloved Karl occasionally threatens me with boiling my tongue if I don't 'shut it' – his words. I somehow think my son will follow in my footsteps in this department. Anyways, whether my sister and Karl like it or not, language is a very human thing. It takes the empty frown and pours meaning into it. I spent a good part of twenty-five years enjoying language, playing with it, making a living from it.

Many philosophers and anthropologists would be happy to stop now and describe language as that all-defining human feature. This isn't good enough for me, though. When I look back, I see that, after mastering language, an intellectual capacity, I also wanted to affect the world around me; to create a change, an outcome that goes beyond survival. It's not that I stopped talking one day and just started doing good deeds, but as I grew older, the outcome of my words and my actions became more important to me, and I also started aiming higher.

From playing with my friends, I moved on to helping my parents set the table for dinner, to taking part in arranging a class party, to getting a job, to setting up a business, to writing recipes, to having a child. Of course, I did many other pointless things and talked a lot of nonsense in between, but my focus shifted gradually from language and the games I played with it to trying, and sometimes also succeeding, in making some changes in the outside world.

So, does that make me human? Tough question. From where I stand now, I'd say yes. What makes us human is our ability to use our unique capacities, language included, to have an effect on the outside world that isn't just about survival; it is wanting to make a mark for the sake of making a mark, nothing else.

So, why a tough question? It may seem like I've just cracked it. Not really, because if I follow my own reasoning so far, I'd have to ask myself, what am I going to be like in twenty years, and then in forty years? And there's no way for me to know now. It could be that in forty years I would be thinking a lot about my mortality and coming to grips with it, so I'd want to conclude that being human is all about having a scope, a perspective, an experience-led understanding of life and death.

I could, again, stop now and conclude that there's no one way to point out to what makes us human, that there isn't such a thing as one definition or understanding of human-ness.

Could it be that all those intellectual and emotional transformations are what being human is all about?

But I actually think that we can, funnily enough, take this dead-end as the answer to the big question. Could it be that all those intellectual and emotional transformations are what being human is all about? That we are given a set of basic tools upon arrival and we use those to constantly change as we carve our own way in this world? Perhaps my tendency to act out, as it were, is another person's tendency to internalise and contemplate?

I tend to think that what makes both my baby and myself human is our propensity for change: the fact that we are both going to turn into different things in twenty years' time, whether we like it or not, that we still don't know what that thing will be, that there is just no certainty for us. Except, maybe, for the fact that probably both of us will still be talking a little bit too much.

BRUCE KENT

Vice President, Campaign for Nuclear Disarmament

Bruce Kent's unique answer considers the qualities of love, compassion and imagination in struggles both big and small, and provides insight into how, even in our most personal struggles, we depend on the kindness and wisdom of others.

This question must mean – what makes us human as a separate part of the animal world? We share a great deal with the rest of creation. We also need food, shelter, warmth and some sort of companionship. We breed as animals do, but we love as well.

So what makes us human? To start with, we have vivid imaginations. Which small boy has not guided lost pilgrims across desert wastes or captained boats on raging seas? Who hasn't bravely entered a burning building to rescue trapped and helpless victims? I never used to pass Marble Arch and the place of the Tyburn gallows without imagining my brave speech to the crowd before they sent me swinging.

Imagination, yes. But what about awe? The other day, I saw a travel advert which showed some Egyptian temple, thousands of years old, with its massive towers. Who put those stones in place? Where did they come from? How were they brought there? How many slaves died while building it? The same goes for the cathedrals and palaces. How did they get erected? Who built and designed those soaring pillars? No engines, no scaffolding. Just crude ropes and wooden ladders.

And what about the time span? I remember someone once saying that if all creation was reduced to the height of Nelson's Trafalgar Square column, a penny put on top would represent all life and a postage stamp on the penny would be the measure of human life . . . That is enough to fill me with awe.

So, too, with the order and regularity of our world and universe. Without them, there could be no science or history. All science does is to pick out the pattern of things. That there is a pattern to start with is the staggering fact. The natural world on which all depend is a wonder – even in my own back garden. No one exists apart from what the earth provides.

We humans have so much in common, yet at the same time depend so much on each other's gifts, creativity and curiosity. I marvel at the ingenuity of those who invent new technology, medical scientists, explorers, or those who can write poetry or perform music.

**We humans have so much in common, yet
at the same time depend so much on each
other's gifts, creativity and curiosity.**

Most important of all for humans is love and compassion. Our world is full of pain and suffering, often, but by no means always, inflicted by humans on humans. For most of us, most of the time, it is not the main feature of our lives. But it is there, not to be dismissed as a small matter. We humans, if we are really human, do what we can in our time to bring love and compassion to our bit of the world. But we are not here for very long.

'Away down the river, a hundred miles or more, other little children shall bring my boats ashore.' So wrote the poet Robert Louis Stevenson. But we cannot leave everything to 'other little children'. We experience compassion and love now. They are qualities as real as earth and water. They exist. But how, in a world that often seems so hard, do they become reality?

We do our best, despite the divisions we ourselves have created. Why all these national borders which divide us? Why is the border between France and Britain more important than the border between London and Essex? Why are there millionaires in lovely homes while some sleep under railway bridges? One has to be human even to ask such questions.

KEN DODD

Comedian

In his famously surreal style, Ken Dodd (1927–2018) gives us a stream-of-consciousness that takes in his own experiences in show business alongside an optimistic exploration of imagination, humour and happiness.

What makes us human? I have been invited to say a few words. Me? A few words?

The famous French Philosopher and mathematician René Descartes said 'I think, therefore I am'. Now that's a good one-liner to start with.

I believe we have been given by our Creator, free of charge, an abundance of gifts. Some of them tangible, some psychological.

The brain. This amazing human organ, the Head Office, thousands of times more intricate than all the computers, iPads, calculators, googlers and all the other man-made tools for thinking. Your brain is working for you all the time, even when you go to sleep at night. When you switch off, your brain doesn't. Your heart keeps beating, it even keeps your hair growing – well, some of it! You don't control your beard's urge to sprout out looking for fresh air.

Oh, and dreaming: this activity is attended to by another branch of the brain – your mind – a most magical part of your thinking. Imagination – your creative mind tool, it's like your own film studio. In a child's imagination, a box can become a castle, an ocean liner, an airplane.

We humans are very curious. I wanted to know about Show Business. When we were children, my dad would treat us. He would take us, the Dodd family – mother, my brother Bill and sister June

– to the Shakespeare Theatre of Varieties in Liverpool. We would sit in red plush seats in this big dark room. There were lots of other people, aromas of cigar smoke and orange peel. A huge crimson curtain with gold fringes and tassels. An orchestra, musicians with black bow-ties; the conductor waved his stick and they played jolly rumpty tumpty tunes. The curtain would rise and reveal a beautiful garden bathed in a rosy glow. Pretty young ladies would dance and sing; acrobats, gymnasts and jugglers. Men in baggy check suits would tell jokes and the audience would laugh – oh, how Mum and Dad laughed. This was a variety show and I loved every minute of it. I was stage-struck!

My father, Arthur, was a very humorous man. He loved comedians. He would tell us about the great comics he'd seen, Norman Evans, Harry Tate, Will Hey, Wilkie Bard and Dozens More – he was very funny – Dozens Moore!! My dad's favourite was Jack Pleasance, the shy comedian. Pop could tell jokes and funny stories superbly. His timing was brilliant. He would buy gramophone records of fabulous funnymen like Sandy Powell, a hilarious comedian from Yorkshire. I thought I'd like to be like that, a comedian. I asked my dad, 'Dad, how do you comedy?' Other kids in Knotty Ash collected railway engine numbers; I collected comedians. The supermen in My Hall of Fame were Arthur Askey, Ted Ray, Robb Wilton, Frankie Howerd, Frank Randle, Laurel and Hardy, Danny Kaye.

I was a very intellectual child. I avidly read the *Wizard* and *Hotspur*, boys' magazines, full of stories of adventures and heroes. I thought, Yes! I'd like to be a hero. On the back page of the *Wizard* was a full-page advertisement offering itching powder, stink bombs, magic tricks and seebackroscopes. One offer was very enticing: 'Fool your teachers, amaze your friends, send sixpence in stamps, become a ventriloquist', so I did. At the age of eight, I launched into my showbusiness career as a Vent act, a performer.

I joined a teenage concert party. The producer was a wonderful lady called Hylda. I have met two people in my life who have the magical gift of inspiring people, motivating them, encouraging them, making them believe they can succeed and Win! Bill Shankley and Hylda Fallon. Hylda was very kind and supportive with everyone.

Curiosity made me think, why do we laugh, what is a joke? We laugh at our mistakes: 'to err is to be human'; 'to err' is also forgetting your lines! In Liverpool, we have a splendiferous Reference Library and I spent many hours in there looking for answers, researching what great philosophers and psychiatrists thought about humour. Sigmund Freud said, 'Laughter is the result of the conservation of psychic energy.' Mind you, Freud never played second house Friday night at Glasgow Empire.

**Curiosity made me think, why do we laugh,
what is a joke? . . . We humans , we are
the only animal that laughs.**

We humans, we are the only animal that laughs. Dogs wag their tails, cats purr! When did you last hear your dog say, 'Woof, that was a good 'un'? We have a 'sense of humour', seeing the funny side of life, thinking about things from a different angle. Perceiving incongruity and comical concepts.

TO BE HUMAN is to THINK, to wonder how and why, to imagine, to plan, to muse, to daydream. We have been given so many precious gifts: enjoy them. We think! Therefore we are. AMAZING. We are unique, very special. To be human is to love life and be happy.

Happiness is the greatest gift that we possess! THINK about it!

TANNI GREY-THOMPSON

Athlete

In grappling with the challenges of answering the question, Tanni Grey-Thompson takes the reader on a journey through the complications of modern life that can come between people and make us forget the values we share. Through this, she shows us all how we can make space in our lives for love, trust and forgiveness.

When considering the question 'what makes us human?', I was momentarily transported back to my finals, and that dreaded moment when you turn over the paper and realise you can't answer the question – and even if you try, then you're likely to get it wrong. It seems annoyingly easy until you start to put pen to paper.

I asked several people for advice, including my husband, who, as a scientist, told me that it was simply a matter of chromosomes. Another 699 words would have helped me. I did consider writing on sarcasm, or scientific humour. But after much consideration and potential dithering, which I'm now sure counts as a human trait – not just the act of dithering, but the understanding that you are doing it – I came to the conclusion that self-awareness was an important facet. But beyond thinking why we are on this earth and what is our purpose, there are such things as our need to be liked, loved or understood, or even known.

The debate on the similarities and differences between us and the animal kingdom has been extensively covered in both a philosophical and scientific context. The fact that we choose to devote any of our time to trying to explain life, death and everything in between is an interesting concept that marks us as being different.

What Makes Us Human?

If I had one wish, it would be that people would become more engaged in the parliamentary process that has such a major effect on all those aspects of our lives and deaths. It would be a wonderful aspiration if we could use the access we have to education to encourage the articulation of opinions on those matters.

But self-awareness is changing, and it is no longer just an individual thinking about why we exist on this earth, but an increased awareness of how we live in our society. In the way we interact with others, and how we are measured and viewed. We judge and are judged, and not always in a good way, based on things like the brand of shoes or – more disturbingly for girls – whether they are wearing the right size clothes. Technology has meant that the world is getting smaller, but not always easier to navigate. I see it as both potentially socially isolating at the same time that I see huge benefits of being immediately in touch with someone anywhere in the world. Every option we are given and every decision we make is potentially more complicated than it used to be.

Rapidly developing technology has also meant that we are seen, measured and monitored in ways that we weren't ten or even five years ago. An opinion can be formed of a person's behaviour or looks without them always having any influence over it. A mistimed entry or photo on a social networking site now has the ability to propel that individual into unknown territory of extreme hatred or inspiration, depending on your original point of view. Never before has it been so important for people to think about the impact that they have on others, and to be aware of themselves and their interaction with society.

Trust of other individuals in the abstract sense is important, but also the ability we have as humans to decide whom we put our faith in and why, until they mess it up.

Out of this, it was also important to consider the matter of trust. Trust of other individuals in the abstract sense is important, but also the ability we have as humans to decide whom we put our faith in and why, until they mess it up. Then there's forgiveness, which is not easily won. There are a small number of people who I implicitly trust to help me make decisions on the most important matters in my life. I also remember my mother telling me that, until you become a parent, you have no idea of the power of love that you can feel for your child. She was right. When I look into my daughter's eyes, and I know that she places all her trust in me to love, nurture and guide her, it is a massive responsibility, possibly the greatest I have felt. I know without a shadow of doubt that I would do anything within my power to protect her, and I hope I always have her trust and the ability to live up to it.

EVELYN GLENNIE

Musician

Drawing on her unique experiences as a deaf musician, Evelyn Glennie shows how 'listening' doesn't have one strict definition, but can encompass compassion, patience, inclusion, individuality and social awareness.

For all the immense achievements created by mankind through the ages, I cannot help but think that the answer to the question of 'what makes us human?' eludes us.

It is not a simple 'it is this' or 'it is that', and although the enormity of the question ties my brain in knots, I wonder if the fact that we are actually able to think about the question is what makes us human?

We are continually exploring the complexities of neurology and the mechanics of the human body, and how it continues to amaze as it reconnects itself in surprising ways under adversity. We are realising that our senses constitute layers upon layers of sub-senses, as I can personally testify.

The temptation to embrace the sheer scale of human behaviour becomes complex simply because there are no set patterns or traits that fit all human beings.

Globally, I am aware that large groups of people are traumatised due to the atrocities of others. The use of force and oppression appears to be the way conflict is resolved in some territories. If the resolution of these matters means we require others to apply judgement, is that the essence of what makes us human? Clearly some individuals and governments see the need to make judgement and act upon it; to take the decision away from others under the banner of democracy or dictatorship, and put in place a statement of what they think is right or wrong, and then use force to implement those decisions.

Debating is another attribute we use to resolve issues, from which meal to order to the G8 summit, where major discussions are debated to resolve global problems including starvation in places like Africa, where millions continue to lack basic needs, while vast resources are wasted elsewhere. It is hard to consider what it is to be human when we appear to 'allow' these things to happen, or to expect others to solve the problems.

I ask myself, therefore, if the answer is compassion, which is demonstrably a key factor within the charity sectors as they strive to fund improvement and offer hope as a mechanism for ending all manner of misery.

Perhaps prayer is the answer: to look to the omnipresence of a superhuman being to provide resolution and sanctuary from all suffering. Or maybe it is patience? After all, this is the trait I find myself using most of all, from waiting in queues at airports to striving to perfect a piece of music.

As a human being, I have feelings. Therefore, is this what makes me human? If it is, I am presented with a conundrum, because I know other species, such as cats and dogs, clearly have feelings too. Having empathy and sensitivity are essential traits and can make a huge difference to our perception of others. These traits are most notably evident in organisations such as hospitals, hospices and other environments where caring is provided. But there are issues with some organisations, such as individual care homes and hospitals where there appears to be a lack of these traits, with devastating effect.

Curiosity also plays a large part in what defines us as human beings, and has catapulted researchers into the development of the human body on an unimaginable scale, possibly redefining what we envisage a human being to be. The science of modern medicine has overcome major challenges, providing cures and prosthetic substitutes, enabling hope and recovery. Technological advances also play a large part in what makes us human. From the manipulation of human embryos, bringing joy to some and concern to others about the ethics of intervention, to the ability to regenerate cells from living specimens, thus enabling life to continue when part or parts of the body are damaged.

This sense of curiosity is my mainstay. I have found other ways to feel and sense sound using my body as a resonating chamber. I have achieved my hopes and dreams of becoming a musician due to my innate sense of curiosity. I have learned to hear by lip-reading, and I have learned to use my body to feel sound as if it were a giant ear.

Therefore, are hopes and dreams the essence of what makes us human? Or perhaps the key is strength of character and determination; I certainly needed plenty of those traits along the way. But I also feel being open-minded is important, because it leads us to information that allows us to make choices and decisions. It also brings about flexibility and the ability to adapt. When I lost my hearing, I chose to adapt and integrate myself into a mainstream school. From my perspective, the choice was to either be labelled as disabled or enable myself to open up a new career as the world's first full-time solo percussionist – I have never regretted the ability to make choices!

Life begins and ends with listening. Perhaps the fact that I have opened my body to listening in a different way enables me to be more sensitive.

Clearly, the answer is complicated. There is another question frequently asked of me – would I be better musician if I had not lost my hearing? I have no idea, but I do know life begins and ends with listening. Perhaps the fact that I have opened my body to listening in a different way enables me to be more sensitive. In conclusion, I feel compassion, patience, inclusion, individuality and social awareness are all forms of social listening, and that is what predominately makes us human. By engaging your body as a huge ear, I wonder if your view on what makes us human would change.

MASON McQUEEN

London black cab driver

Beginning with an analogy of how life is like a cab ride, Mason McQueen's answer takes in many important lessons from the 'school of life', as we learn and progress towards becoming our best selves.

When asked 'what makes us human?', and to take part in this project, I thought, 'Oh my God! Who, me? What do I know?' The calibre of people that have taken part was quite daunting to me, not being an academic myself, but one thing I do know is us humans come in all different shapes, sizes, genders and abilities. I love a challenge, and being a human, to me, is about how we react to certain conditions, predicaments and situations.

As a licensed London cab driver who works into the night in this fantastic city, I see the human condition in all its glory and different emotions. Happy, angry, sad, stressed, relaxed, confused, even merry, or heavily intoxicated – people from all walks of life, or even staggers.

The human race does exactly what it says on the tin, and working in a big city gives you a feel for that, with the fast-paced, high-tech culture we live in. From birth, we gradually propel ourselves upwards by standing, walking and growing, and we're on our way on our little journey – just like when you jump into my cab. We start a journey that has a beginning and an ending. En route in my cab, we might encounter roadworks, congestion, dangerous conditions, bad drivers and bumpy roads: this reflects our own lives as human beings and the experiences we may encounter. We deal with that in our own lives, with our desire to overcome and ability to endure the worst scenarios, and we also face it with our inner belief and determination.

Being a human being, you never really leave school. From birth, you're enrolled in the school of life, where we are constantly learning from our mistakes – and, if we don't, they're wasted. But, just like school, there has to be discipline: a moral code, if you like, for your actions and their consequences. We live in a beautiful but volatile world, and as humans we have the ability to roam this planet, to live, learn, absorb and progress to become better.

On my travels around the world, I've met many people less fortunate than myself, for whom life is a constant struggle. I've seen first-hand how hard life can be, but they also showed me their warmth, love and hospitality, even though they had nothing. The sacrifices they made to make their families' lives better opened my eyes. 'How would I like to live like this?' Put yourself in their shoes and those of other people less fortunate than yourself. Although they had nothing, they were still giving me something, and in my eyes, that's what makes us human. I'm always trying to be a better person. It's our reaching out to help in life that makes all the difference. They made me realise how lucky I am to have what I have, from my beautiful loving family, to good health and a roof over our heads.

En route in my cab, we might encounter roadworks, bad drivers, bumpy roads: this reflects our own lives as human beings and the experiences we may encounter.

So, what does actually make us human? We're the same as other animals, with flesh and blood, and life stages. I thought it was going to be a lot easier separating the two; however, after serious thought, we're very much alike. Animals reproduce, care for and defend their young; some use tools, or have the ability to navigate across oceans. It's like a mirror image of mankind.

What Makes Us Human?

In my eyes, what sets us apart from animals is the ability to progress, and change the face of the earth with many great inventions. But on the other side of the coin, we are culpable for some of the most heinous crimes against mankind, other species and the world we live in.

Personally, I don't think we know exactly what makes us human, – and I doubt we ever will – it's an ongoing question. But one thing I do know: we have the capability to make ourselves better humans with empathy, compassion and consideration for others.

SIMON WESTON

Veteran

Having overcome severe burn injuries sustained in the Falklands War, Simon Weston knows better than most the challenges life can throw at us. But – perhaps because of these experiences – his view on the key to life is to accept the hand we are dealt and not take ourselves too seriously.

What makes us human? I have pondered the notion in my own indomitable style, and I am as confused now as I was when I was first asked the question. I can't say it caused me sleepless nights or even that it made me think at all really, as I know what makes me human.

My first thoughts revolve around everything I hold closest to my heart: my family. The love of family; my wife Lucy, my astounding children – James the graduate, Stuart the independent, and my youngest and delightful Caitlyn – and of course the newest addition, the future that is Zachary. To be human is to love, and adore, and spoil, and worry, and get angry, and to enjoy all that is the best and worst of us.

My ideas of being human are the visits to the hospital when loved ones are sick. That moment when your parents relish the time you are born and hold you for the first time. The feeling of being loved despite all the bad habits that have grown over the decades. The excuses made on your behalf when your behaviour could have been better and expectations are high. It is these learned experiences you hope to pass on to your children. Your hopes and dreams. The continuation of you. But hopefully better looking and distinctly more talented.

What Makes Us Human?

But then you have to think, hang on, this is not the same for all of us. Not all families share the love and devotion that they should. So, therefore, to be human is to be the same, but also to be different. We are a contradiction in terms. For all that my life is full of compassionate and wonderful people, I am so aware that our breed is full of juxtaposition. For every pound of kindness and love, there is an equal weight of hatred and brutality. I am continuously shocked by the notion that there are those amongst us who continue to believe that there can only be one way of life, one way to love, one righteous argument: their way. That they refuse to make way for our diversity.

> **We are a contradiction in terms. For all that my life is full of compassionate and wonderful people, I am so aware that our breed is full of juxtaposition.**

So the truth of the matter is that we are all human because we are all so different. We are human because we are both generous and greedy, we love and we hate, we are peaceful, yet ready for a punch-up.

And do you know, I even think it is our inhumanity that makes us human. It is inhuman to want to hurt our children, to ignore the needs of our elderly, and to turn our backs on those who need our support and not our condemnation. But even cavemen, who had no consciousness of being human, were ruthless and culled the weak when needed. They clubbed their chosen woman on the head and dragged her off.

But if I was to give just one explanation for what makes us human, it has to be our humour, our sheer enjoyment of 'avin a laff'. Of taking life's darkest moments and turning them into an opportunity for cracking jokes, taking the mick, and simply having some fun. My life has had many a hiccough, where by rights I should have been overwhelmed by the sadness of it all. But in my family, we laugh!

Like the moment when my finger was amputated and someone said, 'I hear you've got a ring to sell!' Or when we were attending a funeral, with almost the whole row taken up by the family, and we were asked to move down. We looked at each other as we did a Mexican wave down the line and started, as one, to silently giggle, with shoulders heaving! There was no disrespect in the gesture, just a tense moment alleviated by humour.

So having given it a lot more thought now, I would have to say what makes us human is our similarities. Oh, and our differences. But most of all, it is the ability that the majority of us have to laugh and not take ourselves too seriously. To take this life we are dealt and turn it into a life worth living, with a head-back bellow of laughter and the chance to share that moment with those around us. Go on, give it a try: you might find you like it!

JOHN LLOYD

TV producer and writer

John Lloyd's wide-ranging and hilarious essay reflects on how asking the question of what makes us human unravels a series of other questions.

This is a big question, but one answer covers it all: we ask questions. There are quite a few human languages – Latin and Irish among them – that don't have words for 'yes' or 'no', but every language on earth has a word for 'why'.

Why is this? Why are we the only species on earth that is concerned about things that don't directly affect our survival or that of our offspring? Porcupines do not look up at the night sky and wonder what all the sparkly bits are; weasels don't worry about what other weasels think of them; and lobsters really don't enjoy pub quizzes.

When my son was about fourteen, I was trying to explain what a hydrogen atom is like. The fact that we have any idea at all is, in itself, an extraordinary testament to human curiosity. People have been wondering what stuff is made of since the beginning of time. Antelopes, by contrast, haven't. And no antelope has ever expressed what Harry said next: 'Dad, why is there something and not nothing?' This is a question first posed by the German philosopher Gottfried Leibniz, often said to be the last man in history who knew everything that could be known. But he didn't know that, it seems.

Stephen Hawking asked the same question in a different way: 'Why does the universe go to all the bother of existing?' He happened to be a friend of Jimmy Carr and it was the most wonderfully moving thing to see Jimmy make him laugh. Laughter,

I would say, is another thing that makes us human, and being able to make people laugh is a high calling. Watching Bill Bailey live on stage, for example, always makes me proud to be a member of the same species.

But why do we laugh? I've been working in comedy for forty years and I still don't know. It's the simple things that don't have answers. What is life? No one knows: biologists can't tell the difference between a live hamster and a dead one. What is the *meaning* of life is even more difficult. Scientists can't agree on the meaning of the word meaning.

Where do ideas come from? What is consciousness? Where is last Thursday? Do they artificially sweeten the delicious glue on the back of envelopes? Once you start asking questions, you become like a five-year-old child. You can't stop. And you become very annoying. When I was that age, I asked my father: 'Daddy, what is the Holy Ghost?' 'M'boy,' he replied, 'St Francis of Assisi struggled with that question for forty years in the wilderness – I cannot help you.'

Where do ideas come from? What is consciousness? Where is last Thursday? Do they artificially sweeten the delicious glue on the back of envelopes?

Andrew Billen, the TV critic of *The Times*, once asked me: 'Why do you think the universe is interesting?' Great question – and to my surprise, I found myself answering without thinking: 'Firstly, to lead us to ask the questions that really matter, and, secondly, to distract us from ever finding them.' As Niels Bohr, the great Danish physicist, used to say: 'At least, gentlemen, we have encountered a paradox – now we have some hope of making progress!' Bohr was a bit of a paradox himself. He kept a lucky horseshoe over his door. When asked, 'Surely you don't believe in that nonsense?', he said:

'Of course I don't believe in it, but I understand it works whether you believe in it or not.'

What do you believe in? What questions really matter? I think there are only two: 'Why are we here?' and 'What should we do about it while we are?' The question of what it means to be human is central to all science fiction, and there is a famous quote from one of the greatest writers in the genre, Robert Heinlein. He lists twenty-one things that 'a human being should be able' to do, from changing a diaper to planning an invasion. As Heinlein says, 'Specialisation is for insects.'

We must get on, there's a lot to do.

ACKNOWLEDGEMENTS

PHIL JONES

What Makes us Human began on *The Jeremy Vine Show* on BBC Radio 2 in 2013. It may have been my idea, but it would never have come to life and been the success it has been, without the work of three brilliant producers: Priya Shah launched the series, handed over to Ellie Kifvel, and it's now in the more than capable hands of Ryan Wilson. I'd also like to thank Berni Botto and Patrick Thomas, who worked so hard on helping with this book.